Hibernate Recipes

Second Edition

Joseph Ottinger

Srinivas Guruzu

Gary Mak

Apress®

Hibernate Recipes

ISBN-13 (pbk): 978-1-4842-0128-2

ISBN-13 (electronic): 978-1-4842-0127-5

Managing Director: Welmoed Spahr
Lead Editor: Steve Anglin
Technical Reviewer: Massimo Nardone
Editorial Board: Steve Anglin, Mark Beckner, Gary Cornell, Louise Corrigan, Jim DeWolf,
    Jonathan Gennick, Robert Hutchinson, Michelle Lowman, James Markham, Matthew Moodie,
    Susan McDermott, Jeffrey Pepper, Douglas Pundick, Ben Renow-Clarke, Gwenan Spearing,
    Matt Wade, Steve Weiss
Coordinating Editor: Melissa Maldonado
Copy Editor: Nancy Sixsmith
Compositor: SPi Global
Indexer: SPi Global
Artist: SPi Global
Cover Designer: Anna Ishchenko

Distributed to the book trade worldwide by Springer Science+Business Media New York, 233 Spring Street, 6th Floor, New York, NY 10013. Phone 1-800-SPRINGER, fax (201) 348-4505, e-mail orders-ny@springer-sbm.com, or visit www.springeronline.com. Apress Media, LLC is a California LLC and the sole member (owner) is Springer Science + Business Media Finance Inc (SSBM Finance Inc). SSBM Finance Inc is a Delaware corporation.

For information on translations, please e-mail rights@apress.com, or visit www.apress.com.

Apress and friends of ED books may be purchased in bulk for academic, corporate, or promotional use. eBook versions and licenses are also available for most titles. For more information, reference our Special Bulk Sales–eBook Licensing web page at www.apress.com/bulk-sales.

Any source code or other supplementary material referenced by the author in this text is available to readers at www.apress.com. For detailed information about how to locate your book's source code, go to www.apress.com/source-code/.

Dedicated to various things that keep distracting me from writi- hey, a squirrel!

.

Contents at a Glance

Contents

About the Authors

Joseph B. Ottinger is a writer, an arranger, and a young boy bearing quotes from Rush albums from the early 1980s. He's also a musician and developer, with interests in machine learning, general systems architecture, and transfer of knowledge—including editing stints at Java Developer Journal and TheServerSide.com, neither of which he's willing to mis-spell.

His interests tend to wander far and wide, but his attention is held by his wife and three sons, unless his feline overlords demand otherwise. He works very hard to prevent his cats from publishing, mostly because what they would write would center around food and, more often, being held in a lap beside a fire. It's dull reading.

Srinivas Guruzu is a developer who has been coding for more than 13 years. After completing his MS in mechanical engineering, Srinivas worked on high-traffic payment systems in the banking domain. He also has experience working in the insurance domain. He's worked with Spring and Hibernate building applications that integrate with other products as part of a large customer-enrollment and file-transmission system.

Gary Mak, founder and chief consultant of Meta-Archit Software Technology Limited, has been a technical architect and application developer on the enterprise Java platform for more than seven years. He is the author of the Apress books *Spring Recipes: A Problem-Solution Approach* and *Pro SpringSource dm Server*. In his career, Gary has developed a number of Java–based software projects, most of which are application frameworks, system infrastructures, and software tools. He enjoys designing and implementing the complex parts of software projects. Gary has a master's degree in computer science. His research interests include object-oriented technology, aspect-oriented technology, design patterns, software reuse, and domain-driven development.

Gary specializes in building enterprise applications on technologies including Spring, Hibernate, JPA, JSF, Portlet, AJAX, and OSGi. He has been using the Spring Framework in his projects since Spring version 1.0. Gary has been an instructor of courses on enterprise Java, Spring, Hibernate, Web Services, and agile development. He has written a series of Spring and Hibernate tutorials as course materials, parts of which are open to the public, and they're gaining popularity in the Java community. In his spare time, he enjoys playing tennis and watching tennis competitions.

About the Technical Reviewer

Massimo Nardone holds a master's of science degree in computing science from the University of Salerno, Italy. He worked as a PCI QSA and Senior Lead IT Security/Cloud/SCADA Architect for many years and currently works as Security, Cloud, and SCADA Lead IT Architect for Hewlett Packard Finland. He has more than 20 years of work experience in IT, including Security, SCADA, Cloud Computing, IT Infrastructure, Mobile, Security, and WWW technology areas for both national and international projects. Massimo has worked as a Project Manager, Cloud/SCADA Lead IT Architect, Software Engineer, Research Engineer, Chief Security Architect, and Software Specialist. He worked as visiting lecturer and supervisor for exercises at the Networking Laboratory of the Helsinki University of Technology (Aalto University). He has been programming and teaching how to program with Perl, PHP, Java, VB, Python, C/C++, and MySQL for more than 20 years. He is the author of *Pro Android Games* (Apress, 2015).

He holds four international patents (PKI, SIP, SAML, and Proxy areas). This book is dedicated to Pia, Luna, Leo e Neve, who are the beautiful reasons for his life.

Acknowledgments

Joseph would like to thank many, many people for many different things, but his editor says that the acknowledgments should be somewhat book-related, so thank you for that, editor! In addition, a heartfelt and earnest ode of appreciation goes to his wife and family; Fender and Gibson, both makers of fine guitars, for providing a set of instruments with which to while away the time; various laptop manufacturers for keeping him guessing as to whether his data will remain available on a day-to-day basis; blue beetles, because they sound so interesting (thanks, Todd!); the entire Hibernate development team, for creating a library that does a very difficult job about as well as it can be done; Jetbrains because development should be fun and efficient; Andrew Lombardi, for serving as a sounding board for what turns out to be a lot of rather silly noise; Scott Balmos, just because; Justin Lee, also just because (and for serving as a balance); and finally, Tracy Snell, for preventing Joseph from going too far off into the weeds, and for helping write some of the code that served as a proof for content. Joseph really wishes he was comfortable writing about himself, and in third person, at that.[1]

---

[1]Dear reader, you're going to endure a lot of footnotes throughout this book, but at least I've somehow managed to save you from having to read one on the acknowledgements page. Oh, wait…

CHAPTER 1

■ ■ ■

Starting with Hibernate

An *object model* uses the principles of abstraction, encapsulation, modularity, hierarchy, typing, concurrency, polymorphism, and persistence. The object model enables you to create well-structured and complex systems. In an object model system, *objects* are the components of the system. Objects are instances of classes, and classes are related to other classes via inheritance relationships. An object has an identity, a state, and a behavior. An object model helps you create reusable application frameworks and systems that can evolve over time. In addition, object-oriented systems are usually smaller than non-object-oriented implementations.

A *relational model* defines the structure of data, data manipulation, and data integrity. Data is organized in the form of tables, and different tables are associated by means of referential integrity (a foreign key). Integrity constraints such as a primary key, unique check constraints, and not null are used to maintain an entity's integrity in the relational model.

A relational data model isn't focused on supporting entity-type inheritance: entity-based polymorphic association from an object model can't be translated into similar entities in a relational model. In an object model, you use the state of the model to define equality between objects. But in a relational model, you use an entity's primary key to define equality of entities. Object references are used to associate different objects in an object model, whereas a foreign key is used to establish associations in a relational model. Object references in the object model facilitate easier navigation through the object graph.

Because these two models are distinctly different, you need a way to persist object entities (Java objects) into a relational database. Figure 1-1 provides a simple representation of the object model and Figure 1-2 shows the relational model.

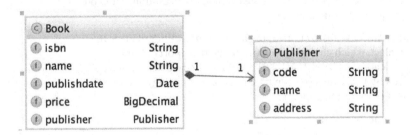

Figure 1-1. The object model

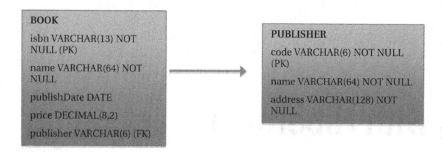

Figure 1-2. *The relational model*

Object/relational mapping (ORM) frameworks help you take advantage of the features present in an object model (such as Java) and a relational model (such as database management systems [DBMSs]). With the help of ORM frameworks, you can persist objects in Java to relational tables using metadata that describes the mapping between the objects and the database. The metadata shields the complexity of dealing directly with SQL and helps you develop solutions in terms of business objects.

An ORM solution can be implemented at various levels:

- *Pure relational*: An application is designed around the relational model.

- *Light object mapping*: Entities are represented as classes and are mapped manually to relational tables.

- *Medium object mapping*: An application is designed using an object model, and SQL is generated during build time using code-generation utilities.

- *Full object mapping*: Supports sophisticated object modeling including composition, inheritance, polymorphism, and persistence by reachability.

The following are the benefits of using an ORM framework:

- *Productivity*: Because you use metadata to persist and query data, development time decreases and productivity increases.

- *Prototyping*: Using an ORM framework is extremely useful for quick prototyping.

- *Maintainability*: Because much of the work is done through configuration, your code has fewer lines and requires less maintenance.

- *Vendor independence*: An ORM abstracts an application from the underlying SQL database and SQL dialect, which gives you the portability to support multiple databases. Java Specification Request 317 (JSR317) defines the Java Persistence API (JPA) specification. Using JPA means you can transparently switch between ORM frameworks such as Hibernate and TopLink.

ORM frameworks also have some disadvantages:

- *Learning curve*: You may experience a steep learning curve as you learn when and how to map and manage objects. You also have to learn a new query language.

- *Overhead*: For simple applications that use a single database and data without many business requirements for complex querying, an ORM framework can be extra overhead.

- *Slower performance*: For large batch updates, performance is slower.

Hibernate is one of the most widely used ORM frameworks in the industry. It provides all the benefits of an ORM solution and implements the JPA defined in the JPA 2.0 specification.

Its main components are as follows:

- *Hibernate Core*: The Core generates SQL and relieves you from manually handling Java Database Connectivity (JDBC) result sets and object conversions. Metadata is defined in simple XML files. The Core offers various options for writing queries: plain SQL; Hibernate Query Language (HQL), which is specific to Hibernate; programmatic criteria, and Query by Example (QBE). It can optimize object loading with various fetching and caching options.

- *Hibernate Annotations*: Hibernate provides the option of defining metadata using annotations. This feature reduces configuration using XML files and makes it easy to define the required metadata directly in the Java source code.

- *Hibernate EntityManager*: The JPA specification defines programming interfaces, life-cycle rules for persistent objects, and query features. The Hibernate implementation for this part of the JPA is available as Hibernate EntityManager.

Hibernate also has Hibernate Search, Hibernate Validator, and Hibernate OGM[1] (No SQL), which are not addressed in this book. This book provides solutions using Hibernate ORM Core and Annotations in a problem-solution approach. The Hibernate version used is 4.3.5.Final.

1-1. Setting Up a Project

Problem

How do you set up a project structure for Hibernate code so that all required libraries are available in the classpath? And how can you build the project and execute unit tests?

Solution

Following are the available build tools that help you build the project and manage the libraries:

- Maven

- Gradle

- SBT

■ **Note**   Although we provide all details to create a project structure, manage libraries, build, and execute tests using Maven, the sample code, downloadable from `Apress.com` includes Gradle and SBT.

Maven is a software project-management and comprehension tool. Based on the concept of a Project Object Model (POM), Maven can manage a project's build, reporting, and documentation from a central piece of information. In Maven, the `POM.XML` file is the central place in which all the information is stored.

---

[1]OGM stands for "Object Graph Model." Hibernate OGM provides an object abstraction for NoSQL databases.

How It Works

The version used here is Java 7, which you can download from http://www.oracle.com/technetwork/java/javase/downloads/jdk7-downloads-1880260.html.

Once you download Java, set the PATH variable to the bin folder in the Java Runtime Environment (JRE). Set the JAVA_HOME variable to the folder in which you installed Java.

■ **Note**   You should be able to execute all code in Java 8 as well.

Installing Eclipse

Eclipse is an integrated development environment (IDE) for developing Java applications. The latest version is Kepler (4.3.2). You can download the latest version from https://www.eclipse.org/downloads/.

The Kepler version specifically for 64bin Win can be downloaded from https://www.eclipse.org/downloads/download.php?file=/technology/epp/downloads/release/kepler/SR2/eclipse-standard-kepler-SR2-win32-x86_64.zip.

Once you extract and start Eclipse, make sure that it is using Java 7. You can see what version of Java is being used by going to Windows ➤ Preferences ➤ Java ➤ JRE in Eclipse. If you have multiple JRE versions, make sure that jre7 is checked.

Installing Maven

Maven can be run both from a command prompt and from Eclipse:

- To run from a command prompt, download the Maven libraries from http://maven.apache.org/download.cgi. Once you unzip into a folder, add the bin folder to the PATH variable. You can then run and build from the command prompt using commands such as mvn package, mvn install, and so on.

- To run Maven from Eclipse, use the M2 plug-in in Eclipse to integrate Eclipse and Maven. This plug-in gives you tremendous flexibility to work with Maven POM files while developing in Eclipse. You can install the M2 plug-in from Eclipse: go to Help ➤ Install New Software and enter http://download.eclipse.org/technology/m2e/releases. Follow the instructions. Once this plug-in is installed, you can create a new Maven project from File ➤ New Project.

Setting Up a Maven Project

This book follows the parent-module project structure instead of a flat project structure. All the common dependencies, library versions, and configurations such as properties and so on can be declared in the parent. Any common code between modules can be placed in a separate module and can be used as a library in the rest of the modules, which enables a cleaner code structure.

The parent project contains only the parent POM and represents the complete book. Each chapter is an individual module under the parent. The dependencies that are common across all chapters are specified in the parent POM, and those that are specific to each chapter are mentioned in the corresponding chapter's POM.

▨ **Note**   For more information on how to create multiple module projects in Maven by using Maven commands, see http://maven.apache.org/plugins/maven-eclipse-plugin/reactor.html.

You can also use Eclipse to create a similar structure. Here are the steps you can use:

1. Create the parent project: go to File ➤ New ➤ Other and select a Maven project. You should see the New Maven Project window shown in Figure 1-3.

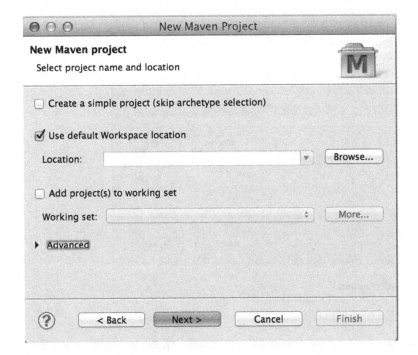

Figure 1-3. *New Maven Project window*

2. Select 'Create A Simple Project'. If you are using the default workspace location, click Next.

3. In the configuration window that displays, specify the Group ID and Artifact ID. The version has a default value. For packaging, choose 'pom'. This book uses the following values (see Figure 1-4):

   - Group ID: com.apress.hibernaterecipes

   - Artifact ID: ver2

   - Version: 1.0.0

   - Packaging: pom

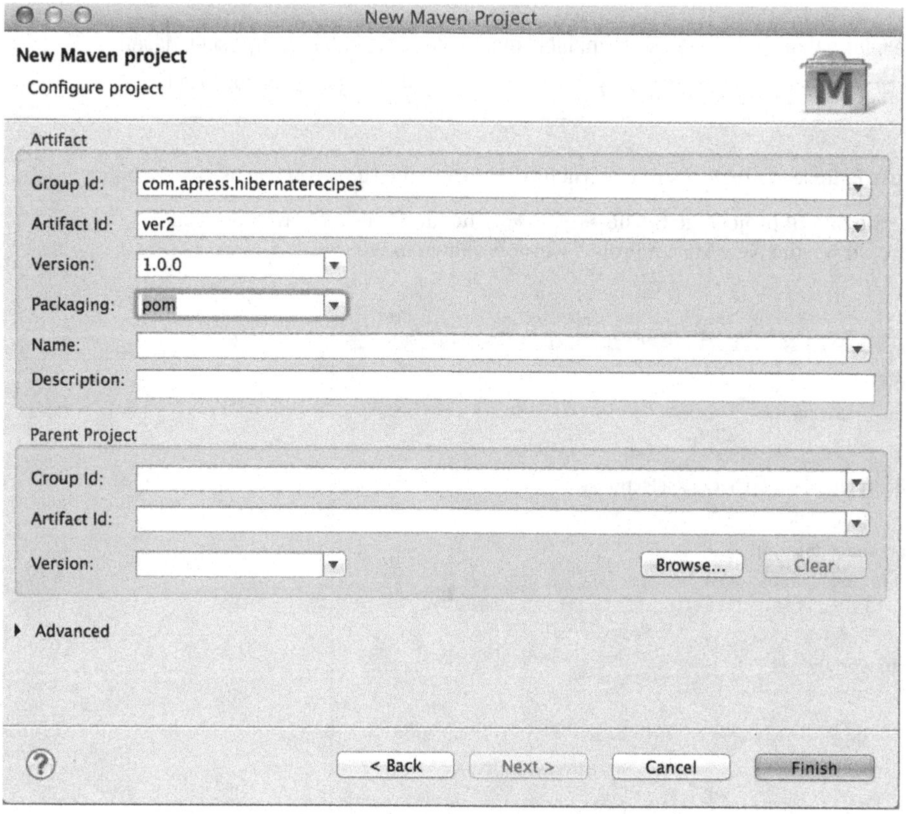

Figure 1-4. *Configuring Maven project values*

4. Click Finish.

A parent project called 'ver2' is created because ver2 was specified as the Artifact ID. When you expand the 'ver2' project in Eclipse, you see only the src folder and a POM file.

Creating a Maven Project Using an Archetype

You can use archetypes to create Maven projects. There are many archetypes available for various kinds of projects such as Java-Spring, Java-Struts, and so on.

Here is how to create a simple Java project using the quickstart archetype:

1. Make sure that the Maven path is set and you can run the mvn command from the command line.

2. Execute the following command:

```
mvn archetype:generate -DgroupId="groupId of your project"
-DartifactId="artifact id of your application" -Dverion="version of your project"
-DarchetypeArtifactId=maven-archetype-quickstart
```

This will create a simple Java project with folders for Java source code and tests. This will not create a folder for resources. You can manually create this folder if it is needed.

Running Unit Tests

All unit tests are written in TestNG, and Eclipse has a plug-in for TestNG that can be installed. Go to Help ➤ Install New Software and enter `http://beust.com/eclipse`. Follow the instructions. Once this plug-in is installed, you should be able to create and execute unit testing with the TestNG application programming interface (API).

You can also execute unit tests for each chapter by accessing the chapter's home folder and running the Maven command `mvn test`.

Creating Modules

Now it's time to create modules for a cleaner code structure and to run individual chapters.

1. Right-click the parent project in Eclipse (ver2, in this case)," and choose New ➤ Other ➤ Maven Module (see Figure 1-5).

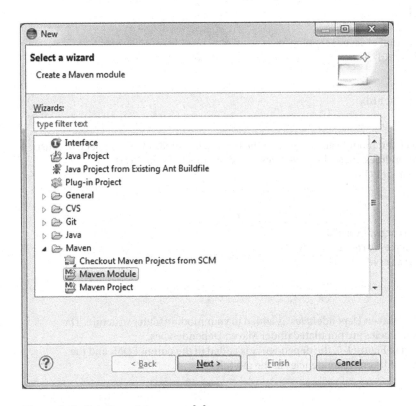

Figure 1-5. *Creating a Maven module*

2. Click Next.

3. In the next window, choose 'Create Simple Project' and a name for your module (we chose chapter1). Your parent project should be selected in the Parent Project field.

4. Click 'Next;' the Group ID, Artifact ID, Version, and Packaging fields should already be populated. In this case, the Group ID is com.apress. hibernaterecipes, which is the same as the Group ID of the parent project. The Artifact ID is the module name. Version is 0.0.1-SNAPSHOT by default, and Packaging should be jar.

Now you have a parent project as well your first module. If you look into the POM of your parent project, you see that a <module> tag is added with the same name that you specified for your module.

The POM in your module has the <parent> tag with the <groupId>, <artifactId>, and <version> tags of the parent project:

```
<modelVersion>4.0.0</modelVersion>
 <parent>
   <groupId>com.apress.hibernaterecipes</groupId>
   <artifactId>ver2</artifactId>
   <version>1.0.0</version>
 </parent>
 <artifactId>chapter1</artifactId>
</project>
```

Now that the parent project and module are set up, add the Hibernate JAR files to the project. Because Hibernate JARs are used by all modules, these dependencies are added to the parent POM.

Add the following to the parent POM:

```
<dependencies>
     <dependency>
         <groupId>org.hibernate</groupId>
         <artifactId>hibernate-core</artifactId>
         <version>4.3.5.Final</version>
     </dependency>
</dependencies>
```

Once you save and refresh, 'Maven Dependencies' is added to your module folder structure. The Hibernate JARs and their dependencies are populated under Maven Dependencies.

If you see the screen shown in Figure 1-6, the dependency is added in the parent POM, and the dependent JARs are added under Maven Dependencies in the module.

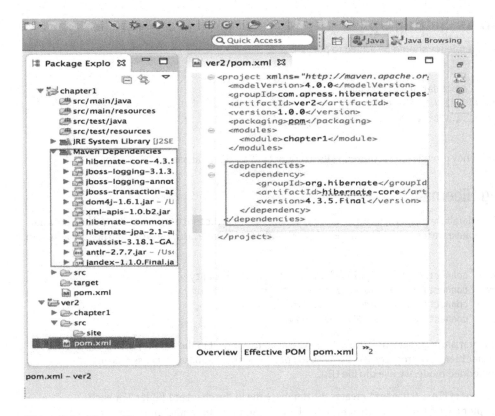

Figure 1-6. Maven Dependencies

■ **Note** Also included in the code repository is the configuration for a project set up using Gradle and SBT (you can download it from the code repository).

1-2. Setting Up a Database

Problem

How do you set up a database to work with Hibernate?

Solution

The H2 database in embedded mode is used for all testing in this book. In addition to instructions on how to set up H2, we provide documentation on how to set up Derby in server mode.

How It Works: Setting Up H2

The following dependency should be added to pom.xml:

```
<dependency>
    <groupId>com.h2database</groupId>
    <artifactId>h2</artifactId>
    <version>1.4.178</version>
</dependency>
```

This dependency provides the required JARs to connect to an H2 database.

Configuring Hibernate

Add the required database properties either to persistence.xml or hibernate.cgf.xml depending on what you are using. Because we test with hibernate.cfg.xml and persistence.xml, these properties are added to both the files:

```
<property name="connection.driver_class">org.h2.Driver</property>
<property name="connection.url">jdbc:h2:file:./chapter1</property>
<property name="connection.username">sa</property>
<property name="connection.password"></property>
```

- The first property sets the driver class to be used to connect to the database. The connection.url property sets the URL to connect to the database. Because it is an embedded mode, we use the file URL.

- jdbc:h2:file:./chapter1 creates the database file in the chapter1 folder. For each chapter the URL to create the database file is the appropriate chapter home folder. The URL for chapter2 is jdbc:h2:file:./chapter2, for example.

- The next two properties are for username and password. By default, H2 uses 'sa' as the username with no password.

- After this configuration is done, you should be able to run the tests that are bundled in the code. Each chapter has its own set of tests in the test folder. If you already installed the TestNG plug-in, go to the test folder, go to a specific test (for example, Recipe1JPATest.java in chapter1), right-click the test file, and click Run As ➤ TestNG Test. When you run the tests in the test folder, two database files are created in the chapter's home folder. For example, if you execute tests for chapter1, the chapter1.mv.db and chapter1.trace.db files are created in the chapter1 folder.

- The .mv.db file is the actual database file that contains all scripts that were executed. Although it is not readable, if you want to view the schema and data, you can view it via the H2 console.

Setting Up the H2 Console to View Data

1. You can download the H2 console from http://www.h2database.com/html/main.html. There are installers for different environments.

2. After you install the console, you see 'H2 Console, which' is a web-based user interface (UI) that opens the connections page in the web browser. By default, the database selected is 'Generic H2(Embedded),' and the driver selected is org.h2.driver.

3. The JDBC URL should be specified to the .mv file in the chapter folder (for example, if your Hibernate recipes code is in C:\HR). You find the chapter1.mv database file inC:\HR\chapter1, so the JDBC URL should be jdbc:h2:file:C:\HR\ chapter1\chapter1.

4. Leave the default values for username and password.

5. Click Connect. You should see the schema on the left pane. When you click a table name, it adds the SELECT SQL statement in the code window. If you execute the statement, you should be able to view the data.

How It Works: Setting Up Derby

The following JAR files are required for the Derby setup:

- Derby.jar.
- Derbyclient.jar.
- Derbynet.jar.
- Derbytools.

Installing Derby

Derby is an open-source SQL relational database engine written in Java. You can go to http://db.apache. org/derby/derby_downloads.html and download the latest version. Derby also provides plug-ins for Eclipse, which provide the required JAR files for development and a command prompt (ij) in Eclipse to execute Data Definition Language (DDL) and Data Manipulation Language (DML) statements.

Creating a Derby Database Instance

To create a new Derby database called BookShopDB at the ij prompt, use the following command:

```
connect 'jdbc:derby://localhost:1527/BookShopDB;create=true;
user=book;password=book';
```

After the database is created, execute the SQL scripts in the next section to create the tables.

Creating the Tables (Relational Model)

These solutions use the example of a bookshop. Books are published by a publisher, and the contents of a book are defined by the chapters. The entities Book and Publisher are stored in the database; you can perform various operations such as reading, updating, and deleting.

Because an ORM is a mapping between an object model and a relational model, you first create the relational model by executing the DDL statements to create the tables/entities in the database. You later see the object model in Java, and finally you see the mapping between the relational and the object models.

Create the tables for the online bookshop using the following SQL statements (Figure 1-7 gives details of the object model and Figure 1-8 shows the relational model):

```
CREATE TABLE publisher (
  code VARCHAR(6) PRIMARY KEY,
  name VARCHAR(64) NOT NULL,
  address VARCHAR(128) NOT NULL,
  UNIQUE (name)
);

CREATE TABLE book (
  isbn VARCHAR(13) PRIMARY KEY,
  name VARCHAR(64) NOT NULL,
  publishDate DATE,
  price DECIMAL(8, 2),
  publisher VARCHAR(6),
  FOREIGN KEY (publisher) REFERENCES publisher (code),
  UNIQUE (name)
);
```

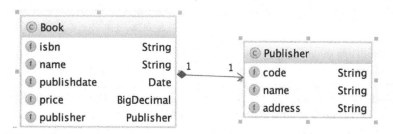

Figure 1-7. *The object model for the bookshop*

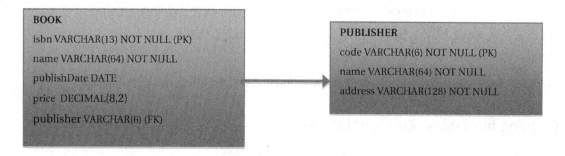

Figure 1-8. *The relational model for the bookshop*

Next, input some data for these tables using the following SQL statements:

```
insert into PUBLISHER(code, name, address)
values ('001', 'Apress', 'New York ,New York');
insert into PUBLISHER(code, name, address)
values ('002', 'Manning', 'San Francisco, CA');
```

```
insert into book(isbn, name, publisher, publishDate, price)
values ('PBN123', 'Spring Recipes', '001', DATE('2008-02-02'), 30);
insert into book(isbn, name, publisher, publishDate, price)
values ('PBN456', 'Hibernate Recipes', '002', DATE('2008-11-02'), 40);
```

1-3. Configuring Hibernate

Problem

How do you configure a Java project that uses an object/relational framework such as Hibernate as a persistence framework? How do you configure Hibernate programmatically?

Solution

Import the required JAR files into your project's classpath and create mapping files that map the state of a Java entity to the columns of its corresponding table. From the Java application, execute Create, Read, Update, Delete (CRUD) operations on the object entities. Hibernate takes care of translating the object state from the object model to the relational model.

How It Works

To configure a Java project to use the Hibernate framework, start by downloading the required JARs and configuring them in the build path.

If you add the following dependency to the Maven pom.xml file, all dependent libraries are downloaded under Maven Dependencies:

```
<dependency>
    <groupId>org.hibernate</groupId>
    <artifactId>hibernate-core</artifactId>
    <version>4.3.5.Final</version>
</dependency>
```

Although we use both annotations and XML configurations for the Hibernate setup wherever possible, the preference is to use annotations instead of XML.

Configuration

Before Hibernate can retrieve and persist objects for you, you have to tell it your application's settings. For example, which kind of objects are persistent objects? What kind of database are you using? How do you connect to the database? You can configure Hibernate in three ways:

- *Programmatic configuration*: Use the API to load the hbm file, load the database driver, and specify the database connection details.

- *XML configuration*: Specify the database connection details in an XML file that's loaded along with the hbm file. The default file name is hibernate.cfg.xml. You can use another name by specifying the name explicitly.

- *Properties file configuration*: Similar to the XML configuration, but uses a .properties file. The default name is hibernate.properties.

This solution introduces only the first two approaches (programmatic and XML configuration). The properties file configuration is much like XML configuration.

Programmatic Configuration

The following code loads the configuration programmatically. If you have a very specific use case to configure programmatically, you can use this method; otherwise, the preferred way is to use annotations.

The Configuration class provides the API to load the hbm files, to specify the driver to be used for the database connection, and to provide other connection details:

```
Configuration configuration = new Configuration()
.addResource("com/metaarchit/bookshop/Book.hbm.xml")
.setProperty("hibernate.dialect", "org.hibernate.dialect.DerbyTenSevenDialect")
.setProperty("hibernate.connection.driver_class", "org.apache.derby.jdbc.EmbeddedDriver")
.setProperty("hibernate.connection.url", "jdbc:derby://localhost:1527/BookShopDB")
.setProperty("hibernate.connection.username", "book")
.setProperty("hibernate.connection.password", "book");

ServiceRegistry serviceRegistry = new StandardServiceRegistryBuilder().applySettings
(configuration.getProperties()).build();
sessionFactory = configuration.buildSessionFactory(serviceRegistry);
```

Instead of using addResource() to add the mapping files, you can also use addClass() to add a persistent class and let Hibernate load the mapping definition for this class:

```
Configuration configuration = new Configuration()
.addClass(com.metaarchit.bookshop.Book.class)
.setProperty("hibernate.dialect", "org.hibernate.dialect.DerbyDialect")
.setProperty("hibernate.connection.driver_class", "org.apache.derby.jdbc.EmbeddedDriver")
.setProperty("hibernate.connection.url", "jdbc:derby://localhost:1527/BookShopDB")
.setProperty("hibernate.connection.username", "book")
.setProperty("hibernate.connection.password", "book");

ServiceRegistry serviceRegistry = new StandardServiceRegistryBuilder().applySettings
(configuration.getProperties()).build();
sessionFactory = configuration.buildSessionFactory(serviceRegistry);
```

If your application has hundreds of mapping definitions, you can pack it in a JAR file and add it to the Hibernate configuration. This JAR file must be found in your application's classpath:

```
Configuration configuration = new Configuration()
.addJar(new File("mapping.jar"))
.setProperty("hibernate.dialect", "org.hibernate.dialect.DerbyDialect")
.setProperty("hibernate.connection.driver_class", "org.apache.derby.jdbc.EmbeddedDriver")
.setProperty("hibernate.connection.url", "jdbc:derby://localhost:1527/BookShopDB")
.setProperty("hibernate.connection.username", "book")
.setProperty("hibernate.connection.password", "book");
ServiceRegistry  serviceRegistry = new StandardServiceRegistryBuilder().applySettings
(configuration.getProperties()).build();
sessionFactory = configuration.buildSessionFactory(serviceRegistry);
```

SESSIONFACTORY

The following statement creates a Hibernate `SessionFactory` to use in the preceding code:

```
SessionFactory factory = configuration.buildSessionFactory(serviceRegistry);
```

A *session factory* is a global object for maintaining `org.hibernate.Session` objects. It i's instantiated once and i's thread-safe. You can look up the `SessionFactory` from a Java Naming and Directory Interface (JNDI) context in an `ApplicationServer` or any other location.

XML Configuration

Another way to configure Hibernate is to use an XML file. You create the file `hibernate.cfg.xml` in the source directory, so Eclipse copies it to the root of your classpath:

```xml
<?xml version="1.0" encoding="UTF-8"?>
<!DOCTYPE hibernate-configuration PUBLIC
        "-//Hibernate/Hibernate Configuration DTD 3.0//EN"
        "http://www.hibernate.org/dtd/hibernate-configuration-3.0.dtd">
<hibernate-configuration>

    <session-factory>
        <!-- H2 Configuration -->

        <property name="connection.driver_class">org.h2.Driver</property>
        <property name="connection.url">jdbc:h2:file:./chapter1</property>
        <property name="connection.username">sa</property>
        <property name="connection.password"></property>

        <property name="hibernate.dialect">org.hibernate.dialect.H2Dialect</property>
        <property name="hibernate.show_sql">true</property>
        <property name="hibernate.hbm2ddl.auto">create</property>
        <mapping resource="com/apress/hibernaterecipes/chapter1/model/Book.hbm.xml"/>
        <mapping resource="com/apress/hibernaterecipes/chapter1/model/Publisher.hbm.xml"/>
    </session-factory>
</hibernate-configuration>
```

Now the code fragment to build up a session factory can be simplified. The configuration loads the `hibernate.cfg.xml` file from the root of the classpath:

```
Configuration configuration = new Configuration().configure();
```

This method loads the default `hibernate.cfg.xml` file from the root classpath. The new `Configuration()` loads the `hibernate.properties` file, and the `configure()` method loads the `hibernate.cfg.xml` file if `hibernate.properties` isn't found. If you need to load another configuration file located elsewhere (not in the root classpath), you can use the following code:

```
new Configuration().configure("/config/recipes.cfg.xml")
```

This code looks for `recipes.cfg.xml` in the `config` subdirectory of the classpath.

Opening and Closing Sessions

A Hibernate Session object represents a unit of work and is bound to the current thread. It also represents a transaction in a database. A session begins when getCurrentSession() is first called on the current thread. The Session object is then bound to the current thread. When the transaction ends with a commit or rollback, Hibernate unbinds the session from the thread and closes it.

Just as with JDBC, you need to do some initial cleanup for Hibernate. First, ask the session factory to open a new session for you. After you finish your work, you must remember to close the session[2]:

```
Session session = factory.openSession();
try {
        // Using the session to retrieve objects
}catch(Exception e)
{
        e.printStackTrace();
} finally {
        session.close();
}
```

Creating Mapping Definitions

First ask Hibernate to retrieve and persist the book objects for you. For simplicity, 'ignore the publisher right now. Create a Book.hbm.xml XML file in the same package as the Book class. This file is called the *mapping definition* for the Book class. The Book objects are called *persistent objects* or *entities* because they can be persisted in a database and represent the real-world entities:

```
<?xml version='1.0' encoding='utf-8'?>
<!DOCTYPE hibernate-mapping PUBLIC
        "-//Hibernate/Hibernate Mapping DTD 3.0//EN"
        "http://www.hibernate.org/dtd/hibernate-mapping-3.0.dtd">
<hibernate-mapping>

    <class name="com.apress.hibernaterecipes.chapter1.model.Book" table="BOOK" lazy="false">
        <id name="isbn">
            <column name="ISBN" sql-type="varchar(13)" not-null="true"/>
        </id>
        <property name="name">
            <column name="NAME" sql-type="varchar(64)" not-null="true" unique="true"/>
        </property>
        <property name="publishdate">
            <column name="PUBLISHDATE" sql-type="date"/>
        </property>
        <property name="price">
            <column name="PRICE" sql-type="decimal" precision="8" scale="2"/>
        </property>
        <many-to-one name="publisher" column="PUBLISHERCODE" cascade="all"/>
    </class>
</hibernate-mapping>
```

---

[2]The sample code rarely includes the exception handling for Hibernate, because we want to focus on how Hibernate is used, rather than on Java's exception mechanism.

Each persistent object must have an identifier, which' is used by Hibernate to uniquely identify that object. Here, you use the ISBN as the identifier for a Book object.

Retrieving and Persisting Objects

Given the ID of a book (an ISBN in this case), you can retrieve the unique Book object from the database. There are multiple ways to do it - session.load() and session.get() are merely two common ones you'll see:

```
Book book = (Book) session.load(Book.class, isbn);
```

and

```
Book book = (Book) session.get(Book.class, isbn);
```

What's the difference between a load() method and a get() method? First, when the given ID can't be found, the load() method throws an org.hibernate.ObjectNotFoundException exception, whereas the get() method returns a null object. Second, the load() method just returns a proxy by default; the database isn't hit until the proxy is first invoked. The get() method hits the database immediately. The load() method is useful when you need only a proxy, not' a database call. You need only a proxy in a given session when you have to associate an entity before persisting.

Just as you can use SQL to query a database, you can use Hibernate to query objects using HQL. For example, note the following code queries for all the Book objects:

```
Query query = session.createQuery("from Book");
List books = query.list();
```

If you're sure that only one object matches, you can use the uniqueResult() method to retrieve the unique result object:

```
Query query = session.createQuery("from Book where isbn = ?");
query.setString(0, isbn);
Book book = (Book) query.uniqueResult();
```

The create() method inserts a new row into the BOOK table. It also loads the object from the database to validate that it exists and is the correct object.

```
@Test
    public void testCreate() {
        Session session = SessionManager.getSessionFactory().openSession();
        Transaction tx = session.beginTransaction();
        Publisher publisher = new Publisher();
        publisher.setCode("apress");
        publisher.setName("Apress");
        publisher.setAddress("233 Spring Street, New York, NY 10013");
        session.persist(publisher);
        tx.commit();
        session.close();

        session = SessionManager.getSessionFactory().openSession();
        tx = session.beginTransaction();
        Publisher publisher1 = (Publisher) session.load(Publisher.class, "apress");
        assertEquals(publisher.getName(), publisher1.getName());
        tx.commit();
        session.close();
    }
```

The Hibernate output is as follows:

```
Hibernate: insert into PUBLISHER (NAME, ADDRESS, CODE) values (?, ?, ?)
Hibernate: select publisher0_.CODE as CODE1_1_0_, publisher0_.NAME as NAME2_1_0_,
publisher0_.ADDRESS as ADDRESS3_1_0_ from PUBLISHER publisher0_ where publisher0_.CODE=?
```

1-4. Using the JPA EntityManager

Problem

Is there a generalized mechanism to configure ORM with less dependency on individual providers such as Hibernate, TopLink, and so on?

Solution

A *persistence context* is defined by the JPA specification as a set of managed entity instances in which the entity instances and their life cycles are managed by an entity manager. Each ORM vendor provides its own entity manager, which is a wrapper around the core API and thus supports the JPA programming interfaces, JPA entity instance life cycles, and query language, providing a generalized mechanism for object/relational development and configuration.

How It Works

You obtain the Hibernate EntityManager from an entity manager factory. When container-managed entity managers are used, the application doesn't interact directly with the entity manager factory. Such entity managers are obtained mostly through JNDI lookup. In the case of application-managed entity managers, the application must use the entity manager factory to manage the entity manager and the persistence context life cycle. This example uses the application-managed entity manager.

Add the following dependency to the pom.xml file:

```
<dependency>
    <groupId>org.hibernate</groupId>
    <artifactId>hibernate-entitymanager</artifactId>
    <version>4.3.5.Final</version>
</dependency>
```

EntityManagerFactory has the same role as SessionFactory in Hibernate. It acts a factory class that provides the EntityManager class to the application. It can be configured either programmatically or by using XML. When you use XML to configure it, the file must be named persistence.xml and must be located in the classpath.

The persistence.xml files should provide a unique name for each persistence unit; this name is the way applications reference the configuration while obtaining a javax.persistence.EntityManagerFactory reference.

Here's the persistence.xml file for the Book and Publisher examples:

```xml
<persistence xmlns="http://java.sun.com/xml/ns/persistence"
             xmlns:xsi="http://www.w3.org/2001/XMLSchema-instance"
             xsi:schemaLocation="http://java.sun.com/xml/ns/persistence http://java.sun.com/
             xml/ns/persistence/persistence_2_0.xsd"
             version="2.0">
    <persistence-unit name="chapter1" transaction-type="RESOURCE_LOCAL">
        <mapping-file>com/apress/hibernaterecipes/chapter1/model/Publisher.hbm.xml</mapping-file>
        <mapping-file>com/apress/hibernaterecipes/chapter1/model/Book.hbm.xml</mapping-file>

        <class>com.apress.hibernaterecipes.chapter1.model.Publisher</class>
        <class>com.apress.hibernaterecipes.chapter1.model.Book</class>

        <properties>
            <property name="javax.persistence.jdbc.driver" value="org.h2.Driver"/>
            <property name="javax.persistence.jdbc.user" value="sa"/>
            <property name="javax.persistence.jdbc.password" value=""/>
            <property name="javax.persistence.jdbc.url" value="jdbc:h2:file:~/chapter1jpa"/>

            <property name="hibernate.dialect" value="org.hibernate.dialect.HSQLDialect"/>
            <property name="hibernate.hbm2ddl.auto" value="create"/>
            <property name="hibernate.show_sql" value="true"/>
        </properties>
    </persistence-unit>
</persistence>
```

The RESOURCE_LOCAL transaction type is used here. Two transaction types define transactional behavior: JTA and RESOURCE_LOCAL. JTA is used in J2EE-managed applications in which the container is responsible for transaction propagation. For application-managed transactions, you can use RESOURCE_LOCAL.

The <provider> tag specifies the third-party ORM implementation you use. In this case, it i's configured to use the Hibernate persistence provider.

The entity instances are configured with the <class> tag.

The rest of the properties are similar to the configuration in the hibernate.cfg.xml file, including the driver class of the database you're connecting to, the connection URL, a username, a password, and the dialect.

Here's the code to create the EntityManagerFactory (EMF) from the configuration and to obtain the EntityManager from the EMF:

```java
package com.hibernaterecipes.annotations.dao;

import javax.persistence.EntityManager;
import javax.persistence.EntityManagerFactory;
import javax.persistence.Persistence;

public class SessionManager {

        public static EntityManager getEntityManager() {
            EntityManagerFactory managerFactory =
Persistence.createEntityManagerFactory("chapter1");
            EntityManager manager = managerFactory.createEntityManager();

            return manager;
        }

}
```

The `Persistence.createEntityManagerFactory()` method creates the EMF. The parameter that it takes is the name of the persistence unit (in this case, `"chapter1"`). It should be the same as the name specified in the `persistence.xml` file's `<persistence-unit>` tag:

```
<persistence-unit name="chapter1"  transaction-type="RESOURCE_LOCAL">
```

The Book entity instance remains the same as defined in the XML config file:

```java
public class Book {
    private String isbn;
    private String name;
    private Date publishdate;
    private BigDecimal price;
    private Publisher publisher;

    //Getters and Setters

    @Override
    public boolean equals(Object o) {
        if (this == o) return true;
        if (o == null || getClass() != o.getClass()) return false;

        Book book = (Book) o;

        if (isbn != null ? !isbn.equals(book.isbn) : book.isbn != null) return false;
        if (name != null ? !name.equals(book.name) : book.name != null) return false;
        if (price != null ? !price.equals(book.price) : book.price != null) return false;
        if (publishdate != null ? !publishdate.equals(book.publishdate) : book.publishdate
        != null) return false;

        return true;
    }

    @Override
    public int hashCode() {
        int result = isbn != null ? isbn.hashCode() : 0;
        result = 31 * result + (name != null ? name.hashCode() : 0);
        result = 31 * result + (publishdate != null ? publishdate.hashCode() : 0);
        result = 31 * result + (price != null ? price.hashCode() : 0);
        return result;
    }
}
```

Here's the Publisher class:

```java
public class Publisher {
    private String code;
    private String name;
    private String address;
```

```
//Getters and setters

@Override
public boolean equals(Object o) {
    if (this == o) return true;
    if (o == null || getClass() != o.getClass()) return false;

    Publisher publisher = (Publisher) o;

    if (address != null ? !address.equals(publisher.address) : publisher.address != null)
    return false;
    if (code != null ? !code.equals(publisher.code) : publisher.code != null)
    return false;
    if (name != null ? !name.equals(publisher.name) : publisher.name != null)
    return false;

    return true;
}

@Override
public int hashCode() {
    int result = code != null ? code.hashCode() : 0;
    result = 31 * result + (name != null ? name.hashCode() : 0);
    result = 31 * result + (address != null ? address.hashCode() : 0);
    return result;
}
}
```

Here's the test code to create and retrieve the object graph of a Publisher and a Book:

```
@Test
    public void testCreateObjectGraph() {
        EntityManager em = emf.createEntityManager();
        em.getTransaction().begin();
        Publisher publisher = new Publisher();
        publisher.setCode("apress");
        publisher.setName("Apress");
        publisher.setAddress("233 Spring Street, New York, NY 10013");

        Book book = new Book();
        book.setIsbn("9781484201282");
        book.setName("Hibernate Recipes");
        book.setPrice(new BigDecimal("44.00"));
        book.setPublishdate(Date.valueOf("2014-10-10"));
        book.setPublisher(publisher);

        em.persist(book);

        em.getTransaction().commit();
        em.close();
```

```
    em = emf.createEntityManager();
    em.getTransaction().begin();
    Book book1 = em.find(Book.class, "9781484201282");
    assertEquals(book.getName(), book1.getName());
    assertNotNull(book.getPublisher());
    assertEquals(book.getPublisher().getName(), publisher.getName());
    em.getTransaction().commit();
    em.close();

    em = emf.createEntityManager();
    em.getTransaction().begin();

    // this changes the publisher back to managed state by
    // returning the managed version of publisher
    publisher = em.merge(publisher);

    book = new Book();
    book.setIsbn("9781430265177");
    book.setName("Beginning Hibernate");
    book.setPrice(new BigDecimal("44.00"));
    book.setPublishdate(Date.valueOf("2014-04-04"));
    book.setPublisher(publisher);

    em.persist(book);
    em.getTransaction().commit();
    em.close();

    em = emf.createEntityManager();
    em.getTransaction().begin();
    book1 = em.find(Book.class, "9781430265177");
    assertEquals(book.getName(), book1.getName());
    assertNotNull(book.getPublisher());
    assertEquals(book.getPublisher().getName(), publisher.getName());
    em.getTransaction().commit();
    em.close();
}
```

Create the publisher object and, when creating the book object with the title *Hibernate Recipes*, set the publisher on the book to the created publisher object. em.persist(book) persists the complete object graph of the publisher and the book. To retrieve the book details from the database, use em.find(Book.class, isbn).

We persist another book with the title *Beginning Hibernate*. Because the same publisher object is used for this book as the first book, now only the new book is inserted. The SQL statements in the Hibernate ouput are shown here.

For book1, *Hibernate Recipes*:

```
Hibernate: insert into PUBLISHER (NAME, ADDRESS, CODE) values (?, ?, ?)

Hibernate: insert into BOOK (NAME, PUBLISHDATE, PRICE, PUBLISHERCODE, ISBN)
values (?, ?, ?, ?, ?)

Hibernate: select book0_.ISBN as ISBN1_0_0_, book0_.NAME as NAME2_0_0_, book0_.
PUBLISHDATE as PUBLISHD3_0_0_, book0_.PRICE as PRICE4_0_0_, book0_.PUBLISHERCODE as
PUBLISHE5_0_0_, publisher1_.CODE as CODE1_1_1_, publisher1_.NAME as NAME2_1_1_, publisher1_.
ADDRESS as ADDRESS3_1_1_ from BOOK book0_ left outer join PUBLISHER publisher1_ on book0_.
PUBLISHERCODE=publisher1_.CODE where book0_.ISBN=?

Hibernate: select publisher0_.CODE as CODE1_1_0_, publisher0_.NAME as NAME2_1_0_,
publisher0_.ADDRESS as ADDRESS3_1_0_ from PUBLISHER publisher0_ where publisher0_.CODE=?
```

You see that there is an insert into the publisher as well.
For book2, *Beginning Hibernate*:

```
Hibernate: insert into BOOK (NAME, PUBLISHDATE, PRICE, PUBLISHERCODE, ISBN)
values (?, ?, ?, ?, ?)

Hibernate: select book0_.ISBN as ISBN1_0_0_, book0_.NAME as NAME2_0_0_, book0_.PUBLISHDATE
as PUBLISHD3_0_0_, book0_.PRICE as PRICE4_0_0_, book0_.PUBLISHERCODE as PUBLISHE5_0_0_,
publisher1_.CODE as CODE1_1_1_, publisher1_.NAME as NAME2_1_1_, publisher1_.ADDRESS
as ADDRESS3_1_1_ from BOOK book0_ left outer join PUBLISHER publisher1_ on book0_.
PUBLISHERCODE=publisher1_.CODE where book0_.ISBN=?
```

1-5. Enabling Logging in Hibernate

Problem

How do you determine what SQL query is being executed by Hibernate? How can you see the Hibernate' internal workings? How do you enable logging to troubleshoot complex issues related to Hibernate?

Solution

You have to enable Hibernate logging in the Hibernate configuration. Hibernate uses Simple Logging Facade for Java (SLF4J) to log various system events. SLF4J, which is distributed as a free software license, abstracts the actual logging framework that an application uses. SLF4J can direct your logging output to several logging frameworks:

- *NOP*: Null logger implementation

- *Simple*: A logging antiframework that is very simple to use and attempts to solve every logging problem in one package

- *Log4j version 1.2*: A widely used open-source logging framework

- *JDK 1.4 logging*: A logging API provided by Java

- *JCL*: An open-source Commons logging framework that provides an interface with thin wrapper implementations for other logging tools

- *Logback*: A serializable logger that logs after its deserialization, depending on the chosen binding

To set up logging, you need the slf4j-api.jar file in your classpath, together with the JAR file for your preferred binding: slf4j-log4j12.jar in the case of log4j. You can also enable a property called showsql to see the exact query being executed. You can configure a logging layer such as Apache log4j to enable Hibernate class- or package-level logging. And you can use the Statistics interface provided by Hibernate to obtain detailed information.

How It Works

You have to configure the Hibernate show_sql property to enable logging.

Inspecting the SQL Statements Issued by Hibernate

Hibernate generates SQL statements that enable you to access the database behind the scene. You can set the show_sql property to true in the hibernate.cfg.xml XML configuration file to print the SQL statements to stdout:

```
<property name="show_sql">true</property>
```

Enabling Live Statistics

You can enable live statistics by setting the hibernate.generate_statistics property in the configuration file:

```
<property name="hibernate.generate_statistics">true</property>
```

You can also access statistics programmatically by using the Statistics interfaces. Hibernate provides SessionStatistics and Statistics interfaces in the org.hibernate.stat package. The following code shows the use of some utility methods:

```
SessionFactory sessionFactory = SessionManager.getSessionFactory();
        session = sessionFactory.openSession();
        SessionStatistics sessionStats = session.getStatistics();
        Statistics stats = sessionFactory.getStatistics();
        tx = session.beginTransaction();
        Publisher publisher = new Publisher();
        publisher.setCode("apress");
        publisher.setName("Apress");
        publisher.setAddress("233 Spring Street, New York, NY 10013");
        session.persist(publisher);
        tx.commit();
        logger.info("getEntityCount- "+sessionStats.getEntityCount());
        logger.info("openCount- "+stats.getSessionOpenCount());
        logger.info("getEntityInsertCount- "+stats.getEntityInsertCount());
        stats.logSummary();
        session.close();
```

The output of this code sample is shown here (the complete log is given for clarity):

```
HCANN000001: Hibernate Commons Annotations {4.0.4.Final}
HHH000412: Hibernate Core {4.3.5.Final}
HHH000206: hibernate.properties not found
HHH000021: Bytecode provider name : javassist
HHH000043: Configuring from resource: /hibernate.cfg.xml
HHH000040: Configuration resource: /hibernate.cfg.xml
HHH000221: Reading mappings from resource: com/apress/hibernaterecipes/chapter1/model/Book.
hbm.xml
HHH000221: Reading mappings from resource: com/apress/hibernaterecipes/chapter1/model/
Publisher.hbm.xml
HHH000041: Configured SessionFactory: null
HHH000402: Using Hibernate built-in connection pool (not for production use!)
HHH000401: using driver [org.hsqldb.jdbcDriver] at URL [jdbc:hsqldb:file:./chapter1;write_
delay=false]
HHH000046: Connection properties: {}
HHH000006: Autocommit mode: false
HHH000115: Hibernate connection pool size: 20 (min=1)
HHH000400: Using dialect: org.hibernate.dialect.HSQLDialect
HHH000399: Using default transaction strategy (direct JDBC transactions)
HHH000397: Using ASTQueryTranslatorFactory
HHH000227: Running hbm2ddl schema export
HHH000230: Schema export complete
Session Metrics {
    14000 nanoseconds spent acquiring 1 JDBC connections;
    0 nanoseconds spent releasing 0 JDBC connections;
    2445000 nanoseconds spent preparing 2 JDBC statements;
    1636000 nanoseconds spent executing 2 JDBC statements;
    0 nanoseconds spent executing 0 JDBC batches;
    0 nanoseconds spent performing 0 L2C puts;
    0 nanoseconds spent performing 0 L2C hits;
    0 nanoseconds spent performing 0 L2C misses;
    0 nanoseconds spent executing 0 flushes (flushing a total of 0 entities and 0
collections);
    59000 nanoseconds spent executing 2 partial-flushes (flushing a total of 0 entities
and 0 collections)
}
getEntityCount- 1
openCount- 2
getEntityInsertCount- 1
HHH000161: Logging statistics....
HHH000251: Start time: 1408349026472
HHH000242: Sessions opened: 2
HHH000241: Sessions closed: 1
HHH000266: Transactions: 2
HHH000258: Successful transactions: 2
HHH000187: Optimistic lock failures: 0
HHH000105: Flushes: 1
HHH000048: Connections obtained: 2
HHH000253: Statements prepared: 3
```

```
HHH000252: Statements closed: 0
HHH000239: Second level cache puts: 0
HHH000237: Second level cache hits: 0
HHH000238: Second level cache misses: 0
HHH000079: Entities loaded: 0
HHH000080: Entities updated: 0
HHH000078: Entities inserted: 1
HHH000076: Entities deleted: 0
HHH000077: Entities fetched (minimize this): 0
HHH000033: Collections loaded: 0
HHH000036: Collections updated: 0
HHH000035: Collections removed: 0
HHH000034: Collections recreated: 0
HHH000032: Collections fetched (minimize this): 0
HHH000438: NaturalId cache puts: 0
HHH000439: NaturalId cache hits: 0
HHH000440: NaturalId cache misses: 0
HHH000441: Max NaturalId query time: 0ms
HHH000442: NaturalId queries executed to database: 0
HHH000210: Queries executed to database: 0
HHH000215: Query cache puts: 0
HHH000433: update timestamps cache puts: 0
HHH000434: update timestamps cache hits: 0
HHH000435: update timestamps cache misses: 0
HHH000213: Query cache hits: 0
HHH000214: Query cache misses: 0
HHH000173: Max query time: 0ms
Session Metrics {
    5000 nanoseconds spent acquiring 1 JDBC connections;
    0 nanoseconds spent releasing 0 JDBC connections;
    262000 nanoseconds spent preparing 1 JDBC statements;
    828000 nanoseconds spent executing 1 JDBC statements;
    0 nanoseconds spent executing 0 JDBC batches;
    0 nanoseconds spent performing 0 L2C puts;
    0 nanoseconds spent performing 0 L2C hits;
    0 nanoseconds spent performing 0 L2C misses;
    8131000 nanoseconds spent executing 1 flushes (flushing a total of 1 entities and 0 collections);
    0 nanoseconds spent executing 0 partial-flushes (flushing a total of 0 entities and 0 collections)
}
```

Summary

This chapter discussed' object/relational mapping and what its benefits are over JDBC. Hibernate is one of the most widely used ORM frameworks in the industry. Using JDBC directly has many disadvantages, including complicated handling of the `ResultSet` and the fact that it isn't portable against different databases. To overcome these issues, you can use ORM for ease of development and to maintain software efficiently.

To configure Hibernate, you need various third-party JAR files that must be specified in the classpath. The configuration to map objects to tables and other details such as connection to databases is done by either using annotations or `.hibernate.cfg.xml` Hibernate Annotations that implement the Java persistence standards defined by the JPA 2.0 specification. You use `org.hibernate.SessionFactory` to create `org.hibernate.Session` objects that represent work units. Other database operations are performed by using the `Session` object.

You can use the `EntityManager` defined by JPA specification to begin, commit, and close transactions. The `EntityManager` uses the `persistence.xml` file for configuration.

■ ■ ■

Basic Mapping and Object Identity

A primary key in a database table is used to uniquely identify a record in that table. The primary key value can't be null and is unique within a table. The primary key is also used to establish a relationship between two tables; it is defined as a foreign key in the associated table. Because the primary key is used to identify a particular record, it can also be called the *database identifier*, which is exposed to the application by Hibernate through an identifier property of the persistent entity. This chapter discusses the various ways to generate an identifier (primary key) for a database record. You learn about metadata configurations and their effect on the persistence mechanism.

First, we discuss creating entities with annotations. Chapter 1 discussed Hibernate configurations using XML; in this chapter, we configure Hibernate mappings within entity classes by using annotations.

2-0. Using JPA Annotations

Problem

How do you manage the metadata required for object/relational mapping (ORM)? Can you use any mechanism other than specifying the metadata in XML files? How do you configure a Hibernate project to use annotations?

Solution

The JPA 2.0 specification defines the Java Persistence API (JPA), which provides ORM using a Java domain model to manage a relational database. Different providers implement this API:

- *TopLink*: A Java ORM solution currently owned by Oracle. See the following web site for more details about TopLink: `www.oracle.com/technology/products/ias/toplink/index.html`.

- *Java Data Objects (JDO)*: A standard interface–based Java model abstraction of persistence developed by the Java Community Process. The current JDO 2.0 is Java Specification Request 243. Beginning with JDO 2.0, the development of the API is taking place within Apache JDO open source.

- *Hibernate*: A very popular ORM framework. Hibernate provides Hibernate Annotations, which implement JPA standards and provide more-advanced mapping features. We will demonstrate configuring a project that uses JPA annotations and Hibernate Annotations.

How It Works

No additional JAR files are required for annotations. The Hibernate Annotations JAR file is added automatically with the Hibernate-core dependency in pom.xml. The classes required for JPA annotations also are added. Generally, JPA annotations are used. For annotations that are not defined in JPA, we use Hibernate Annotations such as GenericGenerator for enhanced ID generators that were introduced in Hibernate 4.

When we use annotations, we do not need the .hbm files, but we still have to use the persistence.xml or hibernate.cfg file. (Refer to Chapter 1 for recipes for each of these configurations.)

Configure the session factory in the hibernate.cfg.xml file or the persistence unit in the persistence.xmlfile. (Note that if you change the name of this file to anything other than hibernate.cfg.xml, you must upload the file programmatically.) The dialect property defines the name of the database, which enables Hibernate to generate SQL optimized for a particular relational database.

H2 is the database in this case, so use the org.hibernate.dialect.H2Dialect property. Also, if you change the database—from H2 to Oracle, for example—you must change the value from org.hibernate. dialect.H2Dialect to org.hibernate.dialect.Oracle9Dialect. This process is the way portability is achieved using Hibernate.

Some of the common dialects that Hibernate supports are as follows:

- DB2Dialect (supports DB2)
- FrontBaseDialect
- HSQLDialect
- InformixDialect
- IngresDialect
- InterbaseDialect
- MySQLDialect
- Oracle8Dialect
- Oracle9Dialect
- Oracle10Dialect
- PointbaseDialect
- PostgreSQLDialect
- ProgressDialect
- ProgressDialect
- SybaseDialect

Here is a sample of persistence.xml when using annotations:

```
<persistence-unit name="chapter2" transaction-type="RESOURCE_LOCAL">
    <properties>
        <property name="javax.persistence.jdbc.driver" value="org.h2.Driver"/>
        <property name="javax.persistence.jdbc.url" value="jdbc:h2:file:./
        chapter2jpa;write_delay=false"/>
        <property name="hibernate.dialect" value="org.hibernate.dialect.H2Dialect"/>
        <property name="hibernate.hbm2ddl.auto" value="create"/>
        <property name="hibernate.show_sql" value="false"/>
    </properties>
</persistence-unit>
```

If you see the persistence.xml file, you don't have to configure the entity classes. Because the classes are annotated, they are recognized as entities representing the tables given in the annotation.

Here's a sample hibernate.cfg file when using annotations:

```xml
<?xml version="1.0" encoding="UTF-8"?>
<!DOCTYPE hibernate-configuration PUBLIC
"-//Hibernate/Hibernate Configuration DTD 3.0//EN"
        "http://www.hibernate.org/dtd/hibernate-configuration-3.0.dtd">
<hibernate-configuration>
        <session-factory>
                <property name="connection.driver_class">org.h2.Driver</property>
                <property name="connection.url">jdbc:h2:file:./chapter2</property>
                <property name="connection.username">sa</property>
                <property name="connection.password"></property>
                <property name="dialect">org.hibernate.dialect.H2Dialect</property>
                <property name="hbm2ddl.auto">create</property>
                <property name="show_sql">true</property>
                <mapping package="com.apress.hibernaterecipes.chapter2.recipe0"/>
                <mapping class="com.apress.hibernaterecipes.chapter2.recipe0.Product"/>
        </session-factory>
</hibernate-configuration>
```

When you use annotations, you don't need the additional mapping file (*.hbm.xml); the metadata for the ORM is specified in the individual classes. You have to add the class mapping only in the hibernate.cfg.xml file. In the previous example, the following line took care of the class mapping:

```xml
<mapping class="com.apress.hibernaterecipes.chapter2.recipe0.Product"/>
```

Next, look at the Product.java file, with annotations for the table name, column names, and other attributes:

```java
@Entity
@Table(name="Product")
public class Product {
    @Id
    long sku;
    @Column
    String title;
    @Column
    String description;

    public long getSku() {
        return sku;
    }

    public void setSku(long id) {
        this.sku = id;
    }

    public String getTitle() {
        return title;
    }
```

```
    public void setTitle(String title) {
        this.title = title;
    }

    public String getDescription() {
        return description;
    }

    public void setDescription(String description) {
        this.description = description;
    }
}
```

The @Entity annotation is defined by the JPA 2.0 specification to annotate an entity bean. An *entity* represents a lightweight persistent domain object or a Plain Old Java Object (POJO). If you are an EJB2.x user and are migrating to Hibernate, the entities are not remotable. The entity object can be allocated with new persistence storage, or it can be attached, detached, and reattached to persistence storage. The entities can be accessed through the JPA javax.persistence.EntityManager or the Hibernate org.hibernate.Session object.

An entity class must have a public or protected no-arg constructor, and it can have other constructors as well. It should be a top-level class and must not be final. If the entity is to be passed by value (that is, through a remote interface), it must implement a Serializable interface.

The state of the entity is represented by the entity's instance variables, which must be accessed only from within the entity class. The client of the entity should not be able to directly access the state of the entity. The instance variables must have private, protected, or package visibility. Every entity must have a primary key that must be declared only once in the entity hierarchy.

You can generate the set and get methods using the Eclipse integrated development environment (IDE). Select the instance variables for which you need to generate the methods, right-click the selection, and select Source ➤ Generate Getters and Setters. Doing so displays all the variables for which the methods must be generated. Select the required variables and click OK. The getter and setter are generated in your source code.

In the previous class, the name of the Product table is specified with the name attribute of the Table annotation. The sku variable is the primary key, which is specified by the @Id tag. The rest of the columns are specified by the @column annotation. If the @column annotation is not specified, the names of the instance variables are considered column names. Every nonstatic and nontransient property of an entity bean is considered persistent unless you specify @Transient. @Transient properties are ignored by the EntityManager when you map persistent properties.

2-1. Providing an ID for Persistence
Problem

How do you generate an identifier for a database entity? What are possible strategies?

Solution

An ID element (<id>) is used to create a mapping in the Hibernate XML file. The ID element has attributes such as column, type, and generator that you use to generate the identifier. The JPA specification requires that every entity must have a primary key. From the JPA perspective, an @id attribute is used to define how an identifier is generated.

When you use inheritance mapping, more than one class can be mapped to a table. These classes (subclass and superclass) are said to be in an *entity hierarchy*. The primary key must be defined exactly once in an entity hierarchy, either on the entity that is the root of the entity hierarchy or on a mapped superclass of the entity hierarchy. Attributes such as @GeneratedValue and @Column are used to define column mapping and strategy.

How It Works

You have to ask Hibernate to generate this ID for you before persisting to the database. Hibernate provides many built-in strategies for ID generation:

- Database sequence
- Native generator
- Increment generator
- Hilo generator

Some of these strategies are available only for specified databases; for instance, the sequence strategy is not supported in MYSQL, but it is provided by Oracle. JPA also provides a way to generate identifiers.

We look at each of these strategies in turn, starting with the database sequence. We have created one class for each identifier and we insert about ten records into each of these entities. The test code is the following:

```
public class Recipe1Test {
    @DataProvider(name = "idClassNames")
    Object[][] getClassNames() {
        return new Object[][]{
                {"com.apress.hibernaterecipes.chapter2.recipe1.AutoIdEntity",},
                {"com.apress.hibernaterecipes.chapter2.recipe1.HiloIdEntity",},
                {"com.apress.hibernaterecipes.chapter2.recipe1.IdentityIdEntity",},
                {"com.apress.hibernaterecipes.chapter2.recipe1.IncrementIdEntity",},
                {"com.apress.hibernaterecipes.chapter2.recipe1.SequenceIdEntity",},
                {"com.apress.hibernaterecipes.chapter2.recipe1.TableIdEntity",},
                {"com.apress.hibernaterecipes.chapter2.recipe1.UUIDIdEntity",},
                {"com.apress.hibernaterecipes.chapter2.recipe1.SequenceStyleIdEntity",},
                {"com.apress.hibernaterecipes.chapter2.recipe1.EnhancedTableIdEntity",},
        };
    }

    /**
     * This method generates forty entities, in ten batches of four. As it
     * generates them, it stores the generated identities in a Set, for
     * validation of uniqueness (which shouldn't be a problem) and for simple
     * visual verification purposes.
     *
     * @param className the entity type to generate
     */
```

```
@Test(dataProvider = "idClassNames")
public void testGeneration(String className) throws Exception {
    Set<Object> generatedKeys = new HashSet<>();
    System.out.println("Testing: " + className);
    Class<?> entityType = Class.forName(className);
    Field idField = entityType.getDeclaredField("id");
    Field fieldField = entityType.getDeclaredField("field");

    for (int i = 0; i < 10; i++) {
        Session session = SessionManager.getSessionFactory().openSession();
        Transaction tx = session.beginTransaction();
        for (int j = 0; j < 4; j++) {
            Object o = entityType.newInstance();
            fieldField.set(o, "" + (char) ('a' + i) + (char) ('b' + j));
            session.persist(o);
            generatedKeys.add(idField.get(o));
        }
        tx.commit();
        session.close();
    }
    for (Object key : generatedKeys) {
        System.out.println(key);
    }
    assertEquals(generatedKeys.size(), 40);
}
}
```

Using the Database Sequence

The most common way to generate an ID uses an autoincremented sequence number. For some kinds of databases, including the Hyper Structured Query Language Database (HSQLDB), you can use a sequence/generator to generate this sequence number. (HSQLDB is a relational database management system written in Java; it supports a large subset of SQL-92 and SQL-2003 standards.) This strategy is called a *sequence* strategy.

We use SequenceIdEntity.java and the @GeneratedValue(strategy = GenerationType.SEQUENCE) annotation:

```
@Entity
public class SequenceIdEntity {
    @Id
    @GeneratedValue(strategy = GenerationType.SEQUENCE)
    public Long id;
    @Column
    public String field;

    public long getId() {
        return id;
    }

    public void setId(long id) {
        this.id = id;
    }
```

```
public String getField() {
    return field;
}

public void setField(String field) {
    this.field = field;
}
}
```

Annotations are the preferred way of development over XML mapping. If you are using XML mapping, however, you can add the following to the <id> tag to specify the generator:

```
<id name="id" column="id" type="long">
    <generator class="sequence">
            <param name="sequence">ID_SEQUENCE</param>
    </generator>
</id>
```

If no sequence name is specified, hibernate_sequence is created.

Using an Increment Generator

The increment generator reads the maximum primary key column value from the table and increments the value by one. It is not advisable to use it when the application is deployed in a cluster of servers because each server generates an ID and it might conflict with the generation on the other server. The increment generator is not available in JPA.

IncrementIdEntity: The following class demonstrates the use of increment strategy for ID generation.

```
@Entity
public class IncrementIdEntity {
    @Id
    @GeneratedValue(generator = "increment")
    public Long id;
    @Column
    public String field;

    public long getId() {
        return id;
    }

    public void setId(long id) {
        this.id = id;
    }

    public String getField() {
        return field;
    }

    public void setField(String field) {
        this.field = field;
    }
}
```

The Identifier is of type long, short, or int.

Using the increment generator, the primary key of the table in which the record is created is incremented, and the database sequence is incremented by using the sequence generator. You can also use a sequence to generate a primary key for multiple tables, whereas an increment generator can be used only to create a primary key for its own table.

Following is the output when you execute the test with IncrementIdEntity:

```
Hibernate: create table IncrementIdEntity (id bigint not null, field varchar(255), primary key (id))
Hibernate: select max(id) from IncrementIdEntity
Hibernate: insert into IncrementIdEntity (field, id) values (?, ?)
```

Once the IncrementIdEntity table is generated by the create statement, the next statement (select max(id) from IncrementIdEntity) selects the maximum value of the ID column. This value is incremented, and when the insert statement is executed, the value is assigned to the ID column.

Using the Hilo Generator

The hilo generator uses the hi/lo algorithm to generate the identifiers that are unique to a particular database. It retrieves the high value from a global source (by default, the hibernate_unique_key table and next_hi column), and the low value from a local source. The max_lo value option is provided to define how many low values are added before a high value is fetched. The two values are added to generate a unique identifier.

HiloIdEntity: The following class uses the hilo for the ID generator:

```java
@Entity
public class HiloIdEntity {
    @Id
    @GeneratedValue(generator = "hilo")
    public Long id;
    @Column
    public String field;

    public long getId() {
        return id;
    }

    public void setId(long id) {
        this.id = id;
    }

    public String getField() {
        return field;
    }

    public void setField(String field) {
        this.field = field;
    }
}
```

The hilo generator is of type long. This generator should *not* be used with a user-supplied connection. The high value *must* be fetched in a separate transaction from the Session transaction, so the generator must be able to obtain a new connection and commit it. Hence, this implementation cannot be used when the user is supplying connections. In that case, a SequenceHiLoGenerator is a better choice (where supported).

The hilo generator is used for batch operations. When Hibernate is using an application server data source to obtain connections enlisted with JTA, you must properly configure the hibernate.transaction. manager_lookup_property, which is the class name of a theTransactionManagerLookup class.

The following is the output of the hilo test case:

```
Hibernate: create table HiloIdEntity (id bigint not null, field varchar(255), primary key (id))
Hibernate: create table hibernate_unique_key ( next_hi integer )
Hibernate: insert into hibernate_unique_key values ( 0 )
Hibernate: select next_hi from hibernate_unique_key for update
Hibernate: update hibernate_unique_key set next_hi = ? where next_hi = ?
Hibernate: insert into HiloIdEntity (field, id) values (?, ?)
```

Enhanced Sequence Style Generator

This generator is one of the enhanced generators introduced for better portability and optimization. Although it is similar to the native generator, the native generator chooses between identity and sequence to generate the identifiers, and the sequence style generator chooses between a table and a sequence to store the increment values. Because the semantics of the table and sequence are the same, portability is achieved.

Optimization allows you to query a bunch of identifiers at a time and store them in local memory. Once they have been exhausted, the database can be queried for the next group of identifiers, which avoids making a call to the database for every new identifier.

Use the GenericGenerator tag for these enhanced generators:

```
@GeneratedValue( generator="IdGen")
@GenericGenerator(strategy="org.hibernate.id.enhanced.SequenceStyleGenerator",name="IdGen",
                parameters = {
        @Parameter(name = "sequence_name", value = "seq_id_gen"),
                @Parameter(name = "optimizer", value = "pooled"),
        @Parameter(name = "initial_value", value = "1000"),
        @Parameter(name = "increment_size", value = "10")
        })
```

The following SequenceStyleIdEntity object uses the IdGen generator. A sequence with the name seq_id_gen is created in the database. If the name is not specified, a sequence with the name hibernate_ sequence is generated by default. The initial value is set to 1000 and the increment size is 10. The optimizer values can be one of the following:

- none does not perform any optimizations and hits the database for every new identifier

- hilo generates the identifiers according to the hi/lo algorithm

- pooled stores the high value in the series as the nextval

- pooled-lo stores the low value in the series as the nextval

```
@Entity
public class SequenceStyleIdEntity {

    @Id
    @GeneratedValue( generator="IdGen")
@GenericGenerator(strategy="org.hibernate.id.enhanced.SequenceStyleGenerator",name="IdGen",
                    parameters = {
            @Parameter(name = "sequence_name", value = "seq_id_gen"),
                        @Parameter(name = "optimizer", value = "pooled"),
            @Parameter(name = "initial_value", value = "1000"),
            @Parameter(name = "increment_size", value = "10")
            })

    public Long id;
    @Column
    public String field;

    public long getId() {
        return id;
    }

    public void setId(long id) {
        this.id = id;
    }

    public String getField() {
        return field;
    }

    public void setField(String field) {
        this.field = field;
    }
}
```

After executing the test for SequenceStyleIdGenerator, the following is the output:

```
Hibernate: create table SequenceStyleIdEntity (id bigint not null, field varchar(255),
primary key (id))
Hibernate: create sequence seq_id_gen start with 1000 increment by 10
Hibernate: call next value for seq_id_gen
Hibernate: call next value for seq_id_gen
Hibernate: insert into SequenceStyleIdEntity (field, id) values (?, ?)
```

Enhanced Table Generator

The second of the enhanced generators is the table generator: `org.hibernate.id.enhanced.TableGenerator`. This generator defines a table that holds the increment values, and the same table can be used by multiple applications for the increment values. Each application is distinguished by the key value.

Here is the configuration:

```
@GeneratedValue( generator="TableIdGen")
@GenericGenerator(strategy="org.hibernate.id.enhanced.TableGenerator",name="TableIdGen",
        parameters = {
            @Parameter(name = "table_name", value = "enhanced_hibernate_sequences"),
            @Parameter(name = "segment_value", value = "id"),
            @Parameter(name = "optimizer", value = "pooled"),
            @Parameter(name = "initial_value", value = "1000"),
            @Parameter(name = "increment_size", value = "10")
        })
```

This configuration uses the GenericGenerator annotation. The segment_value is the key that identifies the object for which increment values are being stored. By default, a table named hibernate_sequences is generated, and the increment values are stored in this table. This same table can be used by another Person object:

```
@GeneratedValue( generator=" TableIdGen ")
@GenericGenerator(strategy="org.hibernate.id.enhanced.TableGenerator",name=" TableIdGen ",
            parameters = {
            @Parameter(name = "table_name", value = "enhanced_hibernate_sequences"),

            @Parameter(name = "segment_value", value = "person_id"),
            @Parameter(name = "optimizer", value = "pooled"),
            @Parameter(name = "initial_value", value = "1000"),
            @Parameter(name = "increment_size", value = "10")
})
```

EnhancedTableIdEntity class: The following class demonstrates how the EnhancedTableId generator is used.

```
@Entity
public class EnhancedTableIdEntity {

    @Id
    @GeneratedValue( generator="TableIdGen")
        @GenericGenerator(strategy="org.hibernate.id.enhanced.TableGenerator",name="TableIdGen",
                        parameters = {
                        @Parameter(name = "table_name", value = "enhanced_hibernate_sequences"),
            @Parameter(name = "segment_value", value = "id"),
            @Parameter(name = "optimizer", value = "pooled"),
            @Parameter(name = "initial_value", value = "1000"),
            @Parameter(name = "increment_size", value = "10")
            })
    public Long id;
    @Column
    public String field;

    public long getId() {
        return id;
    }
}
```

```
    public void setId(long id) {
        this.id = id;
    }

    public String getField() {
        return field;
    }

    public void setField(String field) {
        this.field = field;
    }
}
```

Following is the output of the EnhancedTabledId generator test case:

```
Hibernate: create table EnhancedTableIdEntity (id bigint not null, field varchar(255),
primary key (id))
Hibernate: create table enhanced_hibernate_sequences ( sequence_name varchar(255) not null ,
next_val bigint, primary key ( sequence_name ) )
Hibernate: select tbl.next_val from enhanced_hibernate_sequences tbl where
tbl.sequence_name=? for update
Hibernate: insert into enhanced_hibernate_sequences (sequence_name, next_val) values (?,?)
Hibernate: update enhanced_hibernate_sequences set next_val=?  where next_val=? and
sequence_name=?
Hibernate: select tbl.next_val from enhanced_hibernate_sequences tbl where
tbl.sequence_name=? for update
Hibernate: update enhanced_hibernate_sequences set next_val=?  where next_val=? and
sequence_name=?
Hibernate: insert into EnhancedTableIdEntity (field, id) values (?, ?)
```

2-2. Creating a Composite Key in Hibernate

Problem

How do you create a composite key in Hibernate?

Solution

A table with a composite key can be mapped with multiple properties of the class as identifier properties.
The <composite-id> element accepts <key-property> property mappings and <key-many-to-one>
mappings as child elements. The persistent class must override the equals() and hashCode() method to
implement composite identifier equality. It must also implement the Serializable interface.

How It Works

In some cases, you can use Hibernate to access a legacy database that includes tables by using a *composite key* (a primary key composed of multiple columns). With this kind of legacy table, it is not easy to add an ID column for use as primary key. Suppose that you have a legacy Employee table that was created with the following SQL statement:

```
create table Employee (department bigint not null, idCard bigint not null, name varchar(255)
not null, primary key (department, idCard))
```

You input some data for this table using the following SQL statement:

```
INSERT INTO Employee (department, idCard, name ) VALUES (1, 100, 'Gary', 'Mak');
```

For the object model, you develop the following persistent class for the Employee table:

```java
public class Employee {
  private long department;
  private long idCard;
  private String name;
  // Getters and Setters
}
```

There are three ways to implement a composite identifier:

- Multiple ID properties declared within the entity

- Multiple ID properties as identifier type

- Composite ID as a property using a component type

Multiple ID Properties Declared Within the Entity

Using annotations, you can declare the department and idCard fields as IDs:

```java
@Entity
public class Employee {
    @Id
    Long department;
    @Id
    Long idCard;
    @Column(unique = true, nullable = false)
    String name;

    public Employee(Long department, Long idCard, String name) {
        this.department = department;
        this.idCard = idCard;
        this.name = name;
    }

    public Employee() {
    }
//Getters and setters
}
```

In a mapping file, you can use <composite-id> to define the object ID, which consists of two properties: department and idCard:

```
<hibernate-mapping>
  <class name="Emplyee" table="Employee">
    <composite-id>
      <key-property name="department" type="long" column="department" />
      <key-property name="idCard" type="long" column="idCard "/>
    </composite-id>
    <property name="name" type="string" column=" NAME" />
  </class>
</hibernate-mapping>
```

This method of implementing a composite identifier is not a standard, although Hibernate supports it.

Multiple ID Properties as an Identifier Type

When you use the load() or get() method to retrieve a specified object from the database, you need to provide that object's ID. Which type of object should be passed as the ID? At the moment, you can pass a newly created Employee object with department and idCard set. Note that Hibernate requires any ID class to implement the java.io.Serializable interface:

```
public class Employee implements Serializable {
    ...
}
Employee employeeId = new Employee();
employee.setDepartment(2);
employee.setIdCard (200);
Employee employee = (Employee) session.get(Employee.class, employeeId);
```

It does not make sense to pass a whole persistent object as the ID. A better way is to extract the fields that form the ID as a separate class:

```
public class EmployeeId implements Serializable {
    Long department;
    Long idCard;

    public EmployeeId() {
    }

    public EmployeeId(Long department, Long idCard) {
        this.department = department;
        this.idCard = idCard;
    }

    public Long getDepartment() {
        return department;
    }

    public void setDepartment(Long department) {
        this.department = department;
    }
```

```java
    public Long getIdCard() {
        return idCard;
    }

    public void setIdCard(Long idCard) {
        this.idCard = idCard;
    }

    @Override
    public boolean equals(Object o) {
        if (this == o) return true;
        if (o == null || getClass() != o.getClass()) return false;

        EmployeeId that = (EmployeeId) o;

        if (!department.equals(that.department)) return false;
        if (!idCard.equals(that.idCard)) return false;

        return true;
    }

    @Override
    public int hashCode() {
        int result = department.hashCode();
        result = 31 * result + idCard.hashCode();
        return result;
    }
}
```

Modify the Employee persistent class to use this new ID class:

```java
@Entity
@IdClass(EmployeeId.class)
public class Employee {
    @Id
    Long department;
    @Id
    Long idCard;
    @Column(unique = true, nullable = false)
    String name;

    public Employee(Long department, Long idCard, String name) {
        this.department = department;
        this.idCard = idCard;
        this.name = name;
    }

    public Employee() {
    }
```

```java
    public Long getDepartment() {
        return department;
    }

    public void setDepartment(Long department) {
        this.department = department;
    }

    public Long getIdCard() {
        return idCard;
    }

    public void setIdCard(Long idCard) {
        this.idCard = idCard;
    }

    public String getName() {
        return name;
    }

    public void setName(String name) {
        this.name = name;
    }

}
```

In this case, the department and idCard attributes are declared as IDs in the Employee class. An external class called EmployeeId is created with the same ID property names and types as in the Employee class and is annotated as @IdClass in the Employee object.

The mapping definition should also be modified to use the ID class:

```xml
<hibernate-mapping>
  <class name="Employee" table="employee">
    <composite-id name="id" class=" Employee Id">
      <key-property name="department" type="string" column="department" />
      <key-property name="idCard" type="string" column="IDCARD " />
    </composite-id>
    <property name="name" type="string" column=" NAME" />
  </class>
</hibernate-mapping>
```

To retrieve an Employee object, you need to specify the ID. This time, pass in an instance of EmployeeId type:

```java
EmployeeId employeeId = new EmployeeId(1,1000);
Employee employee = (Employee) session.get(Employee.class, employeeId);
```

To persist an Employee object, use an instance of EmployeeId type as its ID:

```java
Employee employee = new Employee(1,1, 'Joseph Ottinger');
session.save(employee);
```

For Hibernate caching to work correctly, you need to override the equals() and hashCode() methods of the custom ID class. The equals() method is used to compare two objects for equality, and the hashCode() method provides an object's hashcode. You use EqualsBuilder and HashCodeBuilder to simplify the equals() and hashCode() implementations. These classes are provided by the Apache Commons Lang library; you can download it from http://commons.apache.org/proper/commons-lang/download_lang.cgi. After you download the library, include commons-lang-2.1.jar in your project's Java build path.

Composite ID as a Property Using a Component Type

Using this method, the IDs are declared in an external class that is annotated as embeddable in the entity. We will look at the Book sample. A book is identified by its ISBN, which is defined by the group, publisher, titleRef, and checkDigit attributes:

The ISBN class is defined as follows:

```
@Embeddable
public class ISBN implements Serializable {
    @Column(name = "group_number")
    int group;
    int publisher;
    int titleRef;
    int checkDigit;

    public ISBN() {
    }

    public ISBN(int group, int publisher, int titleRef, int checkDigit) {
        this.group = group;
        this.publisher = publisher;
        this.titleRef = titleRef;
        this.checkDigit = checkDigit;
    }

    public ISBN(int ean, int group, int publisher, int titleRef, int checkDigit) {
        this(group, publisher, titleRef, checkDigit);
    }

    //Getter and setters

    @Override
    public boolean equals(Object o) {
        if (this == o) return true;
        if (!(o instanceof ISBN)) return false;

        ISBN isbn = (ISBN) o;

        if (checkDigit != isbn.checkDigit) return false;
        if (group != isbn.group) return false;
        if (publisher != isbn.publisher) return false;
        if (titleRef != isbn.titleRef) return false;

        return true;
    }
```

```
    @Override
    public int hashCode() {
        int result = group;
        result = 31 * result + publisher;
        result = 31 * result + titleRef;
        result = 31 * result + checkDigit;
        return result;
    }
}
```

The Book entity is defined as follows:

```
@Entity
public class Book {
    @Id
    ISBN id;
    @Column
    String title;

    public Book() {
    }

    public Book(int ean, int group, int publisher, int titleRef, int checkDigit, String
title) {
        // ean is ignored; it's always 978.
        id = new ISBN(ean, group, publisher, titleRef, checkDigit);
        this.title = title;
    }

    public ISBN getId() {
        return id;
    }

    public void setId(ISBN id) {
        this.id = id;
    }

    public String getTitle() {
        return title;
    }

    public void setTitle(String title) {
        this.title = title;
    }
}
```

This is the preferred way of defining a composite key.

2-3. saveOrUpdate() in Hibernate

Problem

How do save and update work for the saveOrUpdate() method in Hibernate?

Solution

Hibernate provides a saveOrUpdate() method for persisting objects, which determines whether an object should be saved or updated. It is also very useful for transitive object persistence, so when you use saveOrUpdate(), Hibernate checks to see whether the object is transient (it has no identifier property); if so, Hibernate makes it persistent by generating the identifier and assigning it to a session. If the object already has an identifier, it performs update():

```
session.saveOrUpdate(MapEntry);
```

MapEntry is an entity with just the key and value columns.

How It Works

If a persistent object using an autogenerated ID type is passed to the saveOrUpdate() method with an empty ID value, it is treated as a new object that should be inserted into the database. Hibernate first generates an ID for this object and then issues an INSERT statement. Otherwise, if the ID value is not empty, Hibernate treats it as an existing object and issues an UPDATE statement for it.

How does Hibernate treat an ID as empty? For the Book class, the isbn type is a primitive long data type. You should assign a number as the unsaved value. Typically, "0" is chosen as unsaved because it is the default value for the long data type, but it is a problem that you can't have an object whose ID value is really "0":

```
<id name="isbn" type="long" column="ISBN" unsaved-value="0">
  <generator class="native"/>
</id>
```

The solution to this problem is to use a primitive wrapper class as your ID type (java.lang.Long, in this case). Then null is treated as the unsaved value.

In the MapEntry entity, the ID is a string:

```
@Entity
public class MapEntry {
    @Id
    String key;
    @Column
    String value;

    public MapEntry() {
    }

    public MapEntry(String key, String value) {
        this.key = key;
        this.value = value;
    }
```

```
public String getKey() {
    return key;
}

public void setKey(String key) {
    this.key = key;
}

public String getValue() {
    return value;
}

public void setValue(String value) {
    this.value = value;
}
}
```

The following code creates a new key-value pair:

```
MapEntry mapEntry = new MapEntry("key1", "value1");
session.saveOrUpdate(mapEntry);
```

The saveOrUpdate() method inserts "key1" and "value1". For the same key, the value is updated to "value2". The saveOrUpdate() method updates the value of "value1" to "value2".

```
mapEntry1 = new MapEntry("key1", "value2");
session.saveOrUpdate(mapEntry1);
```

2-4. Dynamic SQL Generation in Hibernate
Problem

What does dynamic SQL generation mean? Why do you need to enable it and how do you do so?

Solution

On application startup, Hibernate creates SQL statements for each of its persistent classes. That means Hibernate creates SQL statements for the Create, Read, Update, and Delete (CRUD) operations, but doesn't execute these statements. So, on application startup, an insert statement (create), a delete, a read, and an update are created. The update statement is created to update every field. At runtime, if the value isn't changed, it is updated with the old value. The CRUD statements are cached in memory by Hibernate.

Dynamic SQL generation means turning off this Hibernate feature. You may want to do so because the feature can mean a longer startup time for the application. The amount of time depends on the number of entity classes in the application. Caching these SQL statements in memory can impact the performance of sensitive applications more in terms of unnecessary memory.

How It Works

For the class element, add the dynamic-insert and dynamic-update attributes and set them to true. The Book.xml mapping file becomes the following:

```xml
<?xml version="1.0" encoding="UTF-8"?>
<!DOCTYPE hibernate-mapping PUBLIC
"-//Hibernate/Hibernate Mapping DTD 3.0//EN"
"http://hibernate.sourceforge.net/hibernate-mapping-3.0.dtd">
<hibernate-mapping package="com.hibernaterecipes.chapter2" auto-import="false">
  <class name="BookCh2" table="BOOK" dynamic-insert="true" dynamic-update="true">
    <id column="isbn" type="long">
      <generator class="native">
      </generator>
    </id>
    <property name="name" type="string" column="BOOK_NAME" />
    <property name="publishDate" type="date" column="PUBLISH_DATE" />
    <property name="price" type="int" column="PRICE" />
  </class>
</hibernate-mapping>
```

The annotation used is @DynamicInsert, with @DynamicUpdate at the class level.

With the dynamic-insert property set to true, Hibernate does *not* include null values for properties (for properties that are not set by the application) during an INSERT operation. With the dynamic-update property set to true, Hibernate does *not* include unmodified properties in the UPDATE operation.

There are two entities: StandardSQLEnity and DynamicSQLEntity. In the StandardSQLEntity, the dynamicInsert is not set.

```java
import lombok.Data;

import javax.persistence.Column;
import javax.persistence.Entity;
import javax.persistence.GeneratedValue;
import javax.persistence.Id;

@Entity
@Data
public class StandardSQLEntity {
    @Id
    @GeneratedValue
    Long id;
    @Column
    String field1, field2, field3, field4, field5, field6, field7, field8;

}
```

When the value for only "field1" is set:

```
StandardSQLEntity standardSQLEntity = new StandardSQLEntity();
            standardSQLEntity.setField1("field 1");
    session.save(standardSQLEntity);
```

the insert statement looks like this:

```
insert into StandardSQLEntity (id, field1, field2, field3, field4, field5, field6, field7,
field8) values (null, ?, ?, ?, ?, ?, ?, ?, ?)
```

Although fields 2-7 are not set, they are inserted with default values.
Now look at DynamicSQLEntity with dynamicInsert set to true:

```
@Entity
@DynamicInsert
public @Data class DynamicSQLEntity {
    @Id
    @GeneratedValue
    Long id;
    @Column
    String field1, field2, field3, field4, field5, field6, field7, field8;
//Getters and Setters
}
```

If only "field1" is set, it looks like this:

```
DynamicSQLEntity dynamicSQLEntity = new DynamicSQLEntity();
dynamicSQLEntity.setField1("field 1");
session.save(dynamicSQLEntity);
```

Now the insert statement looks like this:

```
insert into DynamicSQLEntity (field1, id) values (?, null)
```

So the insert statement is executed only with the values that are set; here it is only "field1". Because the rest of the fields are not set, they are not executed in the insert statement.

Summary

This chapter showed you how and when to use various identity generators. The chapter also demonstrated the implementation of composite keys. You saw how Hibernate saves persistent entities and creates new records in a database. And you learned how to use metadata such as dynamic-insert and dynamic-update to configure your persistence mechanism.

■ ■ ■

CHAPTER 3

Component Mapping

Hibernate makes it easy to employ a fine-grained domain model so you can have more classes than tables. In other words, you can map a single record in a table to more than one class by having one Entity class type; the others should be Value class types.

Hibernate classifies objects as either entity object types or value object types. An entity object type is an independent entity and has its own life cycle. It has its own primary key and hence its own database identity. A value object type doesn't have an identifier. A value object type belongs to an entity and is bound by the life cycle of the owning entity instance. When a value object type is persisted, its state is persisted in the owning entity's table row. Hibernate uses the component element, and JPA has the @Embeddable and @Embedded annotations to achieve the fine-grained model. This chapter goes through the implementation details.

3-1. Implementing a Value Type as a Component

Problem

How do you create a component? How do you create a fine-grained object model to map to a single row in a relational model?

Solution

A component element (`<Component>`) is used to map the value object type. The name component is from the word *Composition* because the component is contained within an entity. In the case of JPA, @Embeddable and @Embedded annotations are used.

How It Works

We'll look at how Hibernate and JPA solve the problem defined above in the sections that follow. Both solutions need a new orders table, so use the following CREATE statement to create a new table called ORDERS:

```
CREATE TABLE ORDERS (id bigint NOT NULL, WEEKDAY_RECIPIENT varchar(100),WEEKDAY_PHONE
varchar(100),WEEKDAY_ADDRESS varchar(100), HOLIDAY_RECIPIENT varchar(100),HOLIDAY_PHONE
varchar(100),HOLIDAY_ADDRESS varchar(100),PRIMARY KEY (id));
```

Using Hibernate XML Mapping

In the online bookshop application, a customer can place an order to purchase some books. Your staff processes the order and delivers these books. The customer can specify different recipients and contact details for different periods (weekdays and holidays).

Add a new Orders persistent class to the application:

```java
package com.hibernaterecipes.chapter3;

import com.hibernaterecipes.bookstore.Book;

/**
 * @author Guruzu
 *
 */
public class Orders {

    private Long id;
    private BookCh2 book;
    private String weekdayRecipient;
    private String weekdayPhone;
    private String weekdayAddress;
    private String holidayRecipient;
    private String holidayPhone;
    private String holidayAddress;

    //getters and setters
}
```

Create a mapping definition for this persistent class. You map the properties of this class as usual:

```xml
<?xml version="1.0" encoding="UTF-8"?>
<!DOCTYPE hibernate-mapping PUBLIC
"-//Hibernate/Hibernate Mapping DTD 3.0//EN"
"http://hibernate.sourceforge.net/hibernate-mapping-3.0.dtd">
<hibernate-mapping package="com.hibernaterecipes.chapter3">
  <class name="Orders" table="ORDERS">
    <id name="id" type="long" column="ID">
      <generator class="native" />
    </id>
    <property name="weekdayRecipient" type="string" column="WEEKDAY_RECIPIENT" />
    <property name="weekdayPhone" type="string" column="WEEKDAY_PHONE" />
    <property name="weekdayAddress" type="string" column="WEEKDAY_ADDRESS" />
    <property name="holidayRecipient" type="string" column="HOLIDAY_RECIPIENT" />
    <property name="holidayPhone" type="string" column="HOLIDAY_PHONE" />
    <property name="holidayAddress" type="string" column="HOLIDAY_ADDRESS" />
    <many-to-one name="book" class="com.hibernaterecipes.chapter2.BookCh2"
                 column="isbn" cascade="save-update"/>
  </class>
</hibernate-mapping>
```

You might feel that the Orders class isn't well designed because the recipient, phone, and address properties are duplicated for weekdays and holidays. From an object-oriented perspective, you could create a class called Contact to encapsulate them:

```
package com.hibernaterecipes.chapter3;

public class Contact {
  private long id;
  private String recipient;
  private String phone;
  private String address;

  // getters and setters
}

package com.hibernaterecipes.chapter3;

import com.hibernaterecipes.bookstore.Book;

public class Orders {

  private Long id;
  private Book book;
      private Contact weekdayContact;
      private Contact holidayContact;

      // getters and setters
}
```

Now the changes are finished for Java, but how can you modify the Hibernate mapping definition to reflect the changes? According to the techniques you've learned, you can specify Contact as a new persistent class and use a one-to-one association. The simplest way is to use a <many-to-one> association with unique="true") to associate the Orders and Contact classes:

```
<hibernate-mapping package=" com.hibernaterecipes.chapter3">
  <class name="Contact" table="CONTACT">
    <id name="id" type="long" column="ID">
      <generator class="native" />
    </id>
    <property name="recipient" type="string" column="RECIPIENT" />
    <property name="phone" type="string" column="PHONE" />
    <property name="address" type="string" column="ADDRESS" />
  </class>
</hibernate-mapping>

<hibernate-mapping package="com.hibernaterecipes.chapter3">
  <class name="Orders" table="ORDERS">
    ...
    <many-to-one name="weekdayContact" class="Contact" column="CONTACT_ID"
                 unique="true" />
    <many-to-one name="holidayContact" class="Contact" column="CONTACT_ID"
                 unique="true" />
  </class>
</hibernate-mapping>
```

In this case, modeling the Contact class as a stand-alone persistent class is unnecessary because a Contact object is meaningless when it is separated from an Order object. The function of the Contact class is to provide some kind of logical grouping. The contact details are completely dependent on the Orders class. For a bookshop application, it doesn't make much sense to hold contact information as separate entities (entities that have a database identity or primary key). For this kind of requirement, for which you can associate an object with a dependent object, you can use what Hibernate calls *components*:

```xml
<?xml version="1.0" encoding="UTF-8"?>
<!DOCTYPE hibernate-mapping PUBLIC
"-//Hibernate/Hibernate Mapping DTD 3.0//EN"
"http://hibernate.sourceforge.net/hibernate-mapping-3.0.dtd">
<hibernate-mapping package="com.hibernaterecipes.chapter3">
  <class name="Orders" table="ORDERS">
    <id name="id" type="long" column="ID">
      <generator class="native" />
    </id>
    <component name="weekdayContact" class="Contact">
      <property name="recipient" type="string" column="WEEKDAY_RECIPIENT" />
      <property name="phone" type="string" column="WEEKDAY_PHONE" />
      <property name="address" type="string" column="WEEKDAY_ADDRESS" />
    </component>
    <component name="holidayContact" class="Contact">
      <property name="recipient" type="string" column="HOLIDAY_RECIPIENT" />
      <property name="phone" type="string" column="HOLIDAY_PHONE" />
      <property name="address" type="string" column="HOLIDAY_ADDRESS" />
    </component>
  </class>
</hibernate-mapping>
```

No new persistent object is introduced, and all the columns mapped for these components are in the same table as their parent object. Components don't have an identity, and they exist only if their parent does. They're most suitable for grouping several properties as a single object.

Using JPA Annotations

With JPA annotations, you have to annotate the Contact class as @Embeddable. You also map the columns to the regular default database columns:

```java
package com.hibernaterecipes.annotations.domain;

import javax.persistence.Column;
import javax.persistence.Embeddable;
import javax.persistence.Entity;

@Embeddable
@Data
public class EmbeddedContact {
    @Column
    String name;
    @Column
```

```
        String address;
        @Column
        String phone;

/* Getters and Setters*/
// ...

    @Override
    public String toString() {
      return "Contact [address=" + address + ", phone=" + phone
          + ", recipient=" + recipient + "]";
    }

}
```

For the Orders class, you annotate the weekday contact as @Embedded. For the holiday contact, you annotate the access as @Embedded and override the values provided in the Contact class, as follows:

```
@Entity
@Data
public class OrderWithEmbeddedContact {
    @Id
    @GeneratedValue
    Long id;
    @Embedded
    EmbeddedContact weekdayContact;

    @Embedded
    @AttributeOverrides({
            @AttributeOverride(name = "name", column = @Column(name = "holidayname")),
            @AttributeOverride(name = "address", column = @Column(name = "holidayaddress")),
            @AttributeOverride(name = "phone", column = @Column(name = "holidayphone")),
    })
    EmbeddedContact holidayContact;
    /*Getters and Setters*/
}
```

3-2. Nesting Components
Problem

How do you nest a component within another component?

Solution

Components can be defined as *nested* when they are embedded within other components. Per JPA specifications, support for only one level of embedding is required.

How It Works

You can define the Phone property as a component and embed it in the contact component:

```
package com.hibernaterecipes.chapter3;

@Data
@AllArgsConstructor
@NoArgsConstructor
public class Phone {
    int areaCode;
    int exchange;
    int number;

    // Getters and Setters. These are automatically created
    // since we annotated this class with @Data from Lombok library
}
```

Change the phone property from a String type to a Phone type in Contact.

```
package com.hibernaterecipes.chapter3;

@Data
@AllArgsConstructor
@NoArgsConstructor
public class Contact {
    String name;
    String address;
    Phone phone;
    // Getters and Setters. These are automatically created
    // since we annotated this class with @Data from Lombok library
}
```

Create a new XML file named Orders.xml and add the nested component, as shown here:

```
<hibernate-mapping package="com.apress.hibernaterecipes.chapter3.recipe2">
    <class name="Order" table="NestedOrder">
        <id name="id" type="long" column="ID">
            <generator class="native"/>
        </id>
        <component name="weekdayContact" class="Contact">
            <property name="name" column="weekday_name"/>
            <property name="address" column="weekday_address"/>
            <component name="phone" class="Phone">
                <property name="areaCode" column="weekday_area_code"/>
                <property name="exchange" column="weekday_exchange"/>
                <property name="number" column="weekday_number"/>
            </component>
        </component>
        <component name="holidayContact" class="Contact">
            <property name="name" column="holiday_name"/>
            <property name="address" column="holiday_address"/>
```

```
            <component name="phone" class="Phone">
                <property name="areaCode" column="holiday_area_code"/>
                <property name="exchange" column="holiday_exchange"/>
                <property name="number" column="holiday_number"/>
            </component>
        </component>
    </class>
</hibernate-mapping>
```

Add this new XML file to the Hibernate XML mapping file. You can use the nested components as shown here in the test method:

```
public class Recipe2Test {
    @Test
    public void testNestedComponents() {
        Session session = SessionManager.openSession();
        Transaction tx = session.beginTransaction();
        Order order = new Order();
        order.setWeekdayContact(new Contact(
                "Srinivas Guruzu",
                "100 Main Street",
                new Phone(454, 555, 1212)));
        order.setHolidayContact(new Contact(
                "Joseph Ottinger",
                "P. O. Box 0",
                new Phone(978, 555, 1212)));
        session.persist(order);
        tx.commit();
        session.close();
    }
}
```

3-3. Adding References in Components
Problem

How do you add a reference to a component's parent object? How do you provide associations within a component?

Solution

You can add a reference to the parent object by using the <parent> tag. The <component> tag allows for many-to-one and one-to-one associations with other tables.

How It Works

A component can have a reference to its parent object through a <parent> mapping:

```
public class Contact {
  private Orders order;
  private String recipient;
  private Phone phone;
  private String address;
  // Getters and Setters
}
```

```
<hibernate-mapping package="com.apress.hibernaterecipes.chapter3.recipe2">
    <class name="Order" table="NestedOrder">
        <id name="id" type="long" column="ID">
            <generator class="native"/>
        </id>
        <component name="weekdayContact" class="Contact">
        <parent name="order"/>
            <property name="name" column="weekday_name"/>
            <property name="address" column="weekday_address"/>
            <component name="phone" class="Phone">
                <property name="areaCode" column="weekday_area_code"/>
                <property name="exchange" column="weekday_exchange"/>
                <property name="number" column="weekday_number"/>
            </component>
        </component>
        <component name="holidayContact" class="Contact">
        <parent name="order"/>
            <property name="name" column="holiday_name"/>
            <property name="address" column="holiday_address"/>
            <component name="phone" class="Phone">
                <property name="areaCode" column="holiday_area_code"/>
                <property name="exchange" column="holiday_exchange"/>
                <property name="number" column="holiday_number"/>
            </component>
        </component>
    </class>
</hibernate-mapping>
```

In JPA, you add the reference to the parent entity and annotate the accessor() method with @Parent:

```
package com.hibernaterecipes.annotations.domain;

import javax.persistence.Column;
import javax.persistence.Embeddable;
import javax.persistence.Entity;

import org.hibernate.annotations.Parent;
```

```
@Embeddable
public class Contact {

  private String name;
  private String phone;
  private String address;
  private Orders order;
  @Parent
  public Orders getOrder() {
    return order;
  }

  // other getters and setters
}
```

A component can be used to group not only normal properties but also many-to-one and one-to-one associations. Suppose that you want to associate the address of an order to the address in your customer database. To do this, create an address table using the following query:

```
CREATE TABLE ADDRESS (id bigint NOT NULL,STREET_ADDRESS_1 varchar(100),STREET_ADDRESS_2
varchar(100),CITY varchar(100),STATE varchar(2),ZIP_CODE INT,PRIMARY KEY (id))
```

Now create the entity class and the Hibernate mapping XML file:

```
package com.hibernaterecipes.chapter3;

public class Address {
  private Long id;
  private String address1;
  private String address2;
  private String city;
  private String state;
  private Integer zipCode;

  // getters and setters
}
```

```xml
<?xml version="1.0" encoding="UTF-8"?>
<!DOCTYPE hibernate-mapping PUBLIC
"-//Hibernate/Hibernate Mapping DTD 3.0//EN"
"http://hibernate.sourceforge.net/hibernate-mapping-3.0.dtd">
<hibernate-mapping package="com.hibernaterecipes.chapter3">
  <class name="Address" table="ADDRESS">
    <id name="id" type="long" column="ID">
      <generator class="native" />
    </id>
    <property name="address1" type="string" column="STREET_ADDRESS_1" />
    <property name="address2" type="string" column="STREET_ADDRESS_2" />
    <property name="city" type="string" column="CITY" />
    <property name="state" type="string" column="STATE" />
    <property name="zipCode" type="integer" column="ZIP_CODE" />
  </class>
</hibernate-mapping>
```

Edit the Contact class as follows:

```
package com.hibernaterecipes.chapter3;

public class Contact {
  private String recipient;
  private Phone phone;
  private Address address;

      // getters and setters
}
```

Change the Orders XML mapping file to include the association:

```
<?xml version="1.0" encoding="UTF-8"?>
<!DOCTYPE hibernate-mapping PUBLIC
"-//Hibernate/Hibernate Mapping DTD 3.0//EN"
"http://hibernate.sourceforge.net/hibernate-mapping-3.0.dtd">
<hibernate-mapping package="com.hibernaterecipes.chapter3">
  <class name="Orders" table="ORDERS">
    <id name="id" type="long" column="ID">
      <generator class="native" />
    </id>
    <component name="weekdayContact" class="Contact">
      <property name="recipient" type="string" column="WEEKDAY_RECIPIENT" />
      <component name="phone" class="Phone">
        <property name="areaCode" type="string" column="WEEKDAY_AREACODE" />
        <property name="telNo" type="string" column="WEEKDAY_TELEPHONE" />
      </component>
      <many-to-one name="address" class="Address" column="WEEKDAY_ADDRESS_ID" />
    </component>
    <component name="holidayContact" class="Contact">
      <property name="recipient" type="string" column="HOLIDAY_RECIPIENT" />
      <component name="phone" class="Phone">
        <property name="areaCode" type="string" column="HOLIDAY_AREACODE" />
        <property name="telNo" type="string" column="HOLIDAY_TELEPHONE" />
      </component>
      <many-to-one name="address" class="Address" column="HOLIDAY_ADDRESS_ID" />
    </component>
  </class>
</hibernate-mapping>
```

3-4. Mapping a Collection of Components
Problem

Does Hibernate support mapping a collection of dependent objects? How do you map a collection of components?

Solution

Hibernate provides the `<composite-element>` tag for mapping a collection of components. The collection elements/tags `<set>`, `<list>`, `<map>`, `<bag>`, and `<idbag>` can accommodate the `<composite-element>` tag to map a collection of dependent objects.

How It Works

Suppose that you need to support a more flexible contact mechanism for book orders. Customers can specify several contact points for a book delivery because they may not be sure which one is most suitable for a specified time period. Your staff has to try these contact points one by one. You can use a `java.util.Set` class to hold all the addresses for a customer.

Customer is defined as follows:

```
@Entity
@DynamicInsert
@DynamicUpdate
@Table(name="Customer")
public class Customer {

        @Id
        @GenericGenerator(name="customergen" , strategy="increment")
        @GeneratedValue(generator="customergen")
        @Column(name="id")
        private Long id;

        @Column
        private String name;

        @ElementCollection(targetClass=Address.class,fetch=FetchType.EAGER)
        @JoinTable (name = "Address", joinColumns = @JoinColumn(name="Customer_ID"))
        private Set<Address> contacts;

        public Long getId() {
                return id;
        }
        public void setId(Long id) {
                this.id = id;
        }

        public Set<Address> getContacts() {
                return contacts;
        }

        public void setContacts(Set<Address> contacts) {
                this.contacts = contacts;
        }
        public String getName() {
                return name;
        }
```

```
        public void setName(String name) {
                this.name = name;
        }
}
```

This Customer object has a set of addresses defined by the Address type. @JoinTable (name = "Address", joinColumns = @JoinColumn(name="Customer_ID")) defines the join column and the object to which the set maps. Here, the join column is the customer_id. When the address table is created, the customer_id column is added, and the ID from the customer table is referenced:

```
@Embeddable
@Table (name="Address")
public class Address {

    @Column
    private String address1;

    @Column
    private String city;

    @Column
    private String state;

    @Column
    private String zip;

    @Parent
    private Customer parent;

    //Getter and Setters
    @Override
    public boolean equals(Object o) {
        if (this == o) return true;
        if (o == null || getClass() != o.getClass()) return false;

        Address that = (Address) o;

        if (!address1.equals(that.address1)) return false;
        if (!city.equals(that.city)) return false;
        if (!state.equals(that.state)) return false;

        return true;
    }

    @Override
    public int hashCode() {
        int result = address1.hashCode();
        result = 31 * result + city.hashCode();
        result = 31 * result + state.hashCode();
        return result;
    }
}
```

The test method to set the addresses and persist the customer is as follows:

```java
@Test
public void testSetComponents() {
    Session session = SessionManager.openSession();
    Transaction tx = session.beginTransaction();
    Customer customer = new Customer();

    Set<Address> addresses = new HashSet<Address>();

    Address secondary = new Address();
    secondary.setAddress1("100 Main Street");
    secondary.setCity("Astoria");
    secondary.setState("Portland");
    secondary.setZip("97210");

    Address primary = new Address();
    primary.setAddress1("1200 Central Ave");
    primary.setCity("Phoenix");
    primary.setState("Arizona");
    primary.setZip("85221");

    addresses.add(primary);
    addresses.add(secondary);

    customer.setContacts(addresses);
    customer.setName("Guruzu");

    session.persist(customer);
    tx.commit();
    session.close();
}
```

```xml
<?xml version="1.0" encoding="UTF-8"?>
<!DOCTYPE hibernate-mapping PUBLIC
"-//Hibernate/Hibernate Mapping DTD 3.0//EN"
"http://hibernate.sourceforge.net/hibernate-mapping-3.0.dtd">
<hibernate-mapping package="com.hibernaterecipes.chapter3">
  <class name="Customer" table="Customer">
    <id name="id" type="long" column="ID">
      <generator class="increment" />
    </id>
    <set name="addresses" table="Address">
      <key column="customer_ID" />
      <composite-element class="Address">
        <property name="address1" type="string" column="address1" />
        <property name="city" type="string" column="city" />
        <property name="state" type="string" column="state" />
        <property name="zip" type="string" column="zip" />

      </composite-element>
    </set>
  </class>
</hibernate-mapping>
```

In this implementation, you use the `<set>` tag. Because `java.util.Set` doesn't allow for duplicate elements, you have to implement the `equals()` and `hashCode()` methods. The database's primary key should not be the only property used for comparison in the implementation of the `equals()` and `hashCode()` methods. If the database primary key is the only property used in the implementation of `equals()` and `hashCode()`, users can't add multiple addresses to the set because the primary key is `null` before it is persisted.

It is recommended that you also use other properties to obtain uniqueness among objects. Hence, the proper implementation of `equals()` and `hashCode()` is required to ensure that duplicate elements aren't added. Note that the `<composite-element>` tag doesn't allow `null` values when the enclosing collection tag is a `<set>` tag because for delete operations, Hibernate needs to identify each composite element to be able to delete that particular element.

Here is the Hibernate SQL output generated when this test case is executed:

```
Hibernate: create table Address (Customer_ID bigint not null, address1 varchar(255),
city varchar(255), state varchar(255), zip varchar(255))
Hibernate: create table Customer (id bigint not null, name varchar(255), primary key (id))
Hibernate: alter table Address add constraint FK_am1iuiv0eo6t45on1y4m7bfst foreign key
(Customer_ID) references Customer
```

The first two statements create the table structures, and the third statement adds the `Customer_Id` of the `Customer` table as a reference in the `Address` table.

Here are the SQL statements that Hibernate generates for inserting into `Customer` and `Address` tables:

```
Hibernate: insert into Customer (name, id) values (?, ?)
Hibernate: insert into Address (Customer_ID, address1, city, state, zip) values (?, ?, ?, ?, ?)
Hibernate: insert into Address (Customer_ID, address1, city, state, zip) values (?, ?, ?, ?, ?)
```

In addition to normal properties, you can define nested components and associations in a collection. Use the `<nested-composite-element>` tag to define nested components in a collection.

3-5. Using Components as Keys to a Map
Problem

Normally, the key to a map can be a `String` type, a `Long` type, an `Integer` type, and so on. But what if you need to implement your own map key? Does Hibernate allow you to map a component class as a key to a map? If so, how do you map components as keys to a map?

Solution

Hibernate provides a `<composite-map-key>` tag, which lets you use components as map keys.

How It Works

Suppose that you want to extend your collection of contact points to be java.util.Map types. You can use date periods as the keys of the map. Create a Period class to encapsulate the start date and end date of a period, and use it as your map's key type. You then define this period as a component in the Orders class. The customer can now specify the most suitable contact point for a particular date period:

```
public class Period {
  private Date startDate;
  private Date endDate;
  // Getters and Setters
}
<hibernate-mapping package="com.metaarchit.bookshop">
  <class name="Orders" table="ORDERS">
...
    <map name="contacts" table="ORDERS_CONTACT">
      <key column="ORDER_ID" />
      <composite-map-key class="Period">
        <key-property name="startDate" type="date" column="START_DATE" />
        <key-property name="endDate" type="date" column="END_DATE" />
      </composite-map-key>
      <composite-element class="Contact">
        <property name="recipient" type="string" column="RECIPIENT" />
        <nested-composite-element name="phone" class="Phone">
          <property name="areaCode" type="string" column="PHONE_AREA_CODE" />
          <property name="telNo" type="string" column="PHONE_TEL_NO" />
        </nested-composite-element>
        <many-to-one name="address" class="Address" column="ADDRESS_ID" />
      </composite-element>
    </map>
  </class>
</hibernate-mapping>
```

For the map-key component to work properly, you need to override the equals() and hashCode() methods of the component class:

```
public class Period {
  ...
  public boolean equals(Object obj) {
    if (!(obj instanceof Period)) return false;
    Period other = (Period) obj;
    return new EqualsBuilder().append(startDate, other.startDate)
      .append(endDate, other.endDate)
      .isEquals();
  }
  public int hashCode() {
    return new HashCodeBuilder().append(startDate)
      .append(endDate)
      .toHashCode();
  }
}
```

Summary

This chapter showed you a way to achieve a finer-grained object model by using value types as components. You effectively created an object graph for use in an application, but it is represented in the database as a single record in a table.

The chapter also discussed a way to bridge the gap between a relational model and an object model by using simple value types. You learned how to nest components within other components and how to add the parent reference in a component. And you saw how to map a collection of components in an entity and use components as keys to a `java.util.Map`.

CHAPTER 4

■ ■ ■

Inheritance and Custom Mapping

Inheritance, polymorphic associations, and polymorphic queries are supported by entities. The JPA specification says that both concrete and abstract classes can be entities and can be mapped with the Entity annotation. Non-entity classes and entity classes can extend each other. Hibernate provides the MappedSuperclass annotation (@MappedSuperclass) to enable inheritance mapping and to let you map abstract or concrete entity subclasses. The mapped superclass doesn't necessarily have its own separate table.

Hibernate provides four strategies for mapping an inheritance hierarchy:

- *Table per class hierarchy*: The class hierarchy is represented in one table. A discriminator column identifies the type and the subclass.

- *Table per subclass*: The superclass has a table, and each subclass has a table that contains only uninherited properties; the subclass tables have a primary key that is a foreign key of the superclass.

- *Table per concrete class with unions*: The superclass can be an abstract class or even an interface. If the superclass is concrete, an additional table is required to map the properties of that class.

- *Table per concrete class with implicit polymorphism*: Each table contains all the properties of the concrete class and the properties that are inherited from its superclasses. Here, all the subclasses are mapped as separate entities.

This chapter discusses these strategies in detail and shows you how to implement them.

The properties of all persistent entities are of certain types, such as String. Some of the important basic types supported by Hibernate are as follows:

- integer, long, short, float, double, character, byte, boolean, yes_no, *and* true_false: Type mappings for Java primitives and wrapper classes.

- string: Type mappings from java.lang.String to something like a VARCHAR.

- date, time, *and* timestamp: Type mappings from java.util.Date and its subclasses to their appropriate SQL types.

Other basic mappings supported by Hibernate include calendar, calendar_date, big_decimal, big_integer, locale, timezone, currency, class, binary, text, and serializable. Hibernate also provides an API to implement custom types. You can use two packages, org.hibernate.type and org.hibernate. userType, to define object types. You can define your custom types either by implementing org.hibernate. type.Type directly or by extending one of the abstract classes provided in the org.hibernate.type package; or you can implement one of the interfaces in the org.hibernate.userType package. This chapter discusses the custom mapping types available in the Hibernate org.hibernate.userType package and the implementation details of the userType and CompositeUserType extensions.

4-1. Mapping Entities with Table per Class Hierarchy
Problem

How do you map entities using the table per class hierarchy strategy? And when should you use it?

Solution

To use the table per class hierarchy strategy, you need to create a single table that contains the state of the complete class hierarchy. The key is that the subclass state can't have not-null constraints, which can be a disadvantage because data integrity is compromised.[1] Because all the state is in the same table, it is a denormalized model.

With this strategy, you get the advantage of good performance[2] for both polymorphic and nonpolymorphic queries. The denormalization of the class hierarchy in the relational model can cause data stability and maintainability issues, so it's a good idea to run it by your database administrator first.

The audio and video section of the bookshop example can help you learn about inheritance mapping. Suppose that your bookshop sells CDs and DVDs. Figure 4-1 shows the class diagram of the object model you might map as a table per class hierarchy.

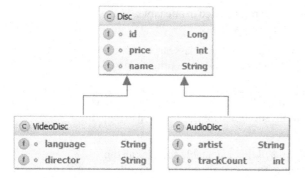

Figure 4-1. *Object model class diagram*

First, let's create a Disc class and provide a mapping definition for it. We use Lombok as in previous chapters to save some boilerplate code—in this case, a constructor, mutators, accessors, and the equals() and hashCode() methods. We leave out the Hibernate configuration until you can see the entire hierarchy.

---

[1]In addition to data integrity being compromised (thanks to the non-null requirement), changes to *any* members of the hierarchy involve changing the data model for *all* members of the hierarchy.
[2]The performance advantage of a single table per hierarchy is based on the fact that a single select can suffice to return many different subclass instances instead of Hibernate having to run many different queries to collect different instance types.

```
@Data
@NoArgsConstructor
public class Disc {
    Long id;
    String name;
    int price;
}
```

Assume there are three kinds of discs to be sold: data (a generic disc), audio, and video,[3] and each type has different properties. From an object-oriented perspective, you should model two more kinds of discs, AudioDisc and VideoDisc, as subclasses of Disc, with additional attributes for each type.

```
@Data
@NoArgsConstructor
public class AudioDisc extends Disc {
    int trackCount;
    String artist;
}
```

```
@Data
@NoArgsConstructor
public class VideoDisc extends Disc {
    String director;
    String language;
}
```

Now let's map these classes into a database structure. We use an inheritance strategy to specify that all objects that are Discs (Disc and all subclasses, meaning VideoDisc and AudioDisc) are represented in a single database table, with an additional column to allow Hibernate to determine what the actual class the database row[4] describes.

Here is the new Disc hierarchy source code, with the annotations to handle the subclass hierarchy in a single table. The key requirement is the @Inheritance annotation, which allows for one of three mapping options: SINGLE_TABLE (as used here), which means that a single table is used for all subclasses, with various columns being ignored if a subclass doesn't need them; TABLE_PER_CLASS, which means that each subclass gets its own table, with the superclass' columns being present in the subclass' tables as well; and JOINED, which means that fields specific to a subclass get mapped to a table specific to that class.

```
@Data
@NoArgsConstructor
@Inheritance(strategy = InheritanceType.SINGLE_TABLE)
@DiscriminatorColumn(name = "disc_type")
@Entity
```

---

[3]In case you're wondering, this model would not work well in the real world. That's okay; we're just using a hypothetical. A good exercise is to actually model a class hierarchy that would consider floppy discs of various sizes and capacities, and CDs, DVDs, Blu-Ray, and other such discs, along with their content types.

[4]A "database row" is also known as a "tuple," which is the term future references will use. Feel the tuple. Love the tuple. Be the tuple. Or don't. That would be a little creepy and probably call your concept of identity into question.

```java
public class Disc {
    @Id
    @GeneratedValue
    Long id;
    @Column(nullable = false)
    String name;
    @Column(nullable = false)
    int price;
}

@Entity
@Data
@EqualsAndHashCode(callSuper = true)
@NoArgsConstructor
public class AudioDisc extends Disc {
    @Column
    int trackCount;
    @Column
    String artist;
}

@Entity
@Data
@EqualsAndHashCode(callSuper = true)
@NoArgsConstructor
public class VideoDisc extends Disc {
    @Column
    String director;
    @Column
    String language;
}
```

Now let's see what all this looks like with a test. Here is hibernate.cfg.xml, which configures the session[5]:

```xml
<?xml version="1.0" encoding="UTF-8"?>
<!DOCTYPE hibernate-configuration PUBLIC
        "-//Hibernate/Hibernate Configuration DTD 3.0//EN"
        "http://www.hibernate.org/dtd/hibernate-configuration-3.0.dtd">
<hibernate-configuration>
    <session-factory>
        <property name="connection.driver_class">org.hsqldb.jdbcDriver</property>
        <property name="connection.url">
            jdbc:hsqldb:file:./chapter4;write_delay=false
        </property>
```

---

[5]Note that we will modify this configuration to add any additional information the rest of this chapter might need.

```
        <property name="hibernate.dialect">org.hibernate.dialect.HSQLDialect</property>
        <property name="hibernate.hbm2ddl.auto">create</property>
        <property name="hibernate.show_sql">true</property>
        <mapping class="com.apress.hibernaterecipes.chapter4.model.Disc"/>
        <mapping class="com.apress.hibernaterecipes.chapter4.model.AudioDisc"/>
        <mapping class="com.apress.hibernaterecipes.chapter4.model.VideoDisc"/>
        <!-- other mappings go here from other recipes -->
    </session-factory>
</hibernate-configuration>
```

Now let's see some code that uses the Disc hierarchy:

```
@Test
public void testHierarchy() {
    Session session = SessionManager.openSession();
    Transaction tx = session.beginTransaction();

    Disc disc = new Disc();
    disc.setName("Blank CDR");
    disc.setPrice(199);
    session.save(disc);

    VideoDisc videoDisc = new VideoDisc();
    videoDisc.setName("Blazing Saddles");
    videoDisc.setPrice(1499);
    videoDisc.setDirector("Mel Brooks");
    videoDisc.setLanguage("english");
    session.save(videoDisc);

    AudioDisc audioDisc = new AudioDisc();
    audioDisc.setName("Grace Under Pressure");
    audioDisc.setPrice(999);
    audioDisc.setArtist("Rush");
    audioDisc.setTrackCount(8);
    session.save(audioDisc);

    tx.commit();
    session.close();

    session=SessionManager.openSession();
    tx=session.beginTransaction();
    Disc disc1= (Disc) session.load(Disc.class, disc.getId());
    assertEquals(disc1.getName(), disc.getName());

    VideoDisc videoDisc2= (VideoDisc) session.load(VideoDisc.class, videoDisc.getId());
    assertEquals(videoDisc2.getName(), videoDisc.getName());

    tx.commit();
    session.close();
}
```

When this code is executed, you see the following information, in addition to various other bits and pieces of data from Hibernate:

```
drop table Disc if exists
create table Disc (disc_type varchar(31) not null, id bigint generated by default as
identity (start with 1), name varchar(255) not null, price integer not null, artist
varchar(255), trackCount integer, director varchar(255), language varchar(255),
primary key (id))
insert into Disc (id, name, price, disc_type) values (default, ?, ?, 'Disc')
insert into Disc (id, name, price, director, language, disc_type) values (default, ?, ?,
?, ?, 'VideoDisc')
insert into Disc (id, name, price, artist, trackCount, disc_type) values (default, ?, ?,
?, ?, 'AudioDisc')
```

Note the table creation, which shows the creation of a single table with name and price not allowing null; then the attributes from VideoDisc and AudioDisc are included as nullable fields. Note that the instance type is included as the discriminator value for each type.

We can use the hierarchy in queries, too. We have to limit the selectors to fields present in the entire hierarchy, but it is not very restrictive. For example, here's some code that shows a query of all discs above a certain price point:

```
@Test
public void showGeneralQueryByPrice() {
    // populate data with our other test method
    testHierarchy();
    Session session=SessionManager.openSession();
    session.setDefaultReadOnly(true);
    Transaction tx=session.beginTransaction();
    Query query=session.createQuery("from Disc d where d.price>:price");
    query.setParameter("price", 1299);
    List<Disc> results=query.list();
    assertEquals(results.size(), 1);
    assertEquals(results.get(0).getName(), "Blazing Saddles");
    tx.commit();
    session.close();
}
```

We can also query for all Disc types with a single query, demonstrating the simple polymorphic nature of the set. We can't do this with all types of inheritance strategies[6]:

```
@Test
public void showGeneralQuery() {
    testHierarchy();
    Session session = SessionManager.openSession();
    session.setDefaultReadOnly(true);
    Transaction tx = session.beginTransaction();
```

---

[6]We can't use a single query to pull back all polymorphic references for some hierarchical strategies because they're not necessarily represented in a simple known set of tables; a single query for all subclasses could theoretically query many, many, *many* more tables than you'd want it to.

```
        Query query = session.createQuery("from Disc d");
        List<Disc> results = query.list();
        assertEquals(results.size(), 3);
        for (Disc d : results) {
            switch (d.getClass().getName()) {
                case "Disc":
                    assertEquals(d.getName(), "Blank CDR");
                    break;
                case "AudioDisc":
                    AudioDisc audioDisc = (AudioDisc) d;
                    assertEquals(audioDisc.getArtist(), "Rush");
                    break;
                case "VideoDisc":
                    VideoDisc videoDisc = (VideoDisc) d;
                    assertEquals(videoDisc.getDirector(), "Mel Brooks");
                    break;
            }
        }
        tx.commit();
        session.close();
}
```

Similarly, we use this feature to clear out all data from prior tests:

```
@BeforeMethod
public void cleanAll() {
    Session session = SessionManager.openSession();
    Transaction tx = session.beginTransaction();
    session.createQuery("delete from Disc").executeUpdate();
    tx.commit();
    session.close();
}
```

The hierarchy acts like a standard Java hierarchy, with a few limits here and there. If you want to create a Reservation, you can refer to Disc; through *polymorphic association*, Hibernate populates the reference with the correct instance type:

```
public class Reservation {
  private Long id;
  private Disc disc;
  private Customer customer;
  private int quantity;
}
```

How It Works

Hibernate uses the discriminator annotation to serve as a description of a field in the table that contains some sort of reference to the actual type. By default, it is a string, using the actual type as the value (thus, you see how a column value of "VideoDisc" and "AudioDisc" were used in the test output.) When the specific type is used, Hibernate looks at the discriminator and builds a reference that reflects the discriminator value.

73

When the table is created, it looks like this:

```
create table Disc (
        disc_type varchar(31) not null,
        id bigint generated by default as identity (start with 1),
        name varchar(255) not null,
        price integer not null,
        artist varchar(255),
        trackCount integer,
        director varchar(255),
        language varchar(255),
        primary key (id)
)
```

The reason why you can't specify the subclass' attributes as non-null should be fairly obvious: if director were non-null, audio discs would have to somehow populate that column before they could be persisted.[7]

Fortunately, there is a workaround—to create the table with meaningful default values for the columns—but the Hibernate default DDL doesn't take this into account (and honestly, neither should most users).

If you want to specify the discriminator value, there's an annotation for that. If we want to use "VIDEO" and "AUDIO" instead of "VideoDisc" and "AudioDisc", we could use the @DiscriminatorValue annotation DiscriminatorValue("VIDEO") //, for example.

4-2. Mapping Entities with Table per Subclass
Problem

How do you map entities using the table per subclass strategy? And when should you use it?

Solution

To use the table per subclass strategy, specify a new inheritance approach: instead of InheritanceType. SINGLE_TABLE, use InheritanceType.JOINED. When the tables are created, one table is created for each type in the hierarchy; the superclass' table contains all attributes managed by the superclass, and each subclass' table has a foreign key pointing to the superclass.

This strategy has an advantage in that it's normalized; conceivably, it uses less space in the database because there aren't wasted fields (VideoDisc doesn't have trackCount, for example, and AudioDisc doesn't have director.) Changing the data model affects only those subclasses being changed.

The table per subclass strategy can have a performance disadvantage compared with some other strategies when relying on polymorphism; it also means that the database runs a join for each query.

---

[7]Plus, all blank discs—the superclass' type—would have to have a director, which would make Hollywood very happy, but blank discs very expensive and make consumers very, very upset.

How It Works

Let's create a duplicate of the data model from Recipe 4.1, except the class names are slightly different. The VideoDisc2 and AudioDisc2 classes are exact analogs of the classes from Recipe 4.1, except the superclass is different; the Disc class is exactly the same, except with a different inheritance strategy:

```
@Data
@NoArgsConstructor
@Inheritance(strategy = InheritanceType.JOINED)
@DiscriminatorColumn(name = "disc_type")
@Entity
public class Disc2 {
    @Id
    @GeneratedValue
    Long id;
    @Column(nullable = false)
    String name;
    @Column(nullable = false)
    int price;
}

@Entity
@Data
@EqualsAndHashCode(callSuper = true)
@NoArgsConstructor
public class AudioDisc2 extends Disc2 {
    @Column
    int trackCount;
    @Column
    String artist;
}

@Entity
@Data
@EqualsAndHashCode(callSuper = true)
@NoArgsConstructor
public class VideoDisc2 extends Disc2 {
    @Column
    String director;
    @Column
    String language;
}
```

We can actually use the test code from Recipe 4.1 almost verbatim, using the new class names as the only changes:

```
@Test
public void testHierarchy() {
    Session session = SessionManager.openSession();
    Transaction tx = session.beginTransaction();
```

```java
Disc2 disc = new Disc2();
disc.setName("Blank CDR");
disc.setPrice(199);
session.save(disc);

VideoDisc2 videoDisc = new VideoDisc2();
videoDisc.setName("Blazing Saddles");
videoDisc.setPrice(1499);
videoDisc.setDirector("Mel Brooks");
videoDisc.setLanguage("english");
session.save(videoDisc);

AudioDisc2 audioDisc = new AudioDisc2();
audioDisc.setName("Grace Under Pressure");
audioDisc.setPrice(999);
audioDisc.setArtist("Rush");
audioDisc.setTrackCount(8);
session.save(audioDisc);

tx.commit();
session.close();

session=SessionManager.openSession();
session.setDefaultReadOnly(true);
tx=session.beginTransaction();
Disc2 disc1= (Disc2) session.load(Disc2.class, disc.getId());
assertEquals(disc1.getName(), disc.getName());

VideoDisc2 videoDisc2= (VideoDisc2) session.load(VideoDisc2.class, videoDisc.getId());
assertEquals(videoDisc2.getName(), videoDisc.getName());

tx.commit();
session.close();
}
```

When Hibernate sees this class hierarchy, it creates the tables with the following SQL:

```sql
create table AudioDisc2 (
        artist varchar(255),
        trackCount integer,
        id bigint not null,
        primary key (id))
create table Disc2 (
        disc_type varchar(31) not null,
        id bigint generated by default as identity (start with 1),
        name varchar(255) not null,
        price integer not null,
        primary key (id))
```

```
create table VideoDisc2 (
        director varchar(255),
        language varchar(255),
        id bigint not null,
        primary key (id))
alter table AudioDisc2
        add constraint FK_i12wsunro63mpv71ko8p1ptyh foreign key (id) references Disc2
alter table VideoDisc2
        add constraint FK_5devgqbkpsmk435tlx12x4fue foreign key (id) references Disc2
```

With this structure, the ID of each subclass table (AudioDisc2 and VideoDisc2) participates in a foreign key relationship with the Disc2 table. Therefore, the VideoDisc2 data is split across both tables, and a VideoDisc2 doesn't take up any more data than is necessary to reproduce the primary key.[8]

You should use this strategy when there is a requirement to use polymorphic associations and polymorphic queries, and when the subclasses' state varies a great deal (that is, the properties that one subclass holds are very different from the properties that other subclasses hold). Also, when the class hierarchy is spread across many classes (depth of inheritance), this strategy can have an impact on performance.

We can still rely on polymorphism in the set: querying for all instance of Disc returns valid instances of VideoDisc and AudioDisc.

4-3. Mapping Entities with Table per Concrete Class
Problem

How do you map entities using the table per concrete class strategy? And when should you use it?

Solution

There are two separate approaches to consider: when the superclass is a valid entity (it is a concrete type; something that exists outside of the context of the subclasses), and when it's not (it is an abstract type).

A Disc has been concrete for our recipes so far (it's been seen as a "blank CDR"). We consider it to be the case for this recipe as well; Recipe 4.4 considers the superclass to be abstract.

This strategy creates tables for every type in the hierarchy, so we end up with a table for Disc3, VideoDisc3, and AudioDisc3. Changes in the hierarchy have to be reflected across each table, and polymorphic queries have to span multiple tables as well. With that said, though, this strategy is very easy to visualize in the database.

Here we map each class into a separate table with a "union" approach, which affects how we generate our primary keys.[9] Apart from that, the code is nearly identical to the previous recipes.

---

[8]Contrast this with the single-table approach. A VideoDisc doesn't have any of the AudioDisc attributes, but the database has to have the AudioDisc data as part of every object descended from Disc. In the joined approach, the primary key—the join field—is duplicated, but nothing else is.

[9]We can't use the IDENTITY strategy with primary keys any longer because each table would have its own identity. Although the *database* could have a Disc3 with identity 2 and a VideoDisc3 with identity 2, the object hierarchy couldn't logically have the two objects with the same identifier.

How It Works

The object hierarchy looks almost identical to our other recipes' models; the main difference is specifying a different identity generation strategy and a different inheritance model:

```
CREATE TABLE "BOOK"."AUDIO_DISC_3"
@Data
@NoArgsConstructor
@Entity
@Inheritance(strategy = InheritanceType.TABLE_PER_CLASS)
public class Disc3 {
    @Id
    @GeneratedValue(strategy = GenerationType.SEQUENCE)
    Long id;
    @Column(nullable = false)
    String name;
    @Column(nullable = false)
    int price;
}
```

The AudioDisc3 and VideoDisc3 classes differ only in name from our other recipes. The validating test is nearly identical to the other recipes' tests as well, differing only in the names of the objects.

```
@BeforeMethod
public void cleanAll() {
    Session session = SessionManager.openSession();
    Transaction tx = session.beginTransaction();
    session.createQuery("delete from Disc3").executeUpdate();
    tx.commit();
    session.close();
}

@Test
public void testHierarchy() {
    Session session = SessionManager.openSession();
    Transaction tx = session.beginTransaction();

    Disc3 disc = new Disc3();
    disc.setName("Blank CDR");
    disc.setPrice(199);
    session.save(disc);

    VideoDisc3 videoDisc = new VideoDisc3();
    videoDisc.setName("Blazing Saddles");
    videoDisc.setPrice(1499);
    videoDisc.setDirector("Mel Brooks");
    videoDisc.setLanguage("english");
    session.save(videoDisc);

    AudioDisc3 audioDisc = new AudioDisc3();
    audioDisc.setName("Grace Under Pressure");
    audioDisc.setPrice(999);
```

```java
        audioDisc.setArtist("Rush");
        audioDisc.setTrackCount(8);
        session.save(audioDisc);

        tx.commit();
        session.close();

        session = SessionManager.openSession();
        session.setDefaultReadOnly(true);
        tx = session.beginTransaction();

        VideoDisc3 videoDisc2 = (VideoDisc3) session.load(VideoDisc3.class, videoDisc.getId());
        assertEquals(videoDisc2.getName(), videoDisc.getName());

        tx.commit();
        session.close();
    }

    @Test
    public void showGeneralQueryByType() {
        // populate data
        testHierarchy();
        Session session=SessionManager.openSession();
        session.setDefaultReadOnly(true);
        Transaction tx=session.beginTransaction();
        Query query=session.createQuery("from Disc3 d where d.price>:price");
        query.setParameter("price", 1299);
        List<Disc3> results=query.list();
        assertEquals(results.size(), 1);
        assertEquals(results.get(0).getName(), "Blazing Saddles");
        tx.commit();
        session.close();
    }

    @Test
    public void showGeneralQuery() {
        testHierarchy();
        Session session = SessionManager.openSession();
        session.setDefaultReadOnly(true);
        Transaction tx = session.beginTransaction();
        Query query = session.createQuery("from Disc3 d");
        List<Disc3> results = query.list();
        assertEquals(results.size(), 3);
        for (Disc3 d : results) {
            switch (d.getClass().getName()) {
                case "Disc":
                    assertEquals(d.getName(), "Blank CDR");
                    break;
                case "AudioDisc":
                    AudioDisc3 audioDisc = (AudioDisc3) d;
                    assertEquals(audioDisc.getArtist(), "Rush");
                    break;
```

```
                case "VideoDisc":
                    VideoDisc3 videoDisc = (VideoDisc3) d;
                    assertEquals(videoDisc.getDirector(), "Mel Brooks");
                    break;
        }
    }
    tx.commit();
    session.close();
}
```

4-4. Mapping Entities with Table per Class with a Mapped Superclass

Problem

What kind of mapping can support a structure in which a superclass contains common attributes, but is abstract?

Solution

As mentioned in Recipe 4.3, Hibernate can support an object hierarchy in which a superclass contains common attributes *without* having to be concrete. For example, we've been using "Disc" as an actual concrete type (you might say that you can buy a disc). However, there are different types of simple discs: Blu-Ray discs, DVDs, and CDs; and that's not even considering the different densities and layers possible for some of these formats. Therefore, we can easily imagine a structure in which Disc is abstract; and we would have DVDRW, DVDR, BluRay, and CDR as concrete types in addition to (or as replacements for) the VideoDisc and AudioDisc examples.

However, rather than replicating an entire and complete hierarchy of disc types and purposes, we stay simple (and illustrative) by simply making the Disc type abstract and retaining the rest of the hierarchy.

Everything in common among the various subclasses can be located in the superclass, which is annotated normally, except that it receives a @MappedSuperclass annotation instead of being marked with @Entity.

```
@Data
@NoArgsConstructor
@MappedSuperclass
public abstract class Disc4 {
    @Id
    @GeneratedValue
    Long id;
    @Column(nullable = false)
    String name;
    @Column(nullable = false)
    int price;
}
```

The AudioDisc4 and VideoDisc4 classes look just like the other examples; here's the VideoDisc4 class, just for clarification:

```
@Entity
@Data
@EqualsAndHashCode(callSuper = true)
@NoArgsConstructor
public class VideoDisc4 extends Disc4 {
    @Column
    String director;
    @Column
    String language;
}
```

The test code is a little different, mostly because we no longer have a simple supertype from which the subclasses are derived. We can't delete all types with a simple session.createQuery("delete from Disc4").executeUpdate(); statement because there is no "Disc4". We have to use two statements: one to delete all AudioDisc4 instances, and the other to delete all VideoDisc4 instances.

In other words, there is no simple polymorphism with this structure. With that said, though, the ability to have a mapped superclass has many benefits in terms of a more general object hierarchy.

How It Works

Here's the test code for the mapped superclass code; note that there is no longer any test data for the simple disc construct because the superclass is abstract (and the "Disc" no longer exists as a simple concrete object type):

```
@BeforeMethod
public void cleanAll() {
    Session session = SessionManager.openSession();
    Transaction tx = session.beginTransaction();
    session.createQuery("delete from VideoDisc4").executeUpdate();
    session.createQuery("delete from AudioDisc4").executeUpdate();
    tx.commit();
    session.close();
}

@Test
public void testHierarchy() {
    Session session = SessionManager.openSession();
    Transaction tx = session.beginTransaction();

    VideoDisc4 videoDisc = new VideoDisc4();
    videoDisc.setName("Blazing Saddles");
    videoDisc.setPrice(1499);
    videoDisc.setDirector("Mel Brooks");
    videoDisc.setLanguage("english");
    session.save(videoDisc);
```

```
        AudioDisc4 audioDisc = new AudioDisc4();
        audioDisc.setName("Grace Under Pressure");
        audioDisc.setPrice(999);
        audioDisc.setArtist("Rush");
        audioDisc.setTrackCount(8);
        session.save(audioDisc);

        tx.commit();
        session.close();

        session = SessionManager.openSession();
        session.setDefaultReadOnly(true);
        tx = session.beginTransaction();

        VideoDisc4 videoDisc2 = (VideoDisc4) session.load(VideoDisc4.class, videoDisc.getId());
        assertEquals(videoDisc2.getName(), videoDisc.getName());

        tx.commit();
        session.close();
}

@Test
public void showGeneralQueryByType() {
        // populate data
        testHierarchy();
        Session session=SessionManager.openSession();
        session.setDefaultReadOnly(true);
        Transaction tx=session.beginTransaction();
        Query query=session.createQuery("from VideoDisc4 d where d.price>:price");
        query.setParameter("price", 1299);
        List<Disc4> results=query.list();
        assertEquals(results.size(), 1);
        assertEquals(results.get(0).getName(), "Blazing Saddles");
        tx.commit();
        session.close();
}
```

With the @MappedSuperclass, Hibernate repeats the attributes in the superclass for each subclass, mapping the columns as necessary in each subclass' database table. However, the hierarchy is tied to the database representation, so a simple expression of polymorphism (as discussed in prior recipes in this chapter) is not possible.[10]

---

[10]Well, let's say that it isn't possible given normal human amounts of effort. You probably could find a way around the polymorphism issue, but it's probably not worth it.

4-5. Custom Mappings

Problem

What are the various extensions that Hibernate provides to implement custom mapping types? How do you create UserType custom mapping?

Solution

Hibernate provides an interface that you can implement to define your own custom mapping types. The extensions are listed in the org.hibernate.usertype package and are as follows:

- CompositeUserType: Exposes the internals of the value type to Hibernate, which allows querying for specific internal properties.

- EnhancedUserType: Used when marshalling value types to and from XML is required. It lets you use the custom type in identifier and discriminator mappings.

- LoggableUserType: Used when you want custom logging of the corresponding value types.

- ParameterizedType: Used when you want to set parameters for a type by using a nested type element for the property element in the mapping file or by defining a typedef.

- UserCollectionType: Used when you want to implement a custom collection mapping type and when you have to persist a non–JDK type collection.

- UserType: A basic extension point that provides a basic framework to implement custom loading and storing of value type instances.

- UserVersionType: Used for a version property.

Modeling a custom type is a simple matter of extending or implementing one of these extensions, along with some specifications of column names, although you can also use @org.hibernate.annotations.Type to specify that a custom type is properly mapped to a default Hibernate type.[11]

You might recognize the similarity with embeddable objects (as discussed in Chapter 3); the strategy you choose depends on your preferences (as in practice, both approaches have similar results in performance and database structure).

How It Works

This example creates an Address entity with an associated geolocation: a single object that represents a longitude and a latitude.

First, let's take a look at Geolocation, which uses Lombok to avoid a lot of boilerplate Java code:

```
@Data
public class Geolocation implements Serializable {
    BigDecimal latitude;
    BigDecimal longitude;
```

---

[11]See http://docs.jboss.org/hibernate/orm/4.3/manual/en-US/html/ch05.html#mapping-types-basictypes for a comprehensive list of the Hibernate internal type mappings.

```
/*
 * We don't use @AllArgsConstructor because we want to make sure our
 * attributes align. No mixups of longitude and latitude for us, no sir!
 */
public Geolocation(BigDecimal latitude, BigDecimal longitude) {
    this.latitude=latitude;
    this.longitude=longitude;
}

public Geolocation(double latitude, double longitude) {
    this(new BigDecimal(latitude),new BigDecimal(longitude));
}
}
```

This is not yet an embedded entity from a Hibernate perspective; it is just an object that represents a longitude and latitude. Because both attributes are the same type, we explicitly specify the constructor because we don't want to run the risk of the attributes being inverted by Lombok.[12]

One way to describe this object to Hibernate is through the CompositeUserType interface, which tells Hibernate how to construct ("assemble") and deconstruct ("disassemble," surprisingly) the type. There is a lot of code here because of the way that the object is handled by Hibernate.[13] We have to make sure the following methods are implemented:

- Assemble(): Reconstructs an object from the cacheable representation. If the object is immutable, you can return the cached object. Mutable objects are expected to at least perform a deep copy.

- Disassemble(): Called when Hibernate is storing the object as a serialized object in second-level memory or cache. (Caching is discussed in more detail in Chapter 12.) For immutable objects, typecast the object as serializable and return it. For mutable objects, return a deep copy. It might not be as easy if the mutable object has other associations. Associations should be cached as identifier values.

- deepCopy(): Returns the persistent state of the object. For immutable objects, it can return the object itself.

- equals(): Checks the equality of two instances for persistent state.

- hashCode(): Performs a hashcode implementation for the instance.

- isMutable(): Specifies whether objects of this type are immutable.

- nullSafeGet(): Retrieves the object from the JDBC result set.

- nullSafeSet(): Writes the object property value to the JDBC prepared statement.

- replace(): Used when merging with a detached instance. For immutable objects, you can return the first parameter (original). For mutable objects, you return a copy of the first parameter. A recursive copy should be performed if the mutable objects have component fields.

---

[12]Lombok uses attribute order in the source file to work out where to place values in parameter lists. If someone were to invert the latitude and longitude, the values would be switched with no warning. This would be ungood. Therefore, we're explicitly including the constructor.

[13]If this looks too long to be worthwhile, remember that embeddable objects work, too; this is really a way of exposing the machinery of embedded objects.

- returnedClass(): Specifies the class returned by the nullSafeGet() method.

- sqlTypes(): Returns the SQL types for the columns mapped by this type. The types are identified as codes, and codes are defined in java.sql.Types.

The implementation is as follows:

```
package com.apress.hibernaterecipes.chapter4.model.recipe5;

import java.io.Serializable;
import java.math.BigDecimal;
import java.sql.PreparedStatement;
import java.sql.ResultSet;
import java.sql.SQLException;

import org.hibernate.HibernateException;
import org.hibernate.engine.spi.SessionImplementor;
import org.hibernate.type.BigDecimalType;
import org.hibernate.type.Type;
import org.hibernate.usertype.CompositeUserType;

public class GeolocationType implements CompositeUserType {

    @Override
    public Class<?> returnedClass() {
        return byte[].class;
    }

    @Override
    public String[] getPropertyNames() {
        return new String[] { "latitude", "longitude" };
    }

    @Override
    public Type[] getPropertyTypes() {
        return new Type[] { BigDecimalType.INSTANCE, BigDecimalType.INSTANCE };
    }

    @Override
    public boolean equals(Object o, Object o2) throws HibernateException {
        return o.equals(o2);
    }

    @Override
    public int hashCode(Object o) throws HibernateException {
        return o.hashCode();
    }
```

```java
@Override
public Object nullSafeGet(ResultSet resultSet, String[] names,
        SessionImplementor sessionImplementor, Object o)
        throws HibernateException, SQLException {
    assert names.length == 2;
    BigDecimal latitude = (BigDecimal) BigDecimalType.INSTANCE.get(
            resultSet, names[0], sessionImplementor);
    BigDecimal longitude = (BigDecimal) BigDecimalType.INSTANCE.get(
            resultSet, names[1], sessionImplementor);
    return latitude == null && longitude == null ? null : new Geolocation(
            latitude, longitude);
}

@Override
public void nullSafeSet(PreparedStatement preparedStatement, Object value,
        int index, SessionImplementor sessionImplementor)
        throws HibernateException, SQLException {
    if (value == null) {
        BigDecimalType.INSTANCE.set(preparedStatement, null, index,
                sessionImplementor);
        BigDecimalType.INSTANCE.set(preparedStatement, null, index + 1,
                sessionImplementor);
    } else {
        Geolocation location = (Geolocation) value;
        BigDecimalType.INSTANCE.set(preparedStatement,
                location.getLatitude(), index, sessionImplementor);
        BigDecimalType.INSTANCE.set(preparedStatement,
                location.getLongitude(), index + 1,
                                    sessionImplementor);
    }
}

@Override
public Object deepCopy(Object value) throws HibernateException {
    return value;
}

@Override
public boolean isMutable() {
    return false;
}

@Override
public Object getPropertyValue(Object component, int property)
        throws HibernateException {
    if (component == null) {
        return null;
    }
```

```java
        Geolocation location = (Geolocation) component;
        switch (property) {
        case 0:
            return location.getLatitude();
        case 1:
            return location.getLongitude();
        default:
            throw new HibernateException("invalid property index " + property);
        }
    }

    @Override
    public void setPropertyValue(Object component, int property, Object value)
            throws HibernateException {
        if (component == null) {
            return;
        }
        Geolocation location = (Geolocation) component;
        // all of our properties are BigDecimal, so this is safe
        BigDecimal val = (BigDecimal) value;
        switch (property) {
        case 0:
            location.setLatitude(val);
            break;
        case 1:
            location.setLongitude(val);
            break;
        default:
            throw new HibernateException("invalid property index " + property);
        }
    }

    @Override
    public Serializable disassemble(Object value, SessionImplementor session)
            throws HibernateException {
        return null;
    }

    @Override
    public Object assemble(Serializable cached, SessionImplementor session,
            Object owner) throws HibernateException {
        return null;
    }

    @Override
    public Object replace(Object original, Object target,
            SessionImplementor session, Object owner) throws HibernateException {
        return null;
    }
}
```

Now you can see how this custom type is used in an Address entity:

```java
@Data
@Entity
@TypeDef(name="Geolocation", typeClass=GeolocationType.class)
public class Address {
    @Id
    @GeneratedValue
    Long id;
    @Column
    String streetAddress;
    @Type(type="com.apress.hibernaterecipes.chapter4.model.recipe5.GeolocationType")
    @Columns(columns={@Column(name="latitude"),@Column(name="longitude")})
    Geolocation geolocation;
}
```

Now you see how the type can be used with a few tests. The first test writes (and queries) an Address; the second uses the geolocation data in a query:

```java
@Test
public void testReadWrite() {
    Session session = SessionManager.openSession();
    Transaction tx = session.beginTransaction();
    Address address=new Address();
    address.setStreetAddress("100 E. Davie Street");
    address.setGeolocation(new Geolocation(35.7754700,-78.6379910));
    session.persist(address);
    tx.commit();
    session.close();

    session = SessionManager.openSession();
    tx = session.beginTransaction();
    Address address2=(Address) session
            .byId(Address.class)
            .load(address.getId());
    assertEquals(address2.getGeolocation().getLongitude().doubleValue(),
            address.getGeolocation().getLongitude().doubleValue(),
            0.01);
    tx.commit();
    session.close();
}

@Test
public void testQueryAttribute() {
    testReadWrite();
    Session session = SessionManager.openSession();
    Transaction tx = session.beginTransaction();
    Address address=new Address();
    address.setStreetAddress("89 E 42nd Street");
    address.setGeolocation(new Geolocation(40.7524710,-73.9772950));
```

```
        session.persist(address);
        tx.commit();
        session.close();

        session = SessionManager.openSession();
        tx = session.beginTransaction();
        Query query=session.createQuery(
                "from Address a where a.geolocation.latitude < :latitude");
        query.setBigDecimal("latitude", new BigDecimal(38));
        List<Address> results=query.list();
        assertEquals(results.size(), 1);
        assertTrue(results.get(0).getStreetAddress().contains("100"));
        tx.commit();
        session.close();
}
```

Summary

In this chapter, you learned the four basic inheritance strategies: table per class hierarchy, table per subclass, table per concrete class with unions, and table per concrete class with implicit polymorphism (see Table 4-1). You saw the implementation of these four inheritance mapping strategies and learned how to choose the appropriate strategy.

Table 4-1. *Polymorphic Associations Supported by Various Inheritance Strategies*

Inheritance Strategy	Polymorphic Many-to-One	Polymorphic One-to-One	Polymorphic One-to-Many	Polymorphic Many-to-Many
Table per class hierarchy	<many-to-one>	<one-to-one>	<one-to-many>	<many-to-many>
Table per subclass	<many-to-one>	<one-to-one>	<one-to-many>	<many-to-many>
Table per concrete class with unions	<many-to-one>	<one-to-one>	<one-to-many> (for Inverse="true" only)	<many-to-many>
Table per concrete class with implicit polymorphism	<any>	Not supported	Not supported	<many-to-any>

You also saw how to explicitly map a user type without establishing an external entity relationship, similar to embeddable mapped objects but with explicit control.

You learned how inheritance mapping enables polymorphic queries; Table 4-2 summarizes the polymorphic query capabilities supported by various inheritance strategies. You also learned about the basic data types that Hibernate supports and the implementation of some custom data types.

Table 4-2. Polymorphic Queries Supported by Various Inheritance Strategies

Inheritance Strategy	Polymorphic load()/get()	Polymorphic Queries	Polymorphic Joins	Outer Join Fetching
Table per class hierarchy	Supported	Supported	Supported	Supported
Table per subclass	Supported	Supported	Supported	Supported
Table per concrete class with unions	Supported	Supported	Supported	Supported
Table per concrete class with implicit polymorphism	Supported	Supported	Not supported	Not supported

Chapter 5 looks at actual object relationships.

CHAPTER 5

■ ■ ■

Many-to-One and One-to-One Mapping

In general, entities are related or associated to each other. For example, a Customer entity is associated with an Address entity. A Customer entity can have one or more than one Address entity (for example, Billing and Shipping).[1] These relationships or associations are represented differently in a relational model and the domain/object model.

In a relational model, a foreign key column represents the dependency of one table on another. The Customer table has an AddressId as the foreign key column, which is the primary key of the Address table.

From the Customer entity perspective, it is a many-to-one relationship because it can have multiple addresses. On the other hand, from the Address entity perspective, it is a one-to-one relationship because one address can belong to only one customer.

The same relationship is represented in terms of classes and attributes in an object model. The Customer class has an attribute to hold multiple addresses belonging to that Customer entity (in Java, it is represented as a collection: List, Set, and so on). The Address class has an attribute of Customer type.

In the case of the Customer and Address entities example, you consider the association from the view of both the Customer entity and the Address entity, so it is a *bidirectional association*. If you use the association from only one entity, it is a *unidirectional association*. In an object/relational mapping (ORM) framework, these relationships are represented using metadata held in either a configuration file or in the source code for the object model.[2]

This chapter shows you how these associations are represented in Hibernate and also discusses the following features:

- Various ways to use many-to-one and one-to-one mappings

- How to make unidirectional associations into bidirectional associations

- How to use features such as lazy initialization and cascade

- How to map an association or a join table

---

[1]Or, as discussed in Chapter 3, we could have holiday contact addresses, too, which much be a *really* nice problem to have to address, so to speak.
[2]There are multiple tools available to help generate a model, including Hibernate Tools (http://hibernate.org/tools/), which is supported and maintained by the Hibernate team.

5-1. Using Many-To-One Associations

Problem

Imagine you are a publisher with many books. Because you value what your readers have to contribute, you allow them to submit errata for a given book, and the errata go through a process by which they're sent to the author or discarded. In this example, Book1[3] has a set of ReaderErrata1.[4] The relationship between ReaderErrata1 and Book1 is a many-to-one relationship. How can this be mapped? How can you cascade changes throughout the hierarchy?

Solution

In this situation, *many-to-one* is a many-to-one relationship, as already mentioned. In a data model, the relationship is expressed in the "child" entity (ReaderErrata in this case). Hibernate uses Java Persistence API (JPA) relationship annotations to create this structure.

How It Works

First, let's take a look at our two object types, Book1 and ReaderErrata1. First, Book1:

```
@Entity
@Data
@NoArgsConstructor
public class Book1 {
    @Id
    @GeneratedValue()
    Long id;
    @Column(nullable = false)
    String title;
}
```

Now let's take a look at ReaderErrata1:

```
@Entity
@Data
@NoArgsConstructor
public class ReaderErrata1 {
    @Id
    @GeneratedValue()
    Long id;
    @ManyToOne
    Book1 book;
    @Temporal(TemporalType.TIMESTAMP)
    Date submitted;
    @Column(nullable = false)
    String content;
}
```

---

[3]Why Book1 and not Book? We may reuse this object model in other recipes in this chapter, and we don't want collisions. We could use namespaces to help, but this naming convention means that we don't have to *try* to avoid collisions; they're avoided by default, at the cost of the names being a touch silly.

[4]Clearly, this example is entirely fabricated and has no bearing on what happens with actual books.

Here's the Hibernate configuration we use for this chapter (missing the other recipes' entities):

```xml
<?xml version="1.0" encoding="UTF-8"?>
<!DOCTYPE hibernate-configuration PUBLIC
        "-//Hibernate/Hibernate Configuration DTD 3.0//EN"
        "http://www.hibernate.org/dtd/hibernate-configuration-3.0.dtd">
<hibernate-configuration>
    <session-factory>
        <property name="connection.driver_class">org.hsqldb.jdbcDriver</property>
        <property name="connection.url">jdbc:hsqldb:file:../chapter4;write_delay=false
        </property>
        <property name="hibernate.dialect">org.hibernate.dialect.HSQLDialect</property>
        <property name="hibernate.hbm2ddl.auto">create</property>
        <property name="hibernate.show_sql">true</property>
        <property name="hibernate.discriminator.ignore_explicit_for_joined">true</property>

        <mapping class="com.apress.hibernaterecipes.chapter5.recipe1.Book1"/>
        <mapping class="com.apress.hibernaterecipes.chapter5.recipe1.ReaderErrata1"/>
        <!-- other mappings go here -->
    </session-factory>
</hibernate-configuration>
```

Now let's take a look at some code to write (and read) an object graph:

```java
@BeforeMethod
public void cleanAll() {
    Session session = SessionManager.openSession();
    Transaction tx = session.beginTransaction();
    session.createQuery("delete from ReaderErrata1 ").executeUpdate();
    session.createQuery("delete from Book1").executeUpdate();
    tx.commit();
    session.close();
}

@Test
public void persistExplicitGraph() {
    Session session = SessionManager.openSession();
    Transaction tx = session.beginTransaction();
    Book1 book1 = new Book1();
    book1.setTitle("Hibernate Recipes");
    session.persist(book1);
    ReaderErrata1 re = new ReaderErrata1();
    re.setBook(book1);
    re.setContent("First chapter is too short");
    session.persist(re);
    tx.commit();
    session.close();

    session = SessionManager.openSession();
    tx = session.beginTransaction();
    ReaderErrata1 re1 = (ReaderErrata1) session.byId(ReaderErrata1.class).load(re.getId());
    assertNotNull(re1);
```

```
    assertNotNull(re1.getBook());
    assertEquals(re1.getBook().getTitle(), book1.getTitle());
    tx.commit();
    session.close();
}
```

If you extrapolate this kind of structure to a large number of entity types (or entities), persisting the entire structure becomes a lot of rather repetitive code, with very little contributing value. We can therefore add a cascade attribute to @ManyToOne to indicate that we want to cascade updates through the entire object graph. Here's the modified ReaderErrata1 class, followed by a test that is virtually identical to persistExplicitGraph(), except that it doesn't include the session.persist(book1) call:

```
@Entity
@Data
@NoArgsConstructor
public class ReaderErrata1 {
    @Id
    @GeneratedValue()
    Long id;
    @ManyToOne(cascade = CascadeType.PERSIST)
    Book1 book;
    @Temporal(TemporalType.TIMESTAMP)
    Date submitted;
    @Column(nullable = false)
    String content;
}

@Test
public void persistImplicitGraph() {
    Session session = SessionManager.openSession();
    Transaction tx = session.beginTransaction();
    Book1 book1 = new Book1();
    book1.setTitle("Hibernate Recipes");
    ReaderErrata1 re = new ReaderErrata1();
    re.setBook(book1);
    re.setContent("First chapter is too short");
    session.persist(re);
    tx.commit();
    session.close();

    session = SessionManager.openSession();
    tx = session.beginTransaction();
    ReaderErrata1 re1 = (ReaderErrata1) session.byId(ReaderErrata1.class).load(re.getId());
    assertNotNull(re1);
    assertNotNull(re1.getBook());
    assertEquals(re1.getBook().getTitle(), book1.getTitle());
    tx.commit();
    session.close();
}
```

The `cascade` parameter takes an array of `CascadeType`s. You can cascade different types of Hibernate operations: persistence (as shown), which persists writes and updates through managed objects; merges, which manage updates to previously persisted objects; deletions; or refreshes (the analog to the merge cascade operation).

5-2. Using a Many-to-One Association with a Join Table

Problem

Sometimes you don't want an association polluting your domain model. In the first recipe, `ReaderErrata1` had a reference to `Book1`, which makes perfect sense because if there were no book, an error wouldn't exist for it. Let's consider a publisher-matching service instead, in which publishers who have published no books can exist, and books can exist without publishers.

For this example, we don't want to pollute the database model for our books with references to publishers; this implies the use of a join table (a table with references to the different participants in the relationship). A join table gives us a more normal schema for our database.

How do you represent this data structure in Hibernate? And what are the additional features that it provides to manage this kind of association?

Solution

Hibernate uses the `@JoinTable` annotation to specify that a reference is external to the entity being joined. The annotation requires that a name for the join table be specified, but the rest is automatic.

How It Works

Figure 5-1 shows an entity-relationship diagram (ERD) of what the database will look like when our model has been persisted. One thing the ERD does not show is that `BOOKS_ID` (in the `PUBLISHER2_BOOK2` join table) is unique, making this a one-to-many relationship.

Figure 5-1. *Entity-relationship drawing showing a many-to-one association with a join table*

Here are our two entities, with the `Publisher2` class first:

```
@Entity
@Data
@NoArgsConstructor
public class Publisher2 {
    @Id
    @GeneratedValue()
    Long id;
```

```
    @Column(nullable = false)
    String name;
    @Column(nullable = false)
    String address;
    @OneToMany
    List<Book2> books;
}
```

Here is the Book2 class, which specifies the join table's characteristics (the name, which is all that is required, although we can control other attributes):

```
@Entity
@Data
@NoArgsConstructor
public class Book2 {
    @Id
    @GeneratedValue()
    Long id;
    @Column(nullable = false)
    String title;
    @Column(nullable = false)
    BigDecimal price;
    @ManyToOne(cascade = CascadeType.ALL)
    @JoinTable(name = "publisher2_book2")
    Publisher2 publisher;
}
```

The BOOKS_ID column in PUBLISHER2_BOOK2 is set as unique, which makes this a one-to-many relationship instead of a many-to-many relationship. The actual SQL from this model might look like the following, depending on the actual database you use:

```
create table Book2 (id bigint generated by default as identity (start with 1),
    price numeric(19,2),
    title varchar(255) not null,
    primary key (id))
create table Publisher2 (id bigint generated by default as identity (start with 1),
    address varchar(255) not null,
    name varchar(255) not null,
    primary key (id))
create table Publisher2_Book2 (Publisher2_id bigint not null, books_id bigint not null)
alter table Publisher2_Book2
    add constraint UK_t935haip50qkt3fdu40degh89  unique (books_id)
alter table Publisher2_Book2
    add constraint FK_t935haip50qkt3fdu40degh89 foreign key (books_id)
        references Book2
alter table Publisher2_Book2
    add constraint FK_19615po0x188x15ct5h0etwmc foreign key (Publisher2_id)
        references Publisher2
```

5-3. Using Lazy Initialization on Many-to-One Associations

Problem

In an association between two entities in an ORM framework, when the data of one entity is loaded from the database, the data of the dependent entity can be fetched along with it or loaded on demand.

For example, in the case of Book1 and ReaderErrata1 from Recipe 5.1, the READERERRATA1 table has the foreign key column book_id. If ReaderErrata1 details are fetched from the database, should the Book1 details be loaded along with them, or should the Book1 details be retrieved only when you explicitly fetch them? When the dependent object's details are loaded only on demand, they're said to be *lazily loaded*. By lazily loading data, you can improve performance because unnecessary queries aren't executed.

How is lazy initialization achieved in Hibernate? What effect does it have when you're retrieving an object graph? And what are the ways to deal with it?

Solution

Enabling lazy initialization defines what objects are available on the detached object. It is defined with the keyword lazy, which is different from the keyword fetch. The keyword fetch is used to define fetching strategies for tuning performance.

Hibernate provides lazy initialization of collections, associations, and even properties or value types. (You will learn more about lazy initialization of collections in the next chapter). The value types of an entity can also be lazily initialized, but it is usually not required; it can be used with databases that have hundreds of columns.

How It Works

Let's look at an object model with three types: Book3, ReaderErrata3Eager, and ReaderErrata3Lazy. The two errata types will be identical, except that we specify eager or lazy initialization for the Book3 type. Here are the entities:

```
// in Book3.java
@Entity
@Data
@NoArgsConstructor
public class Book3 {
    @Id
    @GeneratedValue()
    Long id;
    @Column(nullable = false)
    String title;
}

// in ReaderErrata3Eager.java
@Entity
@Data
@NoArgsConstructor
public class ReaderErrata3Eager {
    @Id
    @GeneratedValue()
    Long id;
```

97

```
    @ManyToOne(fetch = FetchType.EAGER)
    Book3 book;
    @Temporal(TemporalType.TIMESTAMP)
    Date submitted;
    @Column(nullable = false)
    String content;
}

// in ReaderErrata3Lazy.java
@Entity
@Data
@NoArgsConstructor
public class ReaderErrata3Lazy {
    @Id
    @GeneratedValue()
    Long id;
    @ManyToOne(fetch = FetchType.LAZY)
    Book3 book;
    @Temporal(TemporalType.TIMESTAMP)
    Date submitted;
    @Column(nullable = false)
    String content;
}
```

To see what happens and when, let's create a test for this model. First, we create a data set with known data:

```
public class Recipe3 {
    long eagerKey;
    long lazyKey;

    @BeforeMethod
    public void initialize() {
        Session session = SessionManager.openSession();
        Transaction tx = session.beginTransaction();

        session.createQuery("delete from ReaderErrata3Eager").executeUpdate();
        session.createQuery("delete from ReaderErrata3Lazy").executeUpdate();
        session.createQuery("delete from Book1").executeUpdate();

        Book3 book3 = new Book3();
        book3.setTitle("The Dog in the Fog");
        session.persist(book3);

        ReaderErrata3Eager eager = new ReaderErrata3Eager();
        eager.setContent("Test eager data");
        eager.setBook(book3);
        session.save(eager);
        eagerKey = eager.getId();
```

```
        ReaderErrata3Lazy lazy = new ReaderErrata3Lazy();
        lazy.setContent("Test lazy data");
        lazy.setBook(book3);
        session.save(lazy);
        lazyKey = lazy.getId();

        tx.commit();
        session.close();
    }
}
```

Our tests then have access to the primary keys of the errata instances. We can test the loading status by simply starting a session and transaction, fetching the errata, and then closing the session. After the session is closed, accessing the book reference through the errata instance gives us different results based on when the book reference is loaded.

Let's look at the eager test first. *Eager loading* means that it is loaded as soon as possible (i.e., when the ReaderErrata3Eager type is loaded), so we should be able to close the Session and still access the Book3 instance's data:

```
@Test
public void testEager() {
    Session session = SessionManager.openSession();
    Transaction tx = session.beginTransaction();
    ReaderErrata3Eager eager = (ReaderErrata3Eager) session
            .byId(ReaderErrata3Eager.class)
            .load(eagerKey);
    tx.commit();
    session.close();
    assertEquals(eager.getBook().getTitle(), "The Dog in the Fog");
}
```

So far, so good. If we use the same code with the ReaderErrata3Lazy type, though, we expect an exception because the Book3 data is not loadable when the session is closed. Therefore, we need to add an expected exception to the @Test annotation:

```
@Test(expectedExceptions = LazyInitializationException.class)
public void testLazy() {
    Session session = SessionManager.openSession();
    Transaction tx = session.beginTransaction();
    ReaderErrata3Lazy lazy = (ReaderErrata3Lazy) session
            .byId(ReaderErrata3Lazy.class)
            .load(lazyKey);
    tx.commit();
    session.close();
    assertEquals(lazy.getBook().getTitle(), "The Dog in the Fog");
}
```

How do we get around the lazy initialization? Well... there are lots of ways, depending on the runtime environment. You can always keep the session alive (in other words, access the data before closing the Session), for example. There's also a way to initialize the collection without having to specifically access it: Hibernate.initialize(). Here's an example of the lazy test (without the lazy initialization exception):

```
@Test
public void testLazyWorking() {
    Session session = SessionManager.openSession();
    Transaction tx = session.beginTransaction();
    ReaderErrata3Lazy lazy = (ReaderErrata3Lazy) session
            .byId(ReaderErrata3Lazy.class)
            .load(lazyKey);
    Hibernate.initialize(lazy.getBook());
    tx.commit();
    session.close();
    assertEquals(lazy.getBook().getTitle(), "The Dog in the Fog");
}
```

5-4. Creating a One-to-One Association Using a Foreign Key
Problem

Let's say for the sake of an example that one Customer entity has only one Address entity and one Address entity belongs to only one Customer entity.[5] This means there is a one-to-one relationship between a Customer and an Address entity. How can you represent a one-to-one association in Hibernate?

Solution

Hibernate supports the use of @OneToOne. Each entity simply includes a reference for the matching other entity; Hibernate manages the rest. Setting up cascading makes modification and maintenance very easy. The use of a foreign key helps improve query efficiency.

How It Works

Here are the two entity classes: Customer4 and Address4. The relationship is bidirectional in this model; in other words, given an Address4, we automatically have a reference to the Customer4, and vice versa. In a unidirectional relationship between Customer4 and Address4 with Customer4 as the owner, we'd have to run a query to determine the Customer4 matching a given Address4.[6]

```
@Entity
@Data
@NoArgsConstructor
public class Customer4 implements Serializable {
    @Id
    @GeneratedValue(strategy = GenerationType.IDENTITY)
    Integer id;
```

---

[5]Apparently only one person is allowed to live at any given address in this model. Thankfully, it is only an example.
[6]Trust us, this makes sense. If it is confusing, it is because one-to-one relationships like this should be fairly rare.

```
    String name;
    @OneToOne(cascade = CascadeType.ALL)
    private Address4 address4;
}

@Entity
@Data
@NoArgsConstructor
public class Address4 implements Serializable {
    @Id
    @GeneratedValue(strategy = GenerationType.IDENTITY)
    int id;
    @OneToOne
    Customer4 customer;
    String address;
    String city;
}
```

This creates a data model that looks like Figure 5-2:

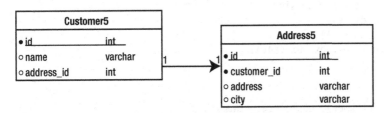

Figure 5-2. *A one-to-one relationship with a foreign key*

The Address4 table has a foreign key relationship with Customer4. Using the data model is fairly straightforward. Note that the one-to-one relationship means we can't just delete all Customer4 entities through the Hibernate Query Language (because it does not follow object relationships):

```
public class Recipe4 {
    @BeforeMethod
    public void clearAll() {
        Session session = SessionManager.openSession();
        Transaction tx = session.beginTransaction();
        Query query = session.createQuery("from Customer4 c");
        List<Customer4> customers = query.list();
        for (Customer4 c : customers) {
            session.delete(c);
        }
        tx.commit();
        session.close();
    }
```

```
@Test
public void testOneToOne() {
    Session session = SessionManager.openSession();
    Transaction tx = session.beginTransaction();
    Customer4 customer4 = new Customer4();
    customer4.setName("Absalom");
    session.persist(customer4);

    Address4 address4 = new Address4();
    address4.setAddress("100 Hebron Way");
    address4.setCity("Tel Aviv");

    address4.setCustomer(customer4);
    customer4.setAddress4(address4);

    tx.commit();
    session.close();

    session = SessionManager.openSession();
    tx = session.beginTransaction();
    Customer4 customer = (Customer4) session
            .byId(Customer4.class)
            .load(Customer4.getId());
    Hibernate.initialize(customer.getAddress4());
    tx.commit();
    session.close();

    assertEquals(customer.getName(), customer4.getName());
    assertEquals(customer.getAddress4().getAddress(),
            customer4.getAddress4().getAddress());
    }
}
```

5-5. Creating a One-to-One Association Using a Join Table

Problem

Another strategy to represent a one-to-one association uses a join table. As explained in Recipe 5.2, the foreign key in a table is null in some scenarios. To avoid storing the rows with null foreign keys, you can create a join table that holds the IDs of both dependent entities. How do you use a join table to establish a one-to-one association in Hibernate?

Solution

The last method of mapping a one-to-one association uses a join-table element with a many-to-one association. The associations would be unique for both join columns (an object could only appear one time in the join table). This method is seldom used.

How It Works

The setup is fairly simple: define the relationships in the objects as you normally would; then specify the join table characteristics. Both sides need to know about the mapping, but the good news is that it is very simple to use. Let's look at the Customer5 and Address5 classes, which look very similar to the prior recipe's versions, except for the highlighted changes:

```java
@Entity
@Data
@NoArgsConstructor
public class Customer5 implements Serializable {
    @Id
    @GeneratedValue(strategy = GenerationType.IDENTITY)
    Integer id;
    String name;
    @OneToOne(cascade = CascadeType.ALL)
    @JoinTable(name = "customer_address",
            joinColumns = @JoinColumn(name = "customer_id"),
            inverseJoinColumns = @JoinColumn(name = "address_id"))
    private Address5 address5;
}

@Entity
@Data
@NoArgsConstructor
public class Address5 implements Serializable {
    @Id
    @GeneratedValue(strategy = GenerationType.IDENTITY)
    int id;
    @OneToOne(mappedBy = "address5")
    Customer5 customer;
    String address;
    String city;
}
```

Our test code can actually be exactly the same, with the difference being the entity type names:

```java
@Test
public void testOneToOne() {
    Session session = SessionManager.openSession();
    Transaction tx = session.beginTransaction();
    Customer5 customer5 = new Customer5();
    customer5.setName("Absalom");
    session.persist(customer5);

    Address5 address5 = new Address5();
    address5.setAddress("100 Hebron Way");
    address5.setCity("Tel Aviv");

    address5.setCustomer(customer5);
    customer5.setAddress5(address5);
```

```
        tx.commit();
        session.close();

        session = SessionManager.openSession();
        tx = session.beginTransaction();
        Customer5 customer = (Customer5) session
                .byId(Customer5.class)
                .load(customer5.getId());
        Hibernate.initialize(customer.getAddress5());
        tx.commit();
        session.close();

        assertEquals(customer.getName(), customer5.getName());
        assertEquals(customer.getAddress5().getAddress(),
                customer5.getAddress5().getAddress());
    }
```

Summary

This chapter showed you how to represent and work with many-to-one and one-to-one associations using Hibernate. For a many-to-one association, you define the <many-to-one> mapping element in the class that has the *many* side of the relationship. When there can be null foreign key values, you use a join table to map between the two dependent objects; the join table contains IDs of both the dependent objects.

You learned that you can use lazy initialization to increase performance because the data of the dependent object is retrieved from the database only on demand. You also learned that shared primary keys are used when rows in two tables are related by a primary key association.

You saw how to map a one-to-one association with a @ManyToOne annotation with a unique constraint on the *one* relationship. A one-to-one association can also be mapped using a join table.

The next chapter addresses collection mapping, one of the forms of representing collections of objects (especially objects that aren't entities).

CHAPTER 6

Collection Mapping

Collection mapping refers to the concept of an object in the database—an entity—that possesses references to a set of other objects, none of which exists outside the context of the owning object. An example is an order line item: an order has many line items, although it might exist without any. However, because a line item does not have any way to exist outside of the context of its order, the order might be said to have a collection of line items.

In Hibernate, this is modeled through the use of the standard Java API collections. An entity merely declares the correct type of collection, along with how to replicate the collection.[1] Each of the major collection types (List, Set, and Map) are supported internally, and their Java declarations are trivial (and idiomatic). As an example, the following code declares chapters to be type java.util.Set (which is an interface) with the matching implementation as java.util.HashSet:

```
private Set<String> chapters = new HashSet<String>();
```

This chapter shows you how to map collections for value types. In Hibernate, collections can be lazily initialized, which means the state of the collection objects is loaded from the database only when the application needs it. This initialization is done transparently from the user. The chapter also deals with sorting collections in memory and at database level. Off we go!

6-1. Mapping a Set
Problem

How do you map value types as collections of type java.util.Set?

Solution

In Java, a Set is a collection of unique elements. For Hibernate, HashSet is probably the best concrete implementation; it is a Set that does *not* provide a specific order of elements. (If you need order, use a List instead.)

How It Works

We will discuss two types of collections to show you how they're declared differently in the entities. Our data model will end up looking like Figure 6-1.

---

[1]A Set and a List might look the same to the database—or they might not. A List might need to include the ordering of each referenced object. A Set means each contained object is referenced only once by that particular collection, which might have implications on the database structure as well.

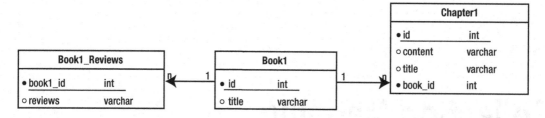

Figure 6-1. *Our data model*

Our object model needs only two entities, though—Book1 and Chapter1—with the reviews being automatically managed by Hibernate. First, let's look at Book1:

```
@Entity
@Data
@NoArgsConstructor
public class Book1 {
    @Id
    @GeneratedValue(strategy = GenerationType.IDENTITY)
    int id;
    String title;
    @OneToMany(cascade = CascadeType.ALL, mappedBy = "book")
    Set<Chapter1> chapters = new HashSet<>();
    @ElementCollection
    @Column(name="review")
    Set<String> reviews=new HashSet<>();
}
```

This is fairly standard and should be familiar based on what you've seen so far, except for @ElementCollection. This annotation is used to define a collection of embeddable objects, which aren't necessarily entities. We could use it to manage our chapters (for example, if we didn't want to mark Chapter1 as an entity).[2]

We use @Column(name="review") to force the actual column name to make sense; otherwise, Hibernate would infer the name from the attribute name, so our table would have book1_id and reviews. It wouldn't *hurt* anything, but it would look silly (because each row wouldn't be a set of reviews; it would be a review). We're angling for grammatical correctness.

Now let's take a look at Chapter1. We can't use @Data as with many entities so far, largely because of the bidirectional relationship between Chapter1 and Book1. hashCode() and toString() would both try to call the Book1 versions of the same methods, which would cause an infinite recursion (and a stack overflow). Because we're using a HashSet, we *know* these methods will be called, so we need to definitely prevent them from recursing into Book1. We also include @Builder and @AllArgsConstructor annotations to simplify working with Chapter1.

```
@Entity
@NoArgsConstructor
@Builder
@AllArgsConstructor
@EqualsAndHashCode(exclude = "book")
@ToString(exclude = "book")
```

---

[2]You will see how this is done in a few pages.

```java
public class Chapter1 {
    @Getter
    @Setter
    @Id
    @GeneratedValue(strategy = GenerationType.IDENTITY)
    int id;
    @Getter
    @Setter
    String title;
    @Getter
    @Setter
    String content;
    @ManyToOne(optional = false)
    @Getter
    @Setter
    Book1 book;
}
```

Because both Chapter1 and Book1 are entities, they need to be included in the hibernate.cfg.xml file:[3]

```xml
<?xml version="1.0" encoding="UTF-8"?>
<!DOCTYPE hibernate-configuration PUBLIC
        "-//Hibernate/Hibernate Configuration DTD 3.0//EN"
        "http://www.hibernate.org/dtd/hibernate-configuration-3.0.dtd">
<hibernate-configuration>
    <session-factory>
        <property name="connection.driver_class">org.h2.Driver</property>
        <property name="connection.url">jdbc:h2:file:./chapter6</property>
        <property name="hibernate.dialect">org.hibernate.dialect.HSQLDialect</property>
        <property name="hibernate.hbm2ddl.auto">create</property>
        <property name="hibernate.show_sql">true</property>
        <property name="hibernate.discriminator.ignore_explicit_for_joined">true</property>
        <property name="connection.username"></property>
        <property name="connection.password"></property>
        <mapping class="com.apress.hibernaterecipes.chapter6.recipe1.Book1"/>
        <mapping class="com.apress.hibernaterecipes.chapter6.recipe1.Chapter1"/>
    </session-factory>
</hibernate-configuration>
```

The good news is that we still can interact with this data model as if it were pure Java. Here's the test code for this iteration of Book1 and Chapter1:

```java
@Test
public void testBook() {
    Session session = SessionManager.openSession();
    Transaction tx = session.beginTransaction();
    Book1 book = new Book1();
    book.setTitle("First book");
```

---

[3]As in previous chapters, this configuration does not yet include the data from other recipes in this chapter.

```
        Chapter1 chapter = Chapter1.builder()
                .book(book)
                .title("first chapter")
                .content("contents")
                .build();
        book.getChapters().add(chapter);

        chapter = Chapter1.builder()
                .book(book)
                .title("second chapter")
                .content("more contents")
                .build();
        book.getChapters().add(chapter);

        book.getReviews().add("This book is great");
        book.getReviews().add("This book is light on content");
        book.getReviews().add("This book is great");

        session.persist(book);
        tx.commit();
        session.close();

        session = SessionManager.openSession();
        tx = session.beginTransaction();

        Book1 book1 = (Book1) session.byId(Book1.class)
                .load(book.getId());
        assertEquals(book1.getReviews().size(), 2);
        assertEquals(book1.getChapters().size(), 2);

        tx.commit();
        session.close();
}
```

What if we don't want Chapter1 to be a separately mapped entity? Let's create Book1Embedded and Chapter1Embedded to show how to do it.

First, we need to mark Chapter1Embedded as @Embeddable, and remove id and book as attributes:[4]

```
@Embeddable
@NoArgsConstructor
@Builder
@AllArgsConstructor
public class Chapter1Embedded {
    @Getter
    @Setter
    String title;
    @Getter
    @Setter
    String content;
}
```

---

[4]An embeddable item doesn't have its own primary key and doesn't need the @ManyToOne relationship included because it doesn't exist outside of the relationship with its containing object.

Next, the Book1Embedded chapters reference should be annotated with @ElementCollection instead of @OneToMany; we no longer need cascade set because an @ElementCollection is automatically managed by the containing object.

```java
@Entity
@Data
@NoArgsConstructor
public class Book1Embedded {
    @Id
    @GeneratedValue(strategy = GenerationType.IDENTITY)
    int id;
    String title;
    @ElementCollection
    Set<Chapter1Embedded> chapters = new HashSet<>();
    @ElementCollection
    @Column(name="review")
    Set<String> reviews = new HashSet<>();
}
```

We need to add Book1Embedded to the hibernate.hbm.xml configuration, but *only* Book1Embedded because Chapter1Embedded is no longer an entity. Once we do that, our test code looks remarkably like the version without the embedded Chapter1 entity, missing only the lines in which we set the chapters' references to the containing Book1.

```java
@Test
public void testEmbedded() {
    Session session = SessionManager.openSession();
    Transaction tx = session.beginTransaction();
    Book1Embedded book = new Book1Embedded();
    book.setTitle("First book");
    Chapter1Embedded chapter = Chapter1Embedded.builder()

            .title("first chapter")
            .content("contents")
            .build();
    book.getChapters().add(chapter);

    chapter = Chapter1Embedded.builder()
            .title("second chapter")
            .content("more contents")
            .build();
    book.getChapters().add(chapter);

    book.getReviews().add("This book is great");
    book.getReviews().add("This book is light on content");
    book.getReviews().add("This book is great");

    session.persist(book);
    tx.commit();
    session.close();

    session = SessionManager.openSession();
    tx = session.beginTransaction();
```

```
Book1Embedded book1 = (Book1Embedded) session
        .byId(Book1Embedded.class)
        .load(book.getId());
assertEquals(book1.getReviews().size(), 2);
assertEquals(book1.getChapters().size(), 2);

tx.commit();
session.close();
}
```

6-2. Mapping a Bag

Problem

A bag is a collection of objects that can have duplicates. It doesn't have any order. It is similar to an ArrayList, but it doesn't retain its index. How do you map value types as collections of type bag? What is the difference between a bag without an ID and a bag with an ID? How do you map a value class in a bag with an associated ID?

Solution

The Java Collections API doesn't have anything called a *bag*. Java developers who want to use bag-like semantics use the java.util.List implementation. Hibernate does the same by requiring the implementation to be an ArrayList. Hibernate recommends using java.util.Collection or java.util.List (which is probably preferable) as the interface to map bag elements. The join table typically doesn't have a primary key when the mapping is done, although one can be added (in which case it becomes a bag with associated ID).

How It Works

The Book2 class has a property called reviews that is of type java.util.List. The property is initialized as an ArrayList:

```
@Entity
@Data
@NoArgsConstructor
public class Book2 {
    @Id
    @GeneratedValue(strategy = GenerationType.IDENTITY)
    int id;
    String title;
    @ElementCollection
    List<String> reviews = new ArrayList<>();
}
```

Our testing code is very straightforward:

```
@Test
public void testBagNoId() {
    Session session=SessionManager.openSession();
    Transaction tx=session.beginTransaction();
    Book2 book2=new Book2();
```

```
book2.setTitle("Title");
book2.getReviews().add("awesome book");
book2.getReviews().add("best ever");
// duplicate is intentional; it's allowed in a bag!
book2.getReviews().add("best ever");

session.persist(book2);
tx.commit();
session.close();

session=SessionManager.openSession();
tx=session.beginTransaction();
Book2 book= (Book2) session.byId(Book2.class)
        .load(book2.getId());
assertEquals(book.getReviews().size(), 3);
book.getReviews().remove(0); // remove the first one
tx.commit();
session.close();

session=SessionManager.openSession();
tx=session.beginTransaction();
book= (Book2) session.byId(Book2.class)
        .load(book2.getId());
assertEquals(book.getReviews().size(), 2);
book.getReviews().set(0, "updated review");
tx.commit();
session.close();}
```

Adding an ID to the reviews property makes modifying the collection more efficient. Ordinarily, changes to bag require removing the entire set and replacing it. Thus, when we remove the first review, Hibernate must clear out the entire bag and repopulate it with multiple SQL INSERT statements. However, bags with associated IDs (known hereafter as "idbags") are most easily mapped with XML rather than with annotations.[5]

The Book2IdBag class looks identical in structure to the Book2 class, except it has no annotations. We will take a look at the mapping file for that class: the test code is identical to the testBagNoId() method, except with a different class being used. Finally, we will take a look at the SQL that is generated, which shows the value of idbag over a plain bag.

The Book2IdBag class definition has no persistence annotations, but uses Lombok to provide mutators, accessors, constructors, equals(), hashCode(), and toString():[6]

```
@Data
@NoArgsConstructor
public class Book2IdBag {
    int id;
    String title;
    List<String> reviews = new ArrayList<>();
}
```

---

[5]Mapping entities with XML rather than annotations is usually mandated for odd mappings or for mappings that leverage specific container features such as idbags. This is noted with some chagrin by one of your authors, who far prefers annotations if there is any possibility to use them for mapping, but uses XML when forced to do so, as in this case.
[6]And lions and tigers and bears, oh my! Imagine the joy in the world if only Lombok were to add annotations for @Lions, @Tigers, and @Bears (and @OhMy). I have no idea what these annotations would do, though.

Now we're faced with the XML configuration, which is fairly straightforward, even with the idbag definition:

```xml
<?xml version='1.0' encoding='utf-8'?>
<!DOCTYPE hibernate-mapping PUBLIC
        "-//Hibernate/Hibernate Mapping DTD 3.0//EN"
        "http://www.hibernate.org/dtd/hibernate-mapping-3.0.dtd">
<hibernate-mapping>
    <class name="com.apress.hibernaterecipes.chapter6.recipe2.Book2IdBag" >
        <id name="id" type="int">
            <generator class="native"/>
        </id>
        <property name="title">
            <column name="title" sql-type="varchar(64)" not-null="true" unique="true"/>
        </property>
        <idbag name="reviews">
            <collection-id column="review_id" type="int">
                <generator class="seqhilo" />
            </collection-id>
            <key column="book_id" />
            <element type="string" column="review" not-null="true"/>
        </idbag>
    </class>
</hibernate-mapping>
```

The hibernate.cfg.xml file needs to reference this file instead of the Book2IdBag class:

```xml
<mapping resource="com/apress/hibernaterecipes/chapter6/Book2IdBag.hbm.xml"/>
```

Now take a look at our test code, which should be identical to the prior test code, except that it uses Book2IdBag instead of Book2:

```java
@Test
public void testIdBag() {
    Session session=SessionManager.openSession();
    Transaction tx=session.beginTransaction();
    Book2IdBag book2=new Book2IdBag();
    book2.setTitle("Title");
    book2.getReviews().add("awesome book");
    book2.getReviews().add("best ever");
    // duplicate is intentional; it's allowed in a bag!
    book2.getReviews().add("best ever");

    session.persist(book2);
    tx.commit();
    session.close();

    session=SessionManager.openSession();
    tx=session.beginTransaction();
    Book2IdBag book= (Book2IdBag) session.byId(Book2IdBag.class)
            .load(book2.getId());
```

```
assertEquals(book.getReviews().size(), 3);
book.getReviews().remove(0); // remove the first one
tx.commit();
session.close();

session=SessionManager.openSession();
tx=session.beginTransaction();
book= (Book2IdBag) session.byId(Book2IdBag.class)
        .load(book2.getId());
assertEquals(book.getReviews().size(), 2);
book.getReviews().set(0, "updated review");
tx.commit();
session.close();
}
```

So what's the actual benefit of using an idbag as opposed to a plain bag? As described—performance. Let's see the SQL that is used when the bag is modified (specifically when it has an element removed):

```
Hibernate: delete from Book2_reviews where Book2_id=?
Hibernate: insert into Book2_reviews (Book2_id, reviews) values (?, ?)
Hibernate: insert into Book2_reviews (Book2_id, reviews) values (?, ?)
```

To remove a single element, it deleted *all* the reviews and repopulated the data with the reviews we didn't delete.

Now let's see what SQL was executed for the same line with Book2IdBag:

```
Hibernate: delete from Book2IdBag_reviews where review_id=?
```

This pattern persists throughout the use of the idbag. When an element is changed, the bag still has to delete all elements and repopulate the database; meanwhile, the idbag can simply issue a SQL update:

```
update Book2IdBag_reviews set review=? where review_id=?
```

In general, use an idbag instead of a bag unless your sets are typically *very* small or you're allergic to the XML.

6-3. Mapping a List

Problem

A *list* is a list of objects. It is an ordered collection. The user of a list has precise control over where in the list each element is inserted. The user can access elements by their integer index (position in the list) and search for elements in the list. How do you map value types as collections of type list?

Solution

The @OrderColumn annotation provides the capability to preserve the order of a List. To add order to our collection, we add the annotation and ordering definition; Hibernate automatically maintains the order of the List.

How It Works

Let's revisit our book class. We rename it Book3 and add the order definition:

```
@Entity
@NoArgsConstructor
@Data
public class Book3 {
    @Id
    @GeneratedValue(strategy = GenerationType.IDENTITY)
    int id;
    @Getter
    @Setter
    String title;
    @ElementCollection
    @OrderColumn(columnDefinition = "int", name = "order_column")
    @Column(name = "review")
    List<String> reviews = new ArrayList<>();
}
```

The @OrderColumn includes the type and name of the column used for ordering the reviews. All we need to do now is exercise the list of reviews to make sure the ordering is preserved. The following test method demonstrates creating the list of reviews and then altering it multiple times to make sure the order is correct:

```
@Test
public void alterElements() {
    Session session = SessionManager.openSession();
    Transaction tx = session.beginTransaction();

    Book3 book1 = new Book3();
    book1.setTitle("First Book");
    book1.getReviews().add("first review");
    book1.getReviews().add("second review");
    session.persist(book1);

    tx.commit();
    session.close();

    session = SessionManager.openSession();
    tx = session.beginTransaction();

    Book3 book = (Book3) session
            .byId(Book3.class)
            .load(book1.getId());

    // let's make sure the order is what we expected
    assertEquals(book.getReviews().size(), 2);
    assertEquals(book.getReviews().get(0), "first review");
    assertEquals(book.getReviews().get(1), "second review");
```

```
// insert a review between the two existing reviews
book.getReviews().add(1, "another review");

tx.commit();
session.close();

// forcibly lose the reference...
// not necessary but let's be explicit
book = null;

session = SessionManager.openSession();
tx = session.beginTransaction();

book = (Book3) session
        .byId(Book3.class)
        .load(book1.getId());

assertEquals(book.getReviews().get(0), "first review");
assertEquals(book.getReviews().get(1), "another review");
assertEquals(book.getReviews().get(2), "second review");

// remove the first, then insert a new one
book.getReviews().remove(0);
book.getReviews().add(1, "new review");

tx.commit();
session.close();

// forcibly lose the reference...
book = null;

session = SessionManager.openSession();
tx = session.beginTransaction();

book = (Book3) session
        .byId(Book3.class)
        .load(book1.getId());
assertEquals(book.getReviews().get(0), "another review");
assertEquals(book.getReviews().get(1), "new review");
assertEquals(book.getReviews().get(2), "second review");

tx.commit();
session.close();
}
```

6-4. Mapping an Array

Problem

How do you map value types as arrays?

Solution

An array has the same use as a List. The only difference is that it corresponds to an array type in Java, not a java.util.List[7] property. It is seldom used unless you're mapping for legacy applications. In most cases, you should use List instead because an array's size can't be increased or decreased dynamically (a list's size can be increased and decreased).

How It Works

Let's look at a version of our book based on Recipe 1: we're concerned only with reviews in this case. Instead of the collection being a List or Set, let's use a String[] instead:

```
@Entity
@NoArgsConstructor
@Data
public class Book4 {
    @Id
    @GeneratedValue(strategy = GenerationType.IDENTITY)
    int id;
    @Getter
    @Setter
    String title;
    @ElementCollection
    @OrderColumn(columnDefinition = "int", name = "order_column")
    @Column(name = "review")
    String[] reviews = new String[0];
}
```

Using the array reference is more work than using a collection (because it is not dynamically sized), but it's fairly straightforward. Here's part of the test code from Recipe 1, using Book4 instead of the original type:

```
@Test
public void testArray() {
    Session session = SessionManager.openSession();
    Transaction tx = session.beginTransaction();
    Book4 book = new Book4();
    book.setTitle("First book");

    String[] reviews = new String[]
            {
                    "This book is great",
                    "This book is light on content"
            };
```

---

[7]This should not be a surprise.

```
    book.setReviews(reviews);

    session.persist(book);
    tx.commit();
    session.close();

    session = SessionManager.openSession();
    tx = session.beginTransaction();

    Book4 book1 = (Book4) session
            .byId(Book4.class)
            .load(book.getId());
    assertEquals(book1.getReviews().length, 2);

    tx.commit();
    session.close();
}
```

6-5. Mapping a Map

Problem

How do you map a set of key/value associations?

Solution

A set of key/value associations is known as a *map, associative array*, or (depending on the type of key) a *sparse array*.[8] In Java, programmers tend to avoid the array labels and just call it a *map*. For Hibernate's purposes, a map is very similar to a list, except that a map uses arbitrary keys to index the collection rather than an integral index. Surprisingly, the Java type used for handling a map is java.util.Map.

How It Works

Using a map as a collection type is very simple: use a reference of type Map and annotate it with @ElementCollection. If you want to change the name of the column used to hold the value of the Map, use the @Column annotation; the @MapKeyColumn is used to control the name of the key of the Map. Here's the Book5 class using annotations to configure the map:

```
@Entity
@NoArgsConstructor
@Data
public class Book5 {
    @Id
    @GeneratedValue(strategy = GenerationType.IDENTITY)
    int id;
    @Getter
```

---

[8]This description of what a set of key/value associations is called is brought to you by the Ghost of Robert Sedgewick, who'd be surprised greatly at its mere existence—because as of this writing, Dr. Sedgewick is still quite alive.

```
    @Setter
    String title;
    @ElementCollection
    @Column(name = "reference")
    @MapKeyColumn(name="topic")
    Map<String, String> topicMap = new HashMap<>();
}
```

Everything about this class works as you'd expect. Here's some test code to show the collection being used:

```
@Test
public void testMappedElements() {
    Session session = SessionManager.openSession();
    Transaction tx = session.beginTransaction();

    Book5 book = new Book5();
    book.setTitle("My World of Stuff");
    book.getTopicMap().put("language", "chapter1");
    book.getTopicMap().put("math", "chapter2");
    book.getTopicMap().put("spellling", "chapter3");
    session.persist(book);

    tx.commit();
    session.close();

    session = SessionManager.openSession();
    tx = session.beginTransaction();

    Book5 book2 = (Book5) session
            .byId(Book5.class)
            .load(book.getId());

    assertTrue(book2.getTopicMap().containsKey("spellling"));
    assertEquals(book2.getTopicMap().get("spellling"), "chapter3");
    book2.getTopicMap().put("reading", "chapter orange");

    tx.commit();
    session.close();

    session = SessionManager.openSession();
    tx = session.beginTransaction();

    book2 = (Book5) session
            .byId(Book5.class)
            .load(book.getId());

    assertTrue(book2.getTopicMap().containsKey("reading"));
    assertEquals(book2.getTopicMap().get("reading"), "chapter orange");

    tx.commit();
    session.close();
}
```

6-6. Sorting Collections

Problem

What are the possible ways to sort collections of objects or entities?

Solution

One way to sort a collection is to use the sorting features provided by the Java Collections Framework. The sorting occurs in the memory of the Java Virtual Machine (JVM) when you run Hibernate after the data is read from the database. Note that for large collections, this kind of sorting might not be efficient. Only Set and Map support this kind of sorting.

You can also sort a collection at the query level using the order-by clause. If your collection is very large, it is more efficient to sort it in the database. You can specify the order-by condition to sort this collection upon retrieval. Notice that the order-by attribute should be a SQL column, not a property name in Hibernate.

How It Works

We now discuss a number of ways to sort a collection, starting with the natural ordering.

Using the Natural Order

Java supports sorted sets, providing a general-purpose interface (SortedSet) and two concrete types that extend SortedSet (ConcurrentSkipListSet and TreeSet). However, when Hibernate populates an object from a database, it doesn't use the specific types that the entity uses. Instead, it uses a series of proxies that fulfill the entity's type requirements.

Therefore, you might construct an entity with a TreeSet<>, as we've done so far, but when Hibernate loads that same entity, you might get an instance of type org.hibernate.collecton.internal. PersistentSortedSet<> instead. Hibernate maps the collection to a database; it doesn't normally serialize the collection to the database, but reconstructs it to a compatible instance.[9]

Therefore, what we need is some way to tell Hibernate how to reconstruct the collection so that it behaves the same way as the default set type.

Let's see how this is done for our book and the contained set of reviews. Our reviews are currently of type String, which implements Comparable; we can use natural sorting for this collection, which works fine for a first example.

```
@Entity
@Data
@NoArgsConstructor
public class Book6NaturalSorting {
    @Id
    @GeneratedValue(strategy = GenerationType.IDENTITY)
    int id;
    String title;
    @ElementCollection(fetch = FetchType.EAGER)
    @SortNatural
    @Column(name = "review")
    Set<String> reviews = new TreeSet<>();
}
```

---

[9]Under most circumstances, this is exactly what you want; after all, having the ability to map an object to a relational database is why you use Hibernate in the first place.

The @SortNatural annotation tells Hibernate to use natural sorting on *reconstruction* of the object. Until it is being reconstructed, the annotation has no effect. Let's see how it works with a test:

```java
@Test
public void testNaturalSorting() {
    Session session = SessionManager.openSession();
    Transaction tx = session.beginTransaction();

    Book6NaturalSorting book6 = new Book6NaturalSorting();

    book6.setTitle("The title");
    book6.getReviews().add("b");
    book6.getReviews().add("c");
    book6.getReviews().add("a");

    session.persist(book6);

    assertEquals(concatenate(book6.getReviews()),
            ":a:b:c");

    tx.commit();
    session.close();

    session=SessionManager.openSession();
    tx=session.beginTransaction();

    Book6NaturalSorting book= (Book6NaturalSorting) session
            .byId(Book6NaturalSorting.class)
            .load(book6.getId());

    assertEquals(concatenate(book.getReviews()),
            ":a:b:c");

    // this may be a brittle test, because future
    // versions of Hibernate might not use the same
    // class name for PersistentSortedSet.
    assertTrue(book.getReviews() instanceof PersistentSortedSet);

    tx.commit();
    session.close();
}
private String concatenate(Collection<String> collection) {
    StringBuilder sb = new StringBuilder();
    for (String s : collection) {
        sb.append(":").append(s);
    }
    return sb.toString();
}
```

The test has an assertion that the type of reviews is an actual Hibernate sorted set as opposed to the natural TreeSet<> because if the TreeSet were what Hibernate used, the behavior would be exactly the same as the instance before it was persisted—which wouldn't illustrate anything.[10]

Writing Your Own Comparator

If you aren't satisfied with the natural ordering, you can write your own comparator instead by implementing the java.util.Comparator interface. The comparing logic should be put inside the overridden compare() method.[11] We can specify the comparator by using the @SortComparator annotation with the custom Comparator class reference. (This sounds a lot more difficult than it is.)

Let's see a simple Comparator first; the following simply inverts the natural ordering for String:

```
public class InvertedStringComparator implements Comparator<String> {
    @Override
    public int compare(String o1, String o2) {
        // natural ordering is o1.compareTo(o2)
        return o2.compareTo(o1);
    }
}
```

The entity definition looks almost identical, differing only in the name of the class and the @SortComparator declaration:

```
@Entity
@Data
@NoArgsConstructor
public class Book6InvertedSorting {
    @Id
    @GeneratedValue(strategy = GenerationType.IDENTITY)
    int id;
    String title;
    @ElementCollection(fetch = FetchType.EAGER)
    @SortComparator(InvertedStringComparator.class)
    @Column(name = "review")
    Set<String> reviews = new TreeSet<>();
}
```

Now our test actually has a better chance of showing us the difference between the original instance and the reconstructed instance.

---

[10]Our example would be a tautology: something that is described in context of itself, such as "a pizza is pizza-shaped." Hopefully, the test for the specific type shows that the instance constructed from the database *acts like* the instance we persisted, but isn't the same. It is like a Stepford Object.

[11]In other words, it should be a Comparator.

If you look carefully at the definition of Book6InvertedSorting, you'll see that reviews is still instantiated with the default TreeSet<> instance, which uses *natural ordering*. However, we are telling Hibernate to reconstruct the instance with InvertedStringComparator, so our test should use natural ordering *before* persistence and inverted ordering *after* reconstruction. Here's the test:

```
@Test
public void testInvertedSorting() {
    Session session = SessionManager.openSession();
    Transaction tx = session.beginTransaction();

    Book6InvertedSorting book6 = new Book6InvertedSorting();

    book6.setTitle("The title");
    book6.getReviews().add("b");
    book6.getReviews().add("c");
    book6.getReviews().add("a");

    session.persist(book6);

    // the entity uses natural ordering
    // before reconstruction through Hibernate.
    assertEquals(concatenate(book6.getReviews()),
            ":a:b:c");

    tx.commit();
    session.close();
    session=SessionManager.openSession();
    tx=session.beginTransaction();

    Book6InvertedSorting book= (Book6InvertedSorting) session
            .byId(Book6InvertedSorting.class)
            .load(book6.getId());

    // the entity should now be using the inverted
    // sort order.
    assertEquals(concatenate(book.getReviews()),
            ":c:b:a");

    tx.commit();
    session.close();
}
```

Sorting in the Database

If your collection is very large, it is more efficient to sort it in the database. You can use the @OrderBy annotation to sort the collection as it is retrieved. Note that the @OrderBy uses the column name, not the attribute name! Hibernate copies the order into the generated SQL, so you need to be precise. But you also can be as specific as you want, including sort order (asc or desc) or multiple columns. Here's our sample class:

```
@Entity
@Data
@NoArgsConstructor
public class Book6DatabaseSorting {
    @Id
    @GeneratedValue(strategy = GenerationType.IDENTITY)
    int id;
```

122

```
    String title;
    @ElementCollection(fetch = FetchType.EAGER)
    @OrderBy("review")
    @Column(name = "review")
    Set<String> reviews = new HashSet<>();
}
```

On to a test that demonstrates the database ordering. We will use the Apache commons-lang3 project[12] to generate random reviews.[13] Our test process has three parts:

- isInOrder() is a method to determine whether a set is ordered

- A test to validate that isInOrder() works properly

- A test to create test data, using isInOrder() to validate that the object constructed by the Hibernate has its reviews ordered alphabetically

```
private boolean isInOrder(Set<String> collection) {
    boolean isInOrder = true;

    Iterator<String> iterator = collection.iterator();
    if (iterator.hasNext()) {
        String j = iterator.next();
        while (isInOrder && iterator.hasNext()) {
            String k = iterator.next();
            //noinspection unchecked
            if (k.compareTo(j) < 1) {
                isInOrder = false;
            }
            j = k;
        }
    }
    return isInOrder;
}

@Test
public void testOrderTest() {
    Set<String> set = new HashSet<>();
    set.add("A");
    set.add("1");
    set.add("a");
    set.add("b");
    set.add("c");
    assertFalse(isInOrder(set));
    set = new TreeSet<>(set);
    assertTrue(isInOrder(set));
}
```

---

[12]http://commons.apache.org/proper/commons-lang/.
[13]Random reviews match what most people expect reviews to be, aside from grammar.

```
@Test(dependsOnMethods = "testOrderTest")
public void testDatabaseSorting() {
    String alphabet = "abcdefghijklmnopqrstuvwxyz";
    Session session = SessionManager.openSession();
    Transaction tx = session.beginTransaction();

    Book6DatabaseSorting book6 = new Book6DatabaseSorting();

    book6.setTitle("The title");
    for (int i = 0; i < 6; i++) {
        // RandomStringUtils is from Apache's commons-lang3 library.
        book6.getReviews().add(RandomStringUtils.random(8, true, true));
    }

    // keep adding reviews until they're not in order,
    // just in case.
    while (isInOrder(book6.getReviews())) {
        book6.getReviews().add(RandomStringUtils.random(8, true, true));
    }

    session.persist(book6);

    tx.commit();
    session.close();

    session = SessionManager.openSession();
    tx = session.beginTransaction();

    Book6DatabaseSorting book = (Book6DatabaseSorting) session
            .byId(Book6DatabaseSorting.class)
            .load(book6.getId());

    assertTrue(isInOrder(book.getReviews()));

    tx.commit();
    session.close();
}
```

6-7. Using Lazy Initialization

Problem

What is lazy initialization? How does lazy initialization work with collections? How do you avoid the LazyInitializationException?

Solution

Lazy initialization occurs when an entity's data is actually retrieved from the database for use by an application. It is referred to as *lazy* because Hibernate might actually transfer data from a database server until the actual point in the code where data is used.

You can easily see this behavior with collections, although it's not limited to collections in any way. When an entity such as our example Book object is accessed, the collections the Book provides aren't loaded from the database until they're being used. This is probably the most efficient way to operate because there's no point in loading data from a database unless the data is used.

The problem with lazy initialization is exposed when an object is accessed outside of the context of the Session from which it was loaded. Lazy initialization uses the Session to query the database, so if the Session isn't available, neither is the data. You then have to handle an exception: the LazyInitializationException.

There are a number of steps to addressing the problem of lazy initialization. First, make sure that you actually *have* a problem. If you received a LazyInitializationException, you probably do, but you should test rigorously and validate that you're actually getting an exception before trying to compensate for it.

Second, you need to address your loading strategy. You can specify an attribute or collection's "fetch mode" to be either eager or lazy; setting the fetch mode to be eager means that as soon as the data *can* be loaded into memory, it *will* be loaded.

Third, consider how you're managing the Session. In our example tests, we explicitly open a Session and Transaction, use them, and then explicitly close them as soon as we finish with them. The LazyInitializationException indicates that we closed the Session and Transaction before we should have.

In some environments, this is less easy to manage than you might think. For example, imagine a web application: a servlet loads an entity from a local Session reference and then forwards the entity to a different class for rendering. The rendering class doesn't have access to the local Session reference from which the entity was loaded; we have a clear susceptibility to lazy initialization errors.

One way to handle this is to use the "session-in-view" strategy, which opens a Session when a request is first received, providing that Session reference through a ThreadLocal for the duration of the request and closing it when the request is finished. (The session-in-view approach is discussed in more detail in Chapter 14).

Another way to handle it is for the service in question (the bit of code that's working with the entity) to make sure that all the elements of the entity are initialized before passing the entity to any *other* code.

How It Works

We use Book7 as our entity, which is effectively a copy of Book1 from this chapter's first recipe, without the references to chapters.[14] We then go to write a test that fails thanks to an issue with lazy initialization:

```
@Entity
@Data
@NoArgsConstructor
public class Book1 {
    @Id
    @GeneratedValue(strategy = GenerationType.IDENTITY)
    int id;
    String title;
    @OneToMany(cascade = CascadeType.ALL, mappedBy = "book")
    Set<Chapter1> chapters = new HashSet<>();
    @ElementCollection(fetch = FetchType.EAGER)
    @Column(name = "review")
    Set<String> reviews = new HashSet<>();
}
```

[14]Chapters? We don't need no stinkin' chapters!

Now let's write a test that expects a LazyInitializationException. This may seem counterintuitive, but it's not; the test had *better* throw an exception, or else something went wrong with the test.

```java
@Test(expectedExceptions = LazyInitializationException.class)
public void testLazyInitialization() {
    Session session = SessionManager.openSession();
    Transaction tx = session.beginTransaction();

    Book7 book7 = new Book7();
    book7.setTitle("Book Title");
    book7.getReviews().add("first");
    book7.getReviews().add("second");

    session.persist(book7);

    tx.commit();
    session.close();

    session = SessionManager.openSession();
    tx = session.beginTransaction();

    Book7 book = (Book7) session
            .byId(Book7.class)
            .load(book7.getId());

    tx.commit();
    session.close();

    // this should throw an exception.
    assertEquals(book.getReviews().size(), 2);
}
```

The reason for this exception is the lazy initialization of the collection. You can initialize it explicitly to access it outside the session with Hibernate.initialize(); let's do that in our next test.

```java
@Test
public void testExplicitInitialization() {
    Session session = SessionManager.openSession();
    Transaction tx = session.beginTransaction();

    Book7 book7 = new Book7();
    book7.setTitle("Book Title");
    book7.getReviews().add("first");
    book7.getReviews().add("second");

    session.persist(book7);

    tx.commit();
    session.close();
```

```
        session = SessionManager.openSession();
        tx = session.beginTransaction();

        Book7 book = (Book7) session
                .byId(Book7.class)
                .load(book7.getId());

        Hibernate.initialize(book.getReviews());

        tx.commit();
        session.close();

        assertEquals(book.getReviews().size(), 2);
}
```

The call to Hibernate.initialize() has the same effect as merely accessing the collection while the Session is available (shown in the next test). However, accessing the collection implies an operation *on* the collection, whereas Hibernate.initialize() simply makes sure the collection is, well, initialized. Conceptually, it's cleaner to use initialize() and it may have performance implications as well. However, the option to access the collection while the Session is still in scope and available is always present:

```
@Test
public void testExplicitUsage() {
    Session session = SessionManager.openSession();
    Transaction tx = session.beginTransaction();

    Book7 book7 = new Book7();
    book7.setTitle("Book Title");
    book7.getReviews().add("first");
    book7.getReviews().add("second");

    session.persist(book7);

    tx.commit();
    session.close();

    session = SessionManager.openSession();
    tx = session.beginTransaction();

    Book7 book = (Book7) session
            .byId(Book7.class)
            .load(book7.getId());

    assertEquals(book.getReviews().size(), 2);

    tx.commit();
    session.close();
}
```

Finally, let's take a look at something similar to a session-in-view approach: we add a ThreadLocal for the Session. Our test method initializes that ThreadLocal and then performs some operations that add and retrieve a Book7 (performing what our other tests have done). The operations manage their own transactions, but the Session is active throughout the test and needs no explicit management by the operations. Note that the operations need to be aware of the lazy initialization of the Book7 collections.

In a web application, the Session would be initialized and cleaned up in a ServletFilter, which can run code both before and after a client request is processed.

Here's the code we use for the session-in-view test:

```
ThreadLocal<Session> session = new ThreadLocal<>();
ThreadLocal<Transaction> tx = new ThreadLocal<>();

@Test
public void testSessionInThreadLocal() throws Exception {
    session.set(SessionManager.openSession());
    tx.set(session.get().beginTransaction());

    Book7 book7 = addBook("Book Title");
    Book7 book = getBook(book7.getId());

    assertEquals(book.getTitle(), book7.getTitle());

    tx.get().commit();
    tx.set(null);
    session.get().close();
    session.set(null);
}

private Book7 getBook(int id) throws Exception {
    if(session.get()==null) {
        throw new Exception("No Session ThreadLocal initialized");
    }
    Book7 book=(Book7)session.get()
            .byId(Book7.class)
            .load(id);
    return book;
}

private Book7 addBook(String title) throws Exception {
    if(session.get()==null) {
        throw new Exception("No Session ThreadLocal initialized");
    }
    Book7 book=new Book7();
    book.setTitle(title);
    session.get().persist(book);
    return book;
}
```

Summary

This chapter showed you how to map a collection of value objects to an entity. You saw the implementation of sets, bags, lists, maps, and arrays. You learned some advantages of each collection-mapping element and when it is a good idea to use each one. You also saw how to sort a collection using a Comparator and using Hibernate to order the collection from the database. Finally, you learned about the implications of lazy initialization and how to manage them.

CHAPTER 7

■ ■ ■

Many-Valued Associations

A many-valued association is by definition a collection of references to entities. The collection can be of type List, Set, Map, and so on in Java.

Why would you have a collection of references? When there is a parent/child relationship, and one parent can be associated to many children, the parent contains a collection of references to the child entities. In a relational model, suppose that two tables are dependent on each other; this relationship can be represented as a foreign key column in the dependent table. For one row in the parent table, many rows exist in the child table.

You saw the use of relationships in earlier chapters[1] where collections were referenced. This chapter discusses one-to-many and many-to-many relationships in detail, including how they're defined and represented in Hibernate. You also learn how data is loaded and updated from/in the database when such relationships are defined.

A one-to-many association is the most common and important type, and a many-to-many association can be represented as two many-to-one associations. This model is more extensible, so it's used more widely in applications. These associations can be unidirectional as well as bidirectional.

7-1. Mapping a One-to-Many Association with a Foreign Key
Problem

How do you map objects using a one-to-many association with a foreign key? Can you establish this association from one direction only (a unidirectional association)? When an operation such as an update is executed on the parent object, users sometimes want the child object to be updated as well; this is called *cascading* in Hibernate. How do you use the cascading feature with a one-to-many association?

Solution

There are two ways to achieve a one-to-many relationship in the database: by having a foreign key column in the dependent table or by creating a join table between the two tables. Each of these relationships can be unidirectional or bidirectional. The one-to-many unidirectional relationship is uncommon and isn't a recommended way to map using Hibernate. (You should probably use bidirectional relationships, even though they can be more verbose.)

---

[1]Chapters 5 and 6, among others; we've seen a few snippets that use relationships in most of our recipes. If we haven't, well, we need to read more closely. Which book do you think you're reading? I know which one I think I'm writing…

131

How It Works

Previous chapters treated a set of reviews as sets of strings and stored them in a collection. We now focus on book chapters by looking at the chapters as separate entities. As discussed in Chapter 6,[2] because one book object can relate to many chapter objects, the association from book to chapter is nominally a one-to-many association. Let's first define this association as unidirectional—navigable from book to chapter only—and we'll make it bidirectional in later recipes.

Let's revisit the Book and Chapter entity definitions with a one-to-many relationship:

```java
@Entity
@NoArgsConstructor
@Data
public class Chapter1 {
    @Id
    @GeneratedValue(strategy = GenerationType.IDENTITY)
    int id;
    String title;
    String content;
}

@Entity
@Data
@NoArgsConstructor
public class Book1 {
    @Id
    @GeneratedValue(strategy = GenerationType.IDENTITY)
    int id;
    String title;
    @OneToMany(cascade = CascadeType.ALL)
    @JoinColumn(name = "book_id")
    Set<Chapter1> chapters = new HashSet<>();
}
```

Now let's take a quick look at the Hibernate configuration file:

```xml
<?xml version="1.0" encoding="UTF-8"?>
<!DOCTYPE hibernate-configuration PUBLIC
        "-//Hibernate/Hibernate Configuration DTD 3.0//EN"
        "http://www.hibernate.org/dtd/hibernate-configuration-3.0.dtd">
<hibernate-configuration>
    <session-factory>
        <property name="connection.driver_class">org.h2.Driver</property>
        <property name="connection.url">jdbc:h2:file:./chapter7</property>
        <property name="hibernate.dialect">org.hibernate.dialect.HSQLDialect</property>
        <property name="hibernate.hbm2ddl.auto">create</property>
        <property name="hibernate.show_sql">true</property>
        <property name="hibernate.discriminator.ignore_explicit_for_joined">true</property>
        <property name="connection.username"></property>
        <property name="connection.password"></property>
```

---

[2]We're revisiting the entity model from Recipe 6.1.

```
        <mapping class="com.apress.hibernaterecipes.chapter7.recipe1.Chapter1" />
        <mapping class="com.apress.hibernaterecipes.chapter7.recipe1.Book1" />
        <!-- we will be adding other mappings here -->
    </session-factory>
</hibernate-configuration>
```

Finally, let's write a test to make sure that the object mapping works:

```
@Test
public void unidirectionalOneToMany() {
    Session session = SessionManager.openSession();
    Transaction tx = session.beginTransaction();

    Book1 book1 = new Book1();
    book1.setTitle("First title");

    Chapter1 chapter1 = new Chapter1();
    chapter1.setTitle("first chapter");
    chapter1.setContent("here's some text");

    book1.getChapters().add(chapter1);
    session.save(book1);

    tx.commit();
    session.close();
    session = SessionManager.openSession();
    tx = session.beginTransaction();

    Book1 book = (Book1) session
            .byId(Book1.class)
            .load(book1.getId());

    assertEquals(book.getTitle(), book1.getTitle());
    assertEquals(book.getChapters().size(),
            book1.getChapters().size());

    tx.commit();
    session.close();

    session = SessionManager.openSession();
    tx = session.beginTransaction();

    book = (Book1) session
            .byId(Book1.class)
            .load(book1.getId());

    session.delete(book);

    tx.commit();
    session.close();
}
```

In Book1, the chapters set is annotated with @JoinColumn(name = "book_id"), which tells Hibernate to use "book_id" as, well, a join column.[3] In this case, because Chapter1 doesn't have a matching column (remember that it is a unidirectional relationship); Hibernate creates the column in the database (in the table for the Chapter1 entities) and uses it to maintain the Chapter1/Book1 relationship.

Using the CascadeType.ALL option on @OneToMany means that when the Book1 is deleted, the chapters are also deleted.

So how can you determine the Book1 associated with a given Chapter1? One fairly easy way is to write a query that navigated from the Book1 side, as shown in the following sample code:

```
@Test
public void findBookGivenChapter() {
    Session session = SessionManager.openSession();
    Transaction tx = session.beginTransaction();

    Book1 book1 = new Book1();
    book1.setTitle("First title");

    Chapter1 chapter1 = new Chapter1();
    chapter1.setTitle("first chapter");
    chapter1.setContent("here's some text");

    book1.getChapters().add(chapter1);
    session.save(book1);

    tx.commit();
    session.close();

    session = SessionManager.openSession();
    tx = session.beginTransaction();

    Chapter1 chapter = (Chapter1) session.byId(Chapter1.class).load(chapter1.getId());
    assertNotNull(chapter);

    Query query = session.createQuery("from Book1 b where :chapter member of b.chapters");
    query.setParameter("chapter", chapter);

    Book1 book = (Book1) query.uniqueResult();
    assertEquals(book.getTitle(), book1.getTitle());

    tx.commit();
    session.close();
}
```

This query includes every Book1 so that its collections of chapters ("b.chapters") includes the reference we're passing in as the query parameter. It's not typically a particularly *efficient* query, but it is one way to get around the unidirectional relationship that doesn't involve making the relationship bidirectional. (Making the relationship bidirectional makes the query far easier, as you'll see in the following recipes.)

---

[3]Surprise, right? But there's a twist: the mapping for Chapter1 in Recipe 7.1 doesn't have book_id as an attribute, which is why the join column is being described specifically.

7-2. Mapping a One-to-Many Bidirectional Association Using a Foreign Key

Problem

How do you map objects using a one-to-many bidirectional association with a foreign key?

Solution

In some (most?) cases, you want your associations to be bidirectional. Recipe 7.1 has chapters that are part of a book, but there's no simple way to figure out which book goes with a given chapter.[4] You can add a bidirectional relationship by adding a reference to the Book inside the Chapter entity while retaining the database structure, providing a bidirectional association.

How It Works

In the previous example, we created Chapter1 as an entity but didn't provide a reference to a Book1; we specified the join column between the two entities as part of the @OneToMany mapping in Book1. An easier way to do this is simply to add a reference to a book inside the Chapter entity, telling the relationship what attribute to use as the relationship.

Here is the source for our new Book2 object. It doesn't have the @JoinColumn annotation, but it *does* specify the mappedBy attribute, which refers to the attribute in the Chapter2 entity that contains the Book2 reference:

```
@Entity
@Data
@NoArgsConstructor
public class Book2 {
    @Id
    @GeneratedValue(strategy = GenerationType.IDENTITY)
    int id;
    String title;
    @OneToMany(cascade = CascadeType.ALL,mappedBy = "book2")
    Set<Chapter2> chapters = new HashSet<>();
}
```

Now let's take a look at the Chapter2 entity. We have to specify more of the Lombok annotations here because we don't want to introduce a recursive loop with toString(), equals(), or hashCode().

```
@Entity
@NoArgsConstructor
@EqualsAndHashCode(exclude = "book2")
@ToString(exclude = "book2")
public class Chapter2 {
    @Id
    @GeneratedValue(strategy = GenerationType.IDENTITY)
    @Getter
    @Setter
    int id;
```

---

[4]As shown at the end of Recipe 1, you generally have to walk the relationship from the owning entity. It can be done in that (and other) ways, but it's not really convenient or efficient.

```
    @Getter
    @Setter
    String title;
    @Getter
    @Setter
    String content;
    @ManyToOne(optional = false)
    @Getter
    @Setter
    Book2 book2;
}
```

The database structure looks *exactly* the same as in Recipe 7.1 (with different table names); the main difference is that we have to explicitly set the relationship in Chapter2 when using the entities. We also have the bidirectional relationship available to us, so getting the Book2 reference given a Chapter2 entity is marvelously easy.

```
@Test
public void bidirectionalOneToMany() {
    Session session = SessionManager.openSession();
    Transaction tx = session.beginTransaction();

    Book2 book2 = new Book2();
    book2.setTitle("First title");

    Chapter2 chapter2 = new Chapter2();
    chapter2.setTitle("first chapter");
    chapter2.setContent("here's some text");
    chapter2.setBook2(book2);
    book2.getChapters().add(chapter2);

    session.save(book2);

    tx.commit();
    session.close();

    session = SessionManager.openSession();
    tx = session.beginTransaction();

    Book2 book = (Book2) session
            .byId(Book2.class)
            .load(book2.getId());

    assertEquals(book.getTitle(), book2.getTitle());
    assertEquals(book.getChapters().size(),
            book2.getChapters().size());

    tx.commit();
    session.close();

    session = SessionManager.openSession();
    tx = session.beginTransaction();
```

```java
        book = (Book2) session
                .byId(Book2.class)
                .load(book2.getId());

        session.delete(book);

        tx.commit();
        session.close();
    }

    @Test
    public void findBookGivenChapter() {
        Session session = SessionManager.openSession();
        Transaction tx = session.beginTransaction();

        Book2 book2 = new Book2();
        book2.setTitle("First title");

        Chapter2 chapter2 = new Chapter2();
        chapter2.setTitle("first chapter");
        chapter2.setContent("here's some text");
        chapter2.setBook2(book2);

        book2.getChapters().add(chapter2);
        session.save(book2);

        tx.commit();
        session.close();

        session = SessionManager.openSession();
        tx = session.beginTransaction();

        Chapter2 chapter = (Chapter2) session.byId(Chapter2.class).load(chapter2.getId());
        assertNotNull(chapter);

        // if we need the book, we have it!
        Book2 book = chapter.getBook2();
        assertEquals(book.getTitle(), book2.getTitle());

        tx.commit();
        session.close();
    }
```

7-3. Mapping a One-to-Many Bidirectional Association Using a Join Table

Problem

How do you map objects using a one-to-many association with a join table?

Solution

We can model our book and chapter relationship as being bidirectional and with a join table by simply not specifying a mapping column. Hibernate then creates (and manages) a join table between our entities.

How It Works

We can take the Book2 from the previous recipe and change the specification for the @OneToMany relationship. Without a specific mappingBy attribute, Hibernate creates a join table, referencing the two primary key columns of the Book and Chapter entities.

The Book3 entity looks like this, with changes from Book2 in bold:

```
@Entity
@Data
@NoArgsConstructor
public class Book3 {
    @Id
    @GeneratedValue(strategy = GenerationType.IDENTITY)
    int id;
    String title;
    @OneToMany(cascade = CascadeType.ALL)
    @JoinTable(name = "book3_chapter3")
    Set<Chapter3> chapters = new HashSet<>();
}
```

The Chapter3 class is identical to the Chapter2 class, except that it refers to Book3 instead of Book2:

```
@Entity
@NoArgsConstructor
@EqualsAndHashCode(exclude = "book3")
@ToString(exclude = "book3")
public class Chapter3 {
    @Id
    @GeneratedValue(strategy = GenerationType.IDENTITY)
    @Getter
    @Setter
    int id;
    @Getter
    @Setter
    String title;
    @Getter
    @Setter
    String content;
```

```
    @ManyToOne(optional = false)
    @Getter
    @Setter
    Book3 book3;
}
```

@JoinTable(name = "book3_chapter3"), which is entirely optional, simply specifies the name of the join table. Hibernate generates a name based on the entities involved in the relationship ("book3_chapter3" in this case, so we didn't need the annotation) if a join table name isn't specified.

The test code is identical to the Recipe 7.2 test code; only the class names and the instance names are different:[5]

```
@Test
public void bidirectionalOneToMany() {
    Session session = SessionManager.openSession();
    Transaction tx = session.beginTransaction();

    Book3 book3 = new Book3();
    book3.setTitle("First title");

    Chapter3 chapter3 = new Chapter3();
    chapter3.setTitle("first chapter");
    chapter3.setContent("here's some text");
    chapter3.setBook3(book3);
    book3.getChapters().add(chapter3);

    session.save(book3);

    tx.commit();
    session.close();

    session = SessionManager.openSession();
    tx = session.beginTransaction();

    Book3 book = (Book3) session
            .byId(Book3.class)
            .load(book3.getId());

    assertEquals(book.getTitle(), book3.getTitle());
    assertEquals(book.getChapters().size(),
            book3.getChapters().size());

    tx.commit();
    session.close();

    session = SessionManager.openSession();
    tx = session.beginTransaction();
```

---

[5]If we were willing to play some tricks with reflection, we could have used the same test for all three recipes, passing around Callable objects to change behavior in small ways. However, that would make the example code *much* harder to read, harder to rely upon, and much more a sample of some author's coding prowess rather than a useful example of how to test some behavior.

```
        book = (Book3) session
                .byId(Book3.class)
                .load(book3.getId());

        session.delete(book);

        tx.commit();
        session.close();
    }

    @Test
    public void findBookGivenChapter() {
        Session session = SessionManager.openSession();
        Transaction tx = session.beginTransaction();

        Book3 book2 = new Book3();
        book2.setTitle("First title");

        Chapter3 chapter3 = new Chapter3();
        chapter3.setTitle("first chapter");
        chapter3.setContent("here's some text");
        chapter3.setBook3(book2);

        book2.getChapters().add(chapter3);
        session.save(book2);

        tx.commit();
        session.close();

        session = SessionManager.openSession();
        tx = session.beginTransaction();

        Chapter3 chapter = (Chapter3) session.byId(Chapter3.class).load(chapter3.getId());
        assertNotNull(chapter);

        // if we need the book, we have it!
        Book3 book = chapter.getBook3();
        assertEquals(book.getTitle(), book2.getTitle());

        tx.commit();
        session.close();
    }
```

7-4. Mapping a Many-to-Many Association with a Join Table

Problem

How do you map objects using a many-to-many unidirectional association with a join table?

Solution

The last type of association discussed in this chapter is the many-to-many association. Suppose that Books and Chapters can have a many-to-many relationship; a chapter can then be a part of more than one book. This example isn't very common,[6] but it is definitely possible to model it in Hibernate. Let's see how it works.

How It Works

We can model the many-to-many relationship between books and chapters in almost the same way as we model one-to-many relationships. All we need to do is model a collection on both entities; Hibernate creates the join table and maintains the data properly, as we'd expect and hope.

Let's take a look at Book4 first. It provides a named query because we want to look up books by their titles in our test. Although there are multiple ways to accomplish it,[7] this method is straightforward:

```
@Entity
@Data
@NoArgsConstructor
@NamedQueries({
        @NamedQuery(name = "Book4.findByTitle",
                query = "from Book4 b where b.title=:title")
})
public class Book4 {
    @Id
    @GeneratedValue(strategy = GenerationType.IDENTITY)
    int id;
    String title;
    @ManyToMany
    Set<Chapter4> chapters = new HashSet<>();
}
```

The Chapter4 uses a Set to map to Book4 instances. We exclude the books references from various annotations to ensure that we're not including the Book4 objects recursively. Just like the Book4 entity, we are using a named query because we want to be able to look up the Chapter4 instances by title.

```
@Entity
@NoArgsConstructor
@EqualsAndHashCode(exclude = "books")
@ToString(exclude = "books")
@NamedQueries({
        @NamedQuery(name = "Chapter4.findByTitle",
                query = "from Chapter4 c where c.title=:title")
})
```

---

[6]How many books share actual chapters?
[7]We could have added the book title as a "natural id," built the query as we needed it, or even used a criteria query… and there are more options I'm not thinking of offhand.

```java
public class Chapter4 {
    @Id
    @GeneratedValue(strategy = GenerationType.IDENTITY)
    @Getter
    @Setter
    int id;
    @Getter
    @Setter
    String title;
    @Getter
    @Setter
    String content;
    @ManyToMany
    @Getter
    @Setter
    Set<Book4> books=new HashSet<>();
}
```

Our test has to do some extra work to lay out the data. First, we want to create a set of Book4 and Chapter4 instances; then we'll use an array to attach chapters and books deterministically (so we know what the data is supposed to look like and can test that it is correct).

```java
@Test
public void testManyToMany() {
    // book, chapter(s)
    int[][] chapterMatrix = new int[][]{{1, 1, 2, 3},
            {2, 4, 5},
            {3, 1, 3, 5},
            {4, 2, 4},
            {5, 1, 2, 4, 5}
    };
    Session session = SessionManager.openSession();
    Transaction tx = session.beginTransaction();
    for (int i = 1; i < 6; i++) {
        Chapter4 c = new Chapter4();
        c.setTitle("title " + i);
        c.setContent("content " + i);

        Book4 b = new Book4();
        b.setTitle("book " + i);

        session.persist(b);
        session.persist(c);
    }
    tx.commit();
    session.close();
    session = SessionManager.openSession();
    tx = session.beginTransaction();
    Query bookQuery = session.getNamedQuery("Book4.findByTitle");
    Query chapterQuery = session.getNamedQuery("Chapter4.findByTitle");
```

```
    for (int[] matrix : chapterMatrix) {
        int bookRef = matrix[0];
        bookQuery.setParameter("title", "book " + bookRef);
        Book4 book = (Book4) bookQuery.uniqueResult();

        assertNotNull(book);

        for (int chapterIndex = 1; chapterIndex < matrix.length; chapterIndex++) {
            chapterQuery.setParameter("title", "title " + matrix[chapterIndex]);
            Chapter4 chapter = (Chapter4) chapterQuery.uniqueResult();

            assertNotNull(chapter);

            book.getChapters().add(chapter);
            chapter.getBooks().add(book);
        }
    }
    tx.commit();
    session.close();

    session = SessionManager.openSession();
    tx = session.beginTransaction();
    bookQuery = session.getNamedQuery("Book4.findByTitle");
    bookQuery.setParameter("title", "book 1");

    Book4 book = (Book4) bookQuery.uniqueResult();

    assertNotNull(book);
    assertNotNull(book.getChapters());
    assertEquals(book.getChapters().size(), 3);

    tx.commit();
    session.close();
}
```

Summary

In this chapter, you learned how to create and use many-valued associations. The two types of many-valued associations are one-to-many and many-to-many. The more widely used of these is the one-to-many association. You can map these relationships by using a foreign key or using a join table.

When you use a foreign key, you map the key in the parent table using a Set with the key attribute as the foreign key column. The class to which it is associated is specified by the <one-to-many> mapping element or, more commonly, the @OneToMany annotation. With the cascade option, operations are cascaded from the parent entity to the associated entity.

A many-to-many association is mapped using a join table. You create a join table to hold the IDs from the parent entity and the associated entity.

A bidirectional association in both one-to-many and many-to-many mappings is represented using inverse="true", which specifies that the inverse directional mapping from the associated entity to the parent entity can be traversed.

CHAPTER 8

HQL and JPA Query Language

When you use JDBC to access databases, you write SQL statements for the query and update tasks. In such cases, you're dealing with tables, columns, and joins. When you use Hibernate, most update tasks can be accomplished through the provided APIs. However, you still need to use a query language for the query tasks, and Hibernate provides a powerful query language called Hibernate Query Language (HQL).

HQL is database independent and translated into SQL by Hibernate at runtime. When you write HQL, you can concentrate on the objects and properties without knowing much detail about the underlying database. You can treat HQL as an object-oriented variant of SQL, with support for concepts such as inheritance, polymorphism, and associations through collections.

In this chapter, you see how to query the database using HQL and JPA Query Language (JPA QL). Hibernate provides three ways to query a database:

- HQL and JPA QL, a subset of HQL

- Criteria API (Criteria and Example)

- Direct SQL

This chapter looks at HQL, JPA QL, and Direct SQL. You see how to form a query, bind parameters (named and position), and execute the query. You also learn how to manipulate the result, which can help you deal with large result sets, and to query associated objects.

8-1. Using the Query Object

Problem

How do you create a Query object in Hibernate? How do you enable pagination? What are the various ways to bind parameters to a query?

Solution

A Query object is an object-oriented representation of an actual query. The Hibernate interface `org.hibernate.Query` and the JPA interface `javax.persistence.Query` provide methods to control the execution of a query and bind values to query parameters. In Hibernate, you can obtain an instance of the Query object by calling `Session.createQuery()`. And in JPA, the `EntityManager` provides an instance of the Query object with a call like `EntityManager.createQuery()`.

How It Works

Let's see how to use the Query object, starting with how to create it.

Creating a Query Object

Previous chapters discussed some basic HQL statements for querying objects. For example, returning to the bookshop example, you can use the following HQL to query for all books and then call the list() method to retrieve the result list that contains book objects:

```
Query query = session.createQuery("from Book");
List books = query.list();
```

from Clause

Now let's look at the from clause, which is the only required part of an HQL statement. The following HQL statement queries for books with the name "Hibernate". Notice that name is a property of the Book object:

```
from Book
where name = 'Hibernate'
```

You can also assign an alias for the object, which is useful when you query multiple objects in one query. You should use the naming conventions for classes and instances in Java. Note that the as keyword is optional:

```
from Book as book
where book.name = 'Hibernate'
```

You can then integrate the alias with this query:

```
Query query = session.createQuery("from Book where book.name='Hibernate'");
List books = query.list();
```

You need to use EntityManager to create a javax.persistence.Query instance in JPA QL. The select clause is required in Java persistence, as shown here:

```
public List<Book> readFromManager() {

    EntityManager manager = SessionManager.getEntityManager();
    EntityTransaction tran = manager.getTransaction();
    tran.begin();
    Query query = manager.createQuery("select b from Book b");
    List<Book> list = query.getResultList();
    return list;
}
```

Note that you need to place the persistence.xml file in the META-INF folder. Also remember to place all the required jars in the classpath.

where Clause

In HQL, you can use where clauses to filter results, just as you do in SQL. For multiple conditions, you can use the and, or, and not operators to combine them. This process is called *applying restrictions*:

```
from Book book
where book.name like '%Hibernate%' and book.price between 100 and 200
```

You can see whether an associated object is null by using is null or is not null:

```
from Book book
where book.publisher is not null
```

Notice that the null check can't be performed on a collection. So if you have a query like the following, you get an exception from Hibernate:

```
from Book8_1 book
where book.chapters is not null
```

Hibernate provides the empty keyword, which you can use to see whether a collection is empty:

```
from Book8_1 book
where book.chapters is not empty
```

Let's say you want to retrieve all books published by the publishers "Apress" and "friendsOfED". In technical terms, you want to retrieve based on a property (publisher's name) of the association (publisher). For this kind of requirement, you can use *implicit joins* in the where clause. You create an implicit join by using the dot (.) operator:

```
from Book book
where book.publisher.name in ('Apress', 'friendsOfED')
```

Remember that for a collection association, if you reference it more than one time, you should use an *explicit join* to avoid duplicated joins. Explicit joins require the use of the join keyword. Querying using joins is described in detail later in this chapter.

Hibernate provides a function that lets you check the size of a collection. You can use the special property size or the special size() function. Hibernate uses a select count(...) subquery to get the size of the collection:

```
from Book book
where book.chapters.size > 10
from Book book
where size(book.chapters) > 10
```

Pagination

When the number of records returned by a query is large, you might want to retrieve only a subset of the actual number of records. The subset is usually equal to the page size (number of records); this feature is called *pagination*. The Hibernate and JPA Query interfaces provide two methods that enable pagination:

- setFirstResult(int beginPoint): Sets the first row with the given beginPoint
- setMaxResult(int size): Sets the returned result-set size

The implementation looks like this:

```
public List<Book> readFromManager() {

    EntityManager manager = SessionManager.getEntityManager();
    EntityTransaction tran = manager.getTransaction();
    tran.begin();
    Query query = manager.createQuery("select b from Book b");
    query.setFirstResult(5);
    query.setMaxResults(15);
    List<Book> list = query.getResultList();
    return list;
}
```

In this example, the records starting with the fifth row and including the next 15 records are retrieved.

Parameter Binding

You use *parameter binding* to bind values to the query parameters. Parameter binding makes the code look cleaner; the code is also safer. It is not recommended that you inject user input into a query using string concatenation; doing so can lead to a security issue called *SQL injection*.

SQL INJECTION

A SQL injection attack is an "injection" of a SQL query into the application via user input. A successful SQL injection exploit can, among other things, read sensitive data from the database, modify database data (insert/update/delete), and execute administrative operations on the database. It can be dangerous—or ruinous—depending on the attractiveness of the application's data (see http://xkcd.com/327/ for a humorous illustration of this).

Let's look at a simple example. The following main() method invokes a method called exampleSQLInjection(), which takes a user input string:

```
public static void main(String[] args) {
    List books = exampleSQLInjection("Hibernate");
    if(books!=null)
    {
      System.out.println("Size- "+books.size());
      Iterator it = books.iterator();
      while(it.hasNext())
      {
        System.out.println("book- "+it.next());
      }
    }
}
```

The implementation of the `exampleSQLInjection()` method is as follows:

```
public static List exampleSQLInjection(String userInput)
{
   Session session = getSession();
   String q="from Book8_1 book where book.bookName='"+userInput+"'";
   Query query = session.createQuery(q);
   List books = query.list();
   return books;
}
```

The `exampleSQLInjection()` method is supposed to return only a list of books with the name "Hibernate". Suppose that the user input changes from "Hibernate" to something like this:

```
Hibernate' or 'x'='x
```

And suppose that the method is invoked like this:

```
List books = exampleSQLInjection("Hibernate' or 'x'='x");
```

All the books in the table are then returned, which violates the query's purpose. Imagine a similar attack on a user table that contains passwords or other secure information.

This is a very basic example of SQL injection. Of course, user input should be validated before it reaches this point, but you should never entirely depend on it being validated properly. It is a very good habit to use parameter binding.

Hibernate and JPA support two types of parameter binding:

- Named parameter binding
- Positional parameter binding

You can specify query parameters the same way you do for SQL queries. If you're sure only one unique object will be returned as a result, you can call the uniqueResult() method to retrieve it. Null is returned if nothing matches:

```
query = session.createQuery("from Book where isbn = ?");
query.setLong(0, 520);
Book bookCh8 = (Book) query.uniqueResult();
```

This example uses ? to represent a query parameter and set it by index (which is zero-based, not one-based as in JDBC). This kind of parameter binding is called *positional* parameter binding. You can also use *named* parameter binding for queries. The advantages of using named parameters are that they're easy to understand and can occur multiple times:

```
Query query = session.createQuery("from Book where isbn =:isbn");
query.setLong("isbn", 520);
Book bookCh8 = (Book) query.uniqueResult();
System.out.println(bookCh8);
```

149

Named Queries

You can put query statements in any mapping definitions[1] and refer to them by name in the code. They are called *named queries*. But for easier maintenance (depending on your preferences), you can centralize all your named queries in one mapping definition in a file of your choosing—NamedQuery.hbm.xml, for example. In addition, setting up a mechanism for naming queries is also beneficial; you need to assign a unique name to each query. You should also put the query string in a <![CDATA[...]]> block to avoid conflicts with special XML characters. Named queries don't have to be HQL or JPA QL strings; they can be native SQL queries:

```
<hibernate-mapping>
  <query name="Book.byIsbn">
    <![CDATA[from Book where isbn = ?]]>
  </query>
</hibernate-mapping>
```

To reference a named query, use the session.getNamedQuery() method:

```
Query query = session.getNamedQuery("Book.byIsbn");
query.setString(0, "1932394419");
Book book = (Book) query.uniqueResult();
```

JPA specifies the @NamedQuery and @NamedNativeQuery annotations.[2] The name and query attributes are required. You can place these annotations in the metadata of a particular entity or into a JPA XML file:

```
@NamedQueries({
  @NamedQuery(
  name="Book.byIsbn",
  query="from Book where isbn = ?"
  )
})
@Entity (name="book")
@Table  (name="BOOK", schema="BOOKSHOP")
public class Book{...}
```

8-2. Using the Select Clause
Problem

How and where do you use the select clause?

Solution

The previous examples query for entire persistent objects. You can instead query for particular fields by using the select clause,[3] which picks the objects and properties to return in the query result set.

---

[1]You can define queries in annotations and in XML files. Because the query annotations are package-level, you can centralize them in a package-info.java as well (see http://docs.oracle.com/javase/specs/jls/se8/html/jls-7.html#jls-7.4.1 for more information).

[2]As usual, one of your authors far prefers the annotations for named queries; your mileage may vary.

[3]Note that with the exception of Java class names and properties, queries are *not* case-sensitive; SeLeCt is the same as select or SELECT. Go nuts. Nobody will care except obsessive-compulsive programmers—and they'll probably care a *lot*.

How It Works

The following query returns all the book names in a list:

```
select book.name
from Book book
```

In HQL, you can use SQL aggregate functions such as count(), sum(), avg(), max(), and min(). They are translated in the resulting SQL:

```
select avg(book.price)
from Book book
```

Implicit joins can also be used in the select clause. In addition, you can use the distinct keyword to return distinct results:

```
select distinct book.publisher.name
from Book book
```

To query multiple fields, use a comma to separate them. The result list contains elements of Object[]:

```
select book.isbn, book.name, book.publisher.name
from Book book
```

You can create custom types and specify them in the select clause to encapsulate the results. For example, let's create a BookSummary class for the bookIsbn, bookName, and publisherName fields. The custom type must have a constructor of all the fields.

To illustrate this, here's a simple model that uses Book2 and Publisher2, with both including named queries (to help our test go more smoothly):

```
@Entity
@Data
@NoArgsConstructor
@NamedQueries({
        @NamedQuery(name = "Book2.byName",
                query = "from Book2 b where b.name=:name")
})
public class Book2 {
    @Id
    @GeneratedValue(strategy = GenerationType.IDENTITY)
    int id;
    @Column(unique = true, nullable = false)
    String name;
    @ManyToOne(optional = false)
    Publisher2 publisher2;

    public Book2(String name) {
        setName(name);
    }
}
```

```
@Entity
@Data
@NoArgsConstructor
@NamedQueries({
        @NamedQuery(name = "Publisher2.byName",
                query = "from Publisher2 p where p.name=:name")
})
public class Publisher2 {
    @Id
    @GeneratedValue(strategy = GenerationType.IDENTITY)
    int id;
    @Column(unique = true, nullable=false)
    String name;

    public Publisher2(String name) {
        setName(name);
    }
}
```

The configuration file (hibernate.cfg.xml) looks like this:

```xml
<?xml version="1.0" encoding="UTF-8"?>
<!DOCTYPE hibernate-configuration PUBLIC
        "-//Hibernate/Hibernate Configuration DTD 3.0//EN"
        "http://www.hibernate.org/dtd/hibernate-configuration-3.0.dtd">
<hibernate-configuration>
    <session-factory>
        <property name="connection.driver_class">org.h2.Driver</property>
        <property name="connection.url">jdbc:h2:file:./chapter8</property>
        <property name="hibernate.dialect">org.hibernate.dialect.HSQLDialect</property>
        <property name="hibernate.hbm2ddl.auto">create</property>
        <property name="hibernate.show_sql">true</property>
        <property name="hibernate.discriminator.ignore_explicit_for_joined">true</property>
        <property name="connection.username"></property>
        <property name="connection.password"></property>
        <mapping class="com.apress.hibernaterecipes.chapter8.recipe2.Book2"/>
        <mapping class="com.apress.hibernaterecipes.chapter8.recipe2.Publisher2"/>
    </session-factory>
</hibernate-configuration>
```

Before we take a look at projections, let's see how the test sets up the data and tests a simple select distinct query:

```java
String[][] data = new String[][][]{
        {"Book1", "Apress"},
        {"Book2", "Apress"},
        {"Book3", "Springer"},
        {"Book4", "Apress"},
        {"Book5", "Springer"},
};
```

```java
@BeforeMethod
public void setup() {
    SessionManager.deleteAll("Book2");
    SessionManager.deleteAll("Publisher2");

    Session session = SessionManager.openSession();
    Transaction tx = session.beginTransaction();
    Query publisherQuery = session.getNamedQuery("Publisher2.byName");
    Query bookQuery = session.getNamedQuery("Book2.byName");
    for (String[] datum : data) {
        publisherQuery.setParameter("name", datum[1]);
        Publisher2 publisher2 = (Publisher2) publisherQuery.uniqueResult();
        if (null == publisher2) {
            publisher2 = new Publisher2(datum[1]);
            session.persist(publisher2);
        }
        bookQuery.setParameter("name", datum[0]);
        Book2 book2 = (Book2) bookQuery.uniqueResult();
        if (null == book2) {
            book2 = new Book2(datum[0]);
            book2.setPublisher2(publisher2);
            session.persist(book2);
        }
    }
    tx.commit();
    session.close();
}

@Test
public void distinctQueries() {
    Session session = SessionManager.openSession();
    Transaction tx = session.beginTransaction();

    Query query = session.createQuery("select b.publisher2.name from Book2 b");
    List results = query.list();
    assertEquals(results.size(), 5);

    // now let's apply distinctness
    query = session.createQuery("select distinct b.publisher2.name from Book2 b");
    results = query.list();
    assertEquals(results.size(), 2);

    tx.commit();
    session.close();
}
```

The simplest kind of projection would return an array of Objects:

```java
@Test
public void testObjectProjection() {
    Session session = SessionManager.openSession();
    Transaction tx = session.beginTransaction();
```

153

```
        Query query = session.createQuery("select " +
                "b.name, b.publisher2.name from Book2 b");
        List<Object[]> results = query.list();
        assertEquals(results.size(), 5);
        for(Object[] o:results) {
            assertEquals(o.length, 2);
        }

        tx.commit();
        session.close();
    }
```

We don't have to use an `Object[]`, though; we can use a custom data type. For illustration, let's use a BookSummary2 class, which simplifies the combined Book2 and Publisher2 data by a tiny margin:

```
@Data
@NoArgsConstructor
@AllArgsConstructor
public class BookSummary2 {
    String bookName;
    String bookPublisher;
}
```

Now we can use the results of the query (as *part of* the query) to construct the objects:

```
@Test
public void testSimpleTypeProjection() {
    Session session = SessionManager.openSession();
    Transaction tx = session.beginTransaction();

    Query query = session.createQuery("select new " +
            "com.apress.hibernaterecipes.chapter8.recipe2.BookSummary2" +
            "(b.name, b.publisher2.name) from Book2 b");
    List results = query.list();
    assertEquals(results.size(), 5);

    tx.commit();
    session.close();
}
```

We can also use collections such as lists and maps as the projected types. The query returns List already, so the result is a List of the collection type. Here's an example of our query using a list as the projection:

```
@Test
public void testListProjection() {
    Session session = SessionManager.openSession();
    Transaction tx = session.beginTransaction();

    Query query = session.createQuery("select new " +
            "list(b.name, b.publisher2.name) from Book2 b");
    List<List> results = query.list();
    assertEquals(results.size(), 5);
```

```
    for (List l : results) {
        assertEquals(l.size(), 2);
    }
    tx.commit();
    session.close();
}
```

We can also use maps, in which case we need to provide aliases for the columns (to serve as keys for the map):

```
@Test
public void testMapProjection() {
    Session session = SessionManager.openSession();
    Transaction tx = session.beginTransaction();

    Query query = session.createQuery("select new " +
            "map(b.name as name, b.publisher2.name as publisher)" +
            " from Book2 b");
    List<Map> results = query.list();
    assertEquals(results.size(), 5);
    for (Map m : results) {
        assertTrue(m.containsKey("name"));
        assertTrue(m.containsKey("publisher"));
    }
    tx.commit();
    session.close();
}
```

8-3. Joining
Problem
How do you create various types of joins in HQL and JPA QL?

Solution
Hibernate and JPA support both inner and outer joins. You use the dot (.) operator to express implicit (inner) association joins.[4]

How It Works
Let's look at all the different types of joins you can take advantage of.

---

[4]In case you're desperately interested, explicit joins are *outer joins* just like implicit joins are *inner joins*.

Explicit Joins

In HQL, you can use the join keyword to join associated objects. The following query finds all the books published by the publisher "Apress". The result contains a list of object pairs in the form of an array of Objects(Object[]). Each pair consists of a book object and a publisher object:

```
from Book book join book.publisher publisher
where publisher.name = 'Apress'
```

In addition to many-to-one associations, all other kinds of associations can be joined. For example, you can join the one-to-many association from book to chapters. The following query finds all the books containing a chapter titled "Hibernate Basics". The result contains a list of object pairs; each pair consists of a book object and a collection of chapters:

```
from Book book join book.chapters chapter
where chapter.title = 'Hibernate Basics'
```

Implicit Joins

In the previous joins, you specify the join keyword to join associated objects. This kind of join is called an *explicit join*. You can also reference an association directly by name, which causes an *implicit join*. For example, the previous two queries can be expressed as follows (the result contains only a list of book objects because no join is specified in the from clause):

```
from Book book
where book.publisher.name = 'Springer'
```

Note that implicit joins are directed along many-to-one or one-to-one associations; they're never directed along many-to-many associations. This means you can never use something like this:

```
String QueryString3 =
  "from Book3 book where book.chapters.title = 'Many-To-Many Association'";
Query query1 = session.createQuery(QueryString3);
List<Chapter3> chptrs = query1.list();
```

The correct usage is as follows:

```
String queryString =
  "from Book3 book join book.chapters chapter where chapter.title=:title";
Query query = session.createQuery(queryString);
query.setString("title", "Many-To-Many Association");
List books = query.list();
```

Outer Joins

If you use the following HQL to query for books joined with publishers, books with a null publisher aren't included. This type of join is called an *inner join*, and it's the default if you don't specify a join type or if you specify inner join. It has the same meaning as an inner join in SQL:

```
from Book book join book.publisher
```

If you want to get all books, regardless of whether the publisher is null, you can use a left join by specifying left join or left outer join:

```
from Book book left join book.publisher
```

HQL supports two other types of joins: right joins and full joins. They have the same meaning as in SQL, but are seldom used.

Matching Text

The following HQL retrieves books and their associated chapters in which at least one of the chapter titles includes the word *Hibernate*. The result contains pairs consisting of a book and a chapter.

```
from Book book join book.chapters chapter
where chapter.title like '%Hibernate%'
```

Fetching Associations

You can use join fetch to force a lazy association to be initialized. It differs from a pure join in that only the parent objects are included in the result:

```
from Book book join fetch book.publisher publisher
```

An inner join fetch query doesn't return book objects with a null publisher. If you want to include them, you must use left join fetch:

```
from Book book left join fetch book.publisher publisher
```

8-4. Creating Report Queries

Problem

How do you create queries that group and aggregate data?

Solution

You use the select clause to generate report queries. The group by and having clauses are used for aggregation. You saw how to use the select clause earlier in this chapter.

How It Works

Let's see how to aggregate and group data.

Projection with Aggregation Functions

HQL and JPA QL support the aggregate functions count(), min(), max(), sum(), and avg(). If you want to know how many books are in your bookshop, you have to do something like this:

```
String q2 = "select count(i) from Book i";
Query query = session.createQuery(q2);
Long count = (Long) query.uniqueResult();
```

To find the minimum and maximum prices of the books in the bookshop, you can use a query like the following:

```
String q3 = "select min(i.price),max(i.price) from Book4 i";
Query query = session.createQuery(q3);
Object[] count = (Object[]) query.uniqueResult();
System.out.println("Minimum price- "+count[0]);
System.out.println("Maximum price- "+count[1]);
```

Note that this query's return type is an Object[] array.

Grouping Aggregated Results

You can sort the result list with an order by clause. Multiple fields and ascending/descending order can be specified:

```
from Book book
order by book.name asc, book.publishDate desc
```

HQL also supports the group by and having clauses. They're translated into SQL by Hibernate:

```
select book.publishDate, avg(book.price)
from Book book
group by book.publishDate
```

```
select book.publishDate, avg(book.price)
from Book book group by book.publishDate
having avg(book.price) > 10
```

Summary

This chapter showed you how to query a database using Hibernate Query Language. You learned how to use the from, select, and where clauses that form the backbone of most queries. And you saw how to bind parameters to the query parameters. You should be able to externalize queries by using named queries. If the result set size is large, you can use pagination to retrieve a subset of the original result set.

You learned to use the dot (.) operator to create implicit joins and the join keyword to create explicit joins. You also saw how to use aggregate functions such as min(), max(), avg(), count(), and sum().

In the next chapter, we show you how to query using the criteria API as well as Query by Example.

CHAPTER 9

Querying with Criteria and Example

In the previous chapter, you saw how to use Hibernate Query Language (HQL) and Java Persistence Query Language (JPA QL). HQL forces you to interact with the database using SQL-like syntax. You must have some knowledge of SQL to create complex queries, which makes it difficult to develop applications that use multicriteria queries.

With HQL and JPA QL, it's easy to make mistakes with string concatenation and SQL syntax.[1] Sometimes, errors occur simply because there is no space between two clauses in SQL. Because these errors are uncovered only at runtime, if you don't have decent unit tests, you must go through the long process of build-and-deploy on an application server to catch them.[2]

Unlike HQL, Hibernate Criteria is completely object oriented; it uses objects and their interfaces to load data from Hibernate-supported databases. It presents an elegant and more clean way to build dynamic queries.[3]

Let's take a look at an example using the Recipe 1 Book1 entity. We'll repeat some of it for Recipe 1, but this serves to illustrate some key differences between the HQL approach and the Criteria API.

There are four methods shown. One sets up the database, and another returns a set of data: the book name, if any; the publisher, if any; and the number of books we expect to see given the criteria. The last two methods offer equivalent functionality, except with the different APIs.

```
@BeforeMethod
public void clear() {
    SessionManager.deleteAll("Book1");

    Session session = SessionManager.openSession();
    Transaction tx = session.beginTransaction();
    for (int i = 1; i < 6; i++) {
        Book1 book = new Book1();
        book.setName("Book " + i);
        book.setPublisher("Publisher " + (i % 2 + 1));
        session.persist(book);
    }
    tx.commit();
    session.close();
}
```

---

[1]This is why one should prefer named queries and proper parameterization of those queries.

[2]And *this* is why most of our example code has been in the form of tests; unit testing is a good habit to have. (And starting a sentence with a conjunction is a *bad* habit to have. But that's okay.)

[3]As usual, "elegant and cleaner" are in the eye of the beholder, and being elegant and more clean is not a guarantee of performance.

```
@DataProvider
Object[][] variedData() {
    return new Object[][] {
            { "Book 1", null, 1},
            { null, "Publisher 2", 3},
            { "Book 1", "Publisher 2", 1},
            { null, null, 5}
    };
}

@Test(dataProvider = "variedData")
public void testRestrictionsCriteria(String name, String publisher, int count) {
    Session session = SessionManager.openSession();
    Transaction tx = session.beginTransaction();

    Criteria criteria = session.createCriteria(Book1.class);
    if(name!=null) {
        criteria.add(Restrictions.eq("name", name));
    }
    if(publisher!=null) {
        criteria.add(Restrictions.eq("publisher", publisher));
    }
    List<Book1> books = criteria.list();
    assertEquals(books.size(), count);

    tx.commit();
    session.close();
}

@Test(dataProvider = "variedData")
public void testRestrictionsHQL(String name, String publisher, int count) {
    Session session = SessionManager.openSession();
    Transaction tx = session.beginTransaction();
    StringBuilder queryText=new StringBuilder("from Book1 b ");

    if(name!=null) {
        queryText.append("where b.name=:name ");
    }
    if(publisher!=null) {
        if(name==null) {
            queryText.append("where ");
        } else {
            queryText.append("and ");
        }
        queryText.append("b.publisher=:publisher ");
    }

    Query query=session.createQuery(queryText.toString());
    if(name!=null) {
        query.setParameter("name", name);
    }
```

```
    if(publisher!=null) {
        query.setParameter("publisher", publisher);
    }

    List<Book1> books = query.list();
    assertEquals(books.size(), count);

    tx.commit();
    session.close();
}
```

The HQL query has to build a valid query and then has to plug the parameters into that query. It is fair to say that the criteria query is far more readable in this case.[4]

In this chapter, you learn how to use Criteria and the Example API. The Java Persistence API version 2.0 introduced a similar Criteria API to support dynamic queries. The documentation for the JPA criteria model can be found in the Java EE tutorial at http://docs.oracle.com/javaee/7/tutorial/doc/persistence-criteria.htm.

The chapter shows how to apply restrictions to Criterion objects to fetch data. These restrictions act like the where clause in HQL or SQL. You learn how to use a Criteria object that isn't in a session, which is called a DetachedCriteria.

9-1. Using Criteria

Problem

How do you create a basic Criteria object and use it to load data from a database?

Solution

As with HQL, you get the Criteria object from the session. If you don't have a session to create a Criteria object, you can use a DetachedCriteria instance. This DetachedCriteria object is later used with the session to get the results. This recipe demonstrates the basic implementation of the Criteria API.

How It Works

A basic Criteria query looks like this:

```
Criteria criteria = session.createCriteria(Book1.class)
List books = criteria.list();
```

This query corresponds to the following HQL query:

```
from Book1 book
```

---

[4]We haven't even looked at Query by Example, which might be even simpler for queries like this. The Criteria API is probably a little more powerful, though.

Most methods in the Criteria class return an instance of themselves, so you can build up your criteria as follows. Here you add a restriction to your criteria, which says that the name of the book should be equal to "Book 1":

```
Criteria criteria = session.createCriteria(Book1.class)
        .add(Restrictions.eq("name", "Book 1"));
List<Book1> books=criteria.list();
```

If you don't have an open session, you can instantiate a detached criteria by using the forClass() method and later attach it to a session for execution. When you have a session to run the query, you call getExecutableCriteria() and pass the session as a method argument. The getExecutableCriteria() method returns an executable instance of Criteria:

```
DetachedCriteria criteria = DetachedCriteria
        .forClass(Book1.class)
        .add(Restrictions.eq("name", "Book 1"));

Session session = SessionManager.openSession();
Transaction tx = session.beginTransaction();

List<Book1> booksFromCriteria = criteria
        .getExecutableCriteria(session)
        .list();
assertEquals(booksFromCriteria.size(), 1);

tx.commit();
session.close();
```

9-2. Using Restrictions

Problem

How do you filter data when using criteria? How do you apply restrictions to criteria?

Solution

You can add a series of restrictions to your Criteria query to filter the results, just as you build up the where clause in HQL. The Restrictions class provides a variety of methods to build restrictions.

How It Works

Each restriction you add is treated as a logical conjunction. The Criterion interface is an object-oriented representation of a query criterion that may be used as a restriction in a Criteria query. The Restrictions class provides static factory methods that return built-in criterion types. The org.hibernate.criterion package provides an API for creating complex queries:

```
Criteria criteria = session.createCriteria(Book.class);
Criterion nameRest = Restrictions.eq("name", "Hibernate Recipes");
criteria.add(nameRest);
List books = criteria.list();
```

This is equivalent to the following HQL:

```
from Book book where name='Hibernate Recipes'
```

eq is an equals implementation that takes two input method arguments: the name of the property of the Book class and the value to be evaluated. To get a unique result, you can use the uniqueResult() method:

```
Criteria criteria = session.createCriteria(Book.class);
Criterion nameRest = Restrictions.eq("name", "Hibernate Recipes");
criteria.add(nameRest);
Book book = (Book)criteria.uniqueResult();
```

You can use the ignoreCase() method to add case insensitivity to the query:

```
Criterion nameRest = Restrictions.eq("name", "Hibernate Recipes").ignoreCase();
```

The Restrictions class has many other methods, including the following:

- gt (greater than)
- lt (less than)
- ge (greater than or equal to)
- idEq (ID is equal to)
- ilike (a case-insensitive like, similar to the PostgreSQL ilike operator)
- isNull
- isNotNull
- isEmpty
- isNotEmpty
- between
- in (applies an "in" constraint to the named property)
- le (less than or equal to)

Here's an example:

```
Criteria criteria = session.createCriteria(Book.class)
        .add(Restrictions.like("name", "%Hibernate%"))
        .add(Restrictions.between("price", new Integer(100), new Integer(200)));
List books = criteria.list();
```

This Criteria query corresponds to the following HQL query:

```
from Book book
where (book.name like '%Hibernate%') and (book.price between 100 and 200)
```

The % character is a wildcard. Because it is added before and after the word *Hibernate*, it enables you to search for all books that have the word *Hibernate* in a book name. If you want to look for all books having a name starting with *Hibernate*, the query is as follows:

```
Criteria criteria = session.createCriteria(Book.class)
        .add(Restrictions.like("name", "Hibernate%"))
        .add(Restrictions.between("price", new Integer(100), new Integer(200)));
List books = criteria.list();
```

Notice that there is no % character before the word *Hibernate* in the search string. You can also group some of the restrictions with logical disjunction. How do you achieve the following query using the Criteria API?

```
from Book book
where (book.name like '%Hibernate%' or book.name like '%Java%') and (book.price between 100
and 200)
```

You can directly translate it into something like this:

```
Criteria criteria = session.createCriteria(Book.class)
        .add(Restrictions.or(
                        Restrictions.like("name", "%Hibernate%"),
                        Restrictions.like("name", "%Java%")
                )
        )
        .add(Restrictions.between("price", new Integer(100), new Integer(200)));
List books = criteria.list();
```

This query can also be written using the Restrictions disjunction() method:

```
Criteria criteria = session.createCriteria(Book.class)
                .add(Restrictions.disjunction()
                                .add(Restrictions.like("name", "%Hibernate%"))
                                .add(Restrictions.like("name", "%Java%"))
                )
                .add(Restrictions.between("price", new Integer(100), new Integer(200)));
List books = criteria.list();
```

If you want to search using wildcards, you can use the MatchMode class, which provides a convenient way to express a substring match without using string manipulation:

```
Criteria criteria = session.createCriteria(Book.class);
Criterion nameRest = Restrictions.like("name", "Hibernate",MatchMode.START);
criteria.add(nameRest);
Book books = (Book)criteria.uniqueResult();
```

This Criteria statement is the same as the following:

```
Criterion nameRest = Restrictions.like("name", "Hibernate%");
```

The following `MatchMode` values are available:

- START: Matches the start of the string with the pattern

- END: Matches the end of the string with the pattern

- ANYWHERE: Matches the pattern anywhere in the string

- EXACT: Matches the complete pattern in the string

Writing Subqueries

Using Criteria, you can also execute subqueries. A *subquery* is a query that is nested inside another query. It is also called an *inner query* or *inner select*.

For example, here's a subquery in SQL:

```
select publisher_name, address from Publisher pub where pub.code=(select publisher_code from
Book book where book.publish_date=current_timestamp)
```

This query fetches the name and address of any publisher whose book was published today. The second `select` query is nested in the main SQL query.

You can write this using Criteria, as follows:

```
DetachedCriteria todaysBook = DetachedCriteria.forClass(Book.class)
.setProjection( (Projection) Property.forName("publishDate").eq("current_timestamp") );
List =manager.createCriteria(Publisher.class)
            .add( Property.forName("publisherCode").eq(todaysBook) )
            .list();
```

9-3. Using Criteria in Associations

Problem

How do you express a join restriction using the Criteria API when there are associated objects? How do you use dynamic fetching?

Solution

When you have associated objects, you need to join them in order to retrieve data from them. In HQL, you use an alias and an equijoin on the foreign key in the where clause:

```
from Book b, Publisher p where b.publisherId = p.publisherId
```

This query joins the `Publisher` object and `Book` object with `publisherId`, which is the foreign key in `Book`.

Let's see how this is achieved using the Criteria API. Hibernate provides two methods to enable joining of associated entities: `createCriteria()` and `createAlias()`. The difference between the two is that `createCriteria()` returns a new instance of `Criteria`, so you can nest calls to `createCriteria()`. The `createAlias()` method doesn't create a new instance of `Criteria` and is very similar to the alias you declare in the HQL from clause.

How It Works

You can reference an association property by its name to trigger an implicit join. For example, suppose that you have an Order class that contains a Price object, which holds details as unitPrice and currency:

```
public class Order {
  ...
  Price price;
}
public class Price {
  ...
  String currency;
  float unitPrice;
}
```

If you need to fetch the unitPrice of an Order, you can use Order.price.unitPrice in HQL:

```
from Order order where order.price.unitPrice > 50
```

Can the same implicit join work using Criteria?

```
Criteria criteria = session.createCriteria(Book.class,"book")
.add(Restrictions.like("name", "%Hibernate%"))
.add(Restrictions.eq("book.publisher.name", "Manning"));
List books = criteria.list();
```

If you execute this code, the following exception is thrown:

```
Exception in thread "main" org.hibernate.QueryException: could not resolve property:
publisher.name of: com.hibernaterecipes.chapter5.Book
    at org.hibernate.persister.entity.AbstractPropertyMapping.propertyException(AbstractProp
ertyMapping.java:67)
```

Hibernate can't resolve the property publisher.name. That means an implicit join isn't supported for Criteria queries. To join an association explicitly, you need to create a new Criteria object for it:

```
Criteria criteria = session.createCriteria(Book.class)
        .add(Restrictions.like("name", "%Hibernate%"))
        .createCriteria("publisher")
        .add(Restrictions.eq("name", "Manning"));
List books = criteria.list();
```

In this example, the createCriteria() method has a string attribute, in which you pass the name of the associated property. Because you're creating a criteria on the publisher property of the Book object, you need to pass "publisher" in this case. You can also use createAlias() to generate the same query:

```
Criteria criteria = session.createCriteria(Book.class)
                .createAlias("publisher", "publisherAlias")
                .add(Restrictions.like("name", "%Hibernate%"))
                .add(Restrictions.eq("publisherAlias.name", "Manning"));
                List books = criteria.list();
```

In HQL, the query is as follows:

```
from Book book
where book.name like '%Hibernate%' and book.publisher.name = 'Manning'
```

As in HQL, you can specify the fetching strategy that Hibernate should follow when it loads data in case of associations. This strategy can also be set in the metadata configuration file. If the configuration needs to be overridden, you can use the FetchMode API when you retrieve data using Criteria.

Following are the FetchMode options that are available:

- DEFAULT: The default setting that is used from the configuration file.

- EAGER: Deprecated. Use FetchMode.JOIN instead.

- JOIN: Retrieves the associated object's data by using an outer join.

- LAZY: Deprecated. Use FetchMode.SELECT instead.

- SELECT: Fetches eagerly using an additional SELECT query. Unless the lazy option is disabled explicitly in the configuration file, the second SELECT query is executed when the association is accessed.

The following code uses the FetchMode.JOIN and FetchMode.SELECT options:

```
Criteria criteria = session.createCriteria(Book.class)
.add(Restrictions.like("name", "%Hibernate%"))
.setFetchMode("publisher", FetchMode.JOIN)
.setFetchMode("chapters", FetchMode.SELECT);
List books = criteria.list();
```

In this case, the associated Publisher object is fetched using an outer join, where Chapters is retrieved with a second SELECT query.

9-4. Using Projections
Problem

What are projections, and how do you use them in the Criteria API?

Solution

Until now, when you retrieved objects using Criteria, you fetched the complete object in the result set. What if you want to fetch only certain fields or columns in a table, and you don't want the complete object?

Projections help you filter data and return only those fields you need. You can use projections when you don't want the entire fetched entity and its associations. You can also use them when there is a requirement to get the results in a flat manner (not in an object graph). This approach improves performance, especially when you're dealing with lot of columns and the object graph is very deep.

How It Works

To customize the fields of the result, you can use projections to specify the fields to be returned:

```
Criteria criteria = session.createCriteria(Book.class)
.setProjection(Projections.property("name"));
List books = criteria.list();
```

This is similar to the following SQL statement:

```
select book.name from Book book
```

It is better than this, which fetches the complete book object although you need only the book name:

```
from Book book
```

Aggregate Functions and Groupings with Projections

Aggregate functions in SQL summarize data and return a single value by calculating it from values in a column. Here are some examples:

- SUM: Returns the summation of the column values on which it is applied

- AVG: Returns the average of the column values

- MIN: Returns the minimum of the specified column values

- MAX: Returns the maximum of the specified column values

In HQL, you can use them directly, just as in SQL:

```
select min(book.price) from Book book
```

This query returns the minimum price of all the books in the BOOK table.

When you're querying with the Criteria API, you can use projections to apply the aggregated functions. These functions are encapsulated in the Projections class as static methods:

```
Criteria criteria = session.createCriteria(Book.class)
.setProjection(Projections.avg("price"));
List books = criteria.list();
```

It is similar to the following:

```
select avg(book.price) from Book book
```

The results can be sorted in ascending or descending order:

```
Criteria criteria = session.createCriteria(Book.class)
.addOrder(Order.asc("name"))
.addOrder(Order.desc("publishDate"));
List books = criteria.list();
```

It is something like this:

```
from Book book
order by book.name asc, book.publishDate desc
```

Grouping is also supported for Criteria queries. You can assign any properties as group properties, and they appear in the group by clause:

```
Criteria criteria = session.createCriteria(Book.class)
.setProjection(Projections.projectionList()
.add(Projections.groupProperty("publishDate"))
.add(Projections.avg("price")));
List books = criteria.list();
```

It results in the following:

```
select book.publishDate, avg(book.price)
from Book book
group by book.publishDate
```

9-5. Querying by Example

Problem

What is Query by Example (QBE) and how do you use it to retrieve data?

Solution

Suppose you need to retrieve data based on different input. The search criteria can be complex, filtering data on various columns. Using Criteria, it might look like this:

```
Criteria criteria = getSession().createCriteria(Book.class);
criteria.add(Restrictions.eq("name", "Hibernate")).
        add(Restrictions.eq("price",100))
```

If you have more columns to be filtered, the list increases. QBE makes this easy for you. QBE returns a result set depending on the properties that were set on an instance of the queried class. You can also specify the properties that need to be excluded. This approach greatly reduces the amount of code you have to write.

Note that QBE is not part of JPA. It is certainly part of Hibernate (which is why it is here, of course), and other JPA implementations provide the capability as well, but it is not part of a standard yet. QBE is also somewhat out of favor as a query technology. It is certainly used, but not often, partially because of the lack of a standard around its use and partially because it is a little bit difficult to get right.

How It Works

Criteria queries can be constructed through an Example object that should be an instance of the persistent class you want to query. All null properties are ignored by default.[5] Here's an example Book5 class for us to use:

```java
@Entity
@Data
public class Book5 {
  @Id
  @GeneratedValue(strategy = GenerationType.IDENTITY)
  int id;
  String name;
  String publisher;
  Double price;
}
```

Now let's take a look at our test, using QBE to find a matching Book5:

```java
@BeforeMethod
  public void clear() {
    SessionManager.deleteAll("Book5");

    Session session = SessionManager.openSession();
    Transaction tx = session.beginTransaction();
    for (int i = 1; i < 6; i++) {
      Book5 book = new Book5();
      book.setName("Book " + i);
      book.setPublisher("Publisher " + (i % 2 + 1));
      book.setPrice(10.0 + i * 2);
      session.persist(book);
    }
    tx.commit();
    session.close();
  }

  @Test
  public void testQueryByExample() {

    Session session = SessionManager.openSession();
    Transaction tx = session.beginTransaction();

    Book5 book5 = new Book5();
    book5.setName("Book 1");
    Example example = Example.create(book5);
    Criteria criteria = session.createCriteria(Book5.class)
        .add(example);
```

---

[5]Query by Example illustrates a good reason to prefer wrapper classes to primitives in entities, even though they require a little more work to use. Because primitives always have a value, there's no way to cleanly say "this field has no value," which means that queries have to explicitly exclude primitives. Alternatively, you can use the wrapper classes and let null serve as a wildcard for you.

```
    List<Book5> books = criteria.list();
    assertEquals(books.size(), 1);
    assertEquals(books.get(0).getPublisher(), "Publisher 2");
    assertEquals(books.get(0).getPrice(), 12.0, 0.01);
    tx.commit();
    session.close();
  }
```

The HQL is similar to the following:

```
from Book book where book.name = 'Book 1'
```

In this next example, the instance of Book5 is created, and the search criteria are set: they include name, publisher, and price. Note two things about our example object: it uses a wildcard ("Publisher%"), and the price is incorrect for this book's title (the price should be 12.00, not 22.00). We then create the example, but enable wildcards (the enableLike() call) and exclude price from the example. Finally, the Criteria interface accepts the Example instance to retrieve the data based on the values set on the Book5 instance.

```
@Test
public void testQueryByExampleLike() {
  Session session = SessionManager.openSession();
  Transaction tx = session.beginTransaction();

  Book5 book5 = new Book5();

  book5.setName("Book 1");
  book5.setPublisher("Publisher%");
  book5.setPrice(22.0);

  Example example = Example.create(book5)
      .enableLike()
      .excludeProperty("price");
  Criteria criteria = session.createCriteria(Book5.class)
      .add(example);
  List<Book5> books = criteria.list();
  assertEquals(books.size(), 1);
  assertEquals(books.get(0).getPublisher(), "Publisher 2");

  tx.commit();
  session.close();
}
```

The corresponding HQL is as follows:

```
from Book5 book where (book.name like 'Book 1' and book.publisher like 'Publisher%')
```

Summary

This chapter introduced the Criteria API and showed how to use it to retrieve data. You can use restrictions to filter data by using the `Restrictions` interface, which has several methods that let you filter data: `equal`, `like`, `greater than`, and `less than`. It also provides disjunctions. The `MatchMode` interface provides variables that you can use for string comparisons. Subqueries also can be implemented using the `DetachedCriteria` object.

You can use the `createCriteria()` and `createAlias()` methods to fetch data when there are associated objects, and you can use projections for aggregated functions and groupings. Finally, QBE makes it easy to fetch data when the data has to be filtered on various search criteria.

In the next chapter, we'll take a closer look at object states in Hibernate.

CHAPTER 10

■ ■ ■

Working with Objects

This chapter discusses the states an object goes through during its life cycle. The session is responsible for managing object state in Hibernate, and the `EntityManager` does the same in Java Persistence. Hibernate provides a persistence mechanism that is transparent to the entities and the application; the application has to know the state of an object.

The chapter also discusses the persistence context provided by Hibernate. The persistence context manages objects and caches object states within a transaction (unit of work). You will learn how to use data filtering and interceptors.

10-1. Identifying Persistent Object States

Problem

What are the states that an object can have in Hibernate? How does the object life cycle work?

Solution

Hibernate defines four object states: transient, persistent, detached, and removed. You will look at each state and learn what methods in Hibernate or JPA take an object to that state.

How It Works

Let's begin with the transient object before moving on to look at the other states.

Transient Objects

Objects instantiated using the `new` operator are called *transient objects*. The Hibernate persistence context isn't aware of operations performed on transient objects. Their state is lost when they aren't referenced by any other object and become available for garbage collection. They don't have any association with any database table row. JPA doesn't have this state. Figure 10-1 provides a graphical representation.

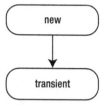

Figure 10-1. *Objects instantiated using the new operator are called transient*

Persistent Objects

An object that has a database identity associated with it is called a *persistent object*. The key for an object to be in a persistent state is to be associated with a *persistent context*. The persistent context caches the object state and can identify changes made, if any.

You can create persistent objects in two ways: you can retrieve a database table row as an entity by calling API methods such as get(), load(), and list(); or you can persist a transient object using API methods such as save() and saveOrUpdate(). Figure 10-2 illustrates several possible ways for an object to become persistent.

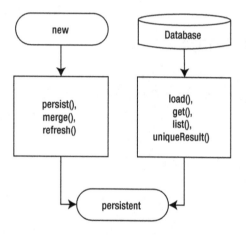

Figure 10-2. *Possible ways for an object to become persistent*

Detached Objects

In the previous section, you learned that a persistent object is associated with a persistent context. The persistent context no longer exists after the transaction is closed. If the application retains a reference to the persistent object, the object is said to be in the *detached state*. The state of a detached object can be modified and can be persisted back to the database, which is very common when you're working with applications that have a multilayered architecture.

Hibernate provides a reattached mode and a merging mode to make a detached object persistent. JPA has a merging mode only. Figure 10-3 illustrates some of the ways by which a persistent object can become *detached* through the Session.

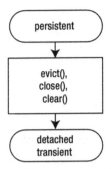

Figure 10-3. *How entities can become detached*

Removed Objects

A persistent object is considered to be in the *removed* state when a delete() or remove() operation is called on it. The delete() method is provided by a Hibernate session, whereas the remove() method is provided by the JPA EntityManager.

Note that when an object is removed, the persistence context then deletes the object from the database. This means you shouldn't use any references to the removed object in the application.[1] For example, in the following code, after the book object has been deleted, the code tries to call the update() method to use the reference to the deleted book, but this isn't correct:

```java
public void deletePersistentObject() {
  Session session = getSession();
  Transaction tx = session.beginTransaction();
  Book book = (Book) session.get(Book.class, new Long(294912));
  session.delete(book);
  tx.commit();
  // cannot use the reference to book as it has been deleted from database.
  tx = session.beginTransaction();
  session.update(book);
  tx.commit();
  session.close();
}
```

Figure 10-4 shows how to reach the removed state.

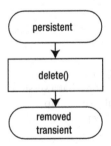

Figure 10-4. *Creating an object in the removed state*

---

[1]The removed reference is still present; you can still work with it in the JVM. It is just seen as being in a *removed state* with respect to the database, and modifications to the instance may not have the effect you intend.

10-2. Working with Persistent Objects

Problem

How do you make a persistent object? How do you perform CRUD operations on it?

Solution

The Session interface provides methods to perform CRUD operations on an entity to make it a persistent object.

How It Works

Let's start by showing how to create a persistent object and then carry out other operations on it.

Creating a Persistent Object

In Hibernate, you need an instance of the session from the application's session factory. The session is a factory for transactions and keeps track of all the changes to an object within its scope. The session factory is an immutable cache of compiled mappings for a single database; it is a factory for providing session instances. So, if your application interacts with two databases, you need to configure two separate session factories.

Here's how to do it in Hibernate:

```
sessionFactory = new Configuration().configure().buildSessionFactory();
Session hibernateSession = sessionFactory.openSession();
```

The first line in this code looks for a hibernate.cfg.xml file in its path. It then compiles and loads the mapping listed in the file. Creating a session factory is an expensive task, so you should create it only once—preferably at application startup. Creating a session is relatively inexpensive; it doesn't even open a database connection.

Let's create the persistent object:

```
Transaction tx = session.beginTransaction();
Book book = new Book();
book.setName("Hibernate Recipes");
book.setPrice(79);
book.setPublishDate(new Date());
Serializable bookId = session.save(book);
tx.commit();
session.close();
```

On the first line, an instance of Transaction is retrieved from the session.[2] By default, the session provides a Java Database Connectivity (JDBC) transaction. The other two types of transactions that a session can provide are the Java Transaction API (JTA) and container-managed transaction. For the session to provide either of these two types, you need to declare the hibernate.transaction_factory property in the hibernate.cfg.xml file.

---

[2]Important note: changes to persistent objects (i.e., managed by the Session, as described in this chapter) will be persisted by the Transaction when it is committed. Rolling back the Transaction avoids any changes to the database.

The next couple of lines create a transient book object using the new keyword. You make the transient object into a persistent object by calling the save() method. The book object is then associated with the session and its persistent context. Note that until this point, a database record hasn't been created.

The save() method returns the primary key of the newly inserted record.[3] Only by calling commit() on the transaction is a database connection created and a record inserted into the database. The last line closes the session, which means its persistent context is no longer active. The book object is now in a detached state.

Next, here's how you do it in JPA:

```
EntityManagerFactory managerFactory = Persistence.createEntityManagerFactory("book");
EntityManager manager = managerFactory.createEntityManager();
```

In JPA, you use the createEntityManagerFactory() method of the javax.persistence.Persistence class to get an instance of the EntityManagerFactory class. This method call looks for a persistence. xml file in the META-INF folder. EntityManagerFactory is similar to the Hibernate sessionFactory class; it provides you with an EntityManager. The EntityManager has a new persistent context, which is used to save and load objects:

```
Book newBook = new Book();
newBook.setBookName("HIbernate Recipes Phase1");
newBook.setPublishDate(new Date());
newBook.setPrice(50l);
EntityTransaction tran = manager.getTransaction();
tran.begin();
manager.persist(book);
tran.commit();
manager.close();
```

In JPA, the EntityManager replaces the session: it is a factory that provides transactions (EntityTransactions in this case). The save() method is replaced by the persist() method, which moves the book object from the transient state to the persistent state. After the persist() method is called, the state of the book object is managed by the persistence context. Note that persist() doesn't return the serializable ID of the newly created record.[4]

Retrieving a Persistent Object

In Hibernate, you need an instance of the session to retrieve an entity by its ID. Hibernate provides two methods for this: get() and load(). Both methods take the entity class and the ID as input parameters:

```
Session session = getSession();
Transaction tx = session.beginTransaction();
//Book book = (Book) session.load(Book.class, new Long(294912));
Book book1 = (Book) session.get(Book.class, new Long(294912));
tx.commit();
session.close();
System.out.println(book1);
```

The get() method makes a call to the database and does a lookup for the primary key. If it finds the primary key, it retrieves and returns the object. If it can't, it returns null.

---

[3]An alternative is using Session.persist(Object), which modifies the instance much as save() does, but doesn't return the primary key, acting just like the JPA persist() method does.
[4]You knew this already, because you already read the previous footnote.

The load() method, on the other hand, looks in the current persistence context. If it can find the entity, it returns the entity object. If the object isn't being managed in the current persistence context, a proxy placeholder is returned without hitting the database. This means if you request an entity object that isn't in the database (or, of course, the current persistence context), the load() method returns a proxy. You get an org.hibernate.ObjectNotFoundException when you try to read/retrieve properties other than the primary key within the same persistence context, and you get an org.hibernate.LazyInitializationException when you try to read/retrieve properties after the session is closed (the persistence context has ended). The load() method is useful when you need only a proxy and don't need to make a database call. You need just a proxy when, in a given persistence context, you need to associate an entity before persisting.[5]

In JPA, you use the EntityManager to read/retrieve persistent entities. JPA provides two methods: find() and getReference(). Both methods take the entity class and the ID as input parameters:

```
EntityManager manager = SessionManager.getEntityManager();
EntityTransaction tran = manager.getTransaction();
tran.begin();
Book book = manager.find(Book.class, new Long(294912));
//Book book1 = manager.getReference(Book.class, new Long(294912));
tran.commit();
manager.close();
```

The find() method is similar to the get() method in Hibernate. A call to the database is made when this method is invoked. If it doesn't find the persistent entity, the find() method returns null. Note that you haven't cast the return value from the find() method. It isn't required because find() is a generic method, and the first parameter is set as the return type.

The getReference() method is similar to the load() method in Hibernate. You should use it when you need only a proxy.

Modifying a Persistent Object

You can modify any persistent object that is associated with a session and a persistence context. Its state is then synchronized with the database:

```
Session session = getSession();
Transaction tx = session.beginTransaction();
Book book = (Book) session.get(Book.class, new Long(294912));
book.setName("Book Name - hibernate 2");
tx.commit();
session.close();
```

The entity is retrieved from the database and modified in the same transaction. The modifications are propagated to the database when the commit() method is called. The persistence context identifies the changes that have been made to the entity's state and synchronizes with the database. This process is called *automatic dirty checking*.

---

[5]You can also use Session.byId() to accomplish the same kind of operation, as some of our previous recipes have done (e.g., Chapter 7, Recipe 3, is only one example). They work effectively the same way as get() and load() do, and, in fact, end up with getReference() and load() method calls in the end. They just offer you a way to specify lock options as part of the instance retrieval process.

The implementation in JPA is as follows:

```
EntityManager manager = SessionManager.getEntityManager();
EntityTransaction tran = manager.getTransaction();
tran.begin();
Book book = manager.find(Book.class, new Long(294912));
book.setBookName("Book Name - hibernate 22");
tran.commit();
manager.close();
```

Deleting a Persistent Object

You can delete from the database any persistent object that is associated with a session and a persistence context. To do so, you call the delete() method:

```
Session session = getSession();
Transaction tx = session.beginTransaction();
Book book = (Book) session.get(Book.class, new Long(294912));
session.delete(book);
tx.commit();
session.close();
```

The entity is in the *removed state* after the call to delete(). The database record is deleted after the transaction is committed, and the object is in the *transient state* after the session is closed.

In JPA, the remove() method performs the same function as the delete() method:

```
EntityManager manager = SessionManager.getEntityManager();
EntityTransaction tran = manager.getTransaction();
tran.begin();
Book book = manager.find(Book.class, new Long(294912));
manager.remove(book);
tran.commit();
manager.close();
```

10-3. Persisting Detached Objects
Problem

How do you persist a detached object?

Solution

You can persist a detached object two ways: by reattaching it or by merging it.

How It Works

You first reattach a detached object and then merge one.

Reattaching a Detached Object

In Hibernate, you use the session's update() method to reattach a detached object to the session and persistence context:

```
Session session = getSession();
Transaction tx = session.beginTransaction();
Book book = (Book) session.get(Book.class, new Long(294912));
tx.commit();
session.close();
book.setName("Detached Hibernate");
Session session2 = getSession();
Transaction tx2 = session2.beginTransaction();
session2.update(book);
tx2.commit();
session2.close();
```

Hibernate keeps track of modifications made to the detached object. Hence, when the update() method is called, it always schedules an update SQL command. If you don't want to make an update call, you can configure the class mapping to have select-before-update='true'. A get() call is then made to check whether the object has been updated before the call to the update() method.

JPA doesn't have an update() method; it supports only merging detached objects.

Merging a Detached Object

In Hibernate, you use the session's merge() method to persist a detached object. The merge() method call results in a complex set of actions. Hibernate first looks to see whether the instance of the entity is in the current persistence context. If it finds an instance of the entity equal to the detached object, it copies the state from the detached object to the instance in the persistence context:

```
Session session = getSession();
Transaction tx = session.beginTransaction();
Book book = (Book) session.get(Book.class, new Long(294912));
tx.commit();
session.close();
book.setName("Detached Hibernate");
Session session2 = getSession();
Transaction tx2 = session2.beginTransaction();
Book book2 = (Book) session2.merge(book);
tx2.commit();
session2.close();
```

If the persistence context doesn't contain an equal instance of the entity, Hibernate makes a get() call internally to load the persistent entity object into the persistence context. The detached object state is then copied onto the newly created persistent entity object.

Note that if a transient object is passed to the merge() method, a new persistent instance is created, and the state is copied to the new instance. The same applies to JPA. Here's the implementation:

```
EntityManager manager = SessionManager.getEntityManager();
EntityTransaction tran = manager.getTransaction();
tran.begin();
Book book = manager.find(Book.class, new Long(262144));
```

```
tran.commit();
manager.close();
book.setBookName("Detached Hibernate merged");
EntityManager manager2 = SessionManager.getEntityManager();
EntityTransaction tran2 = manager2.getTransaction();
tran2.begin();
Book book2 = (Book) manager2.merge(book);
tran2.commit();
manager2.close();
```

10-4. Using Data Filters

Problem

Suppose your bookshop has a lot of children and teenagers as users.[6] You want to add a classification to the books so that you can limit access to certain books for underage readers. (You don't want a child to be able to see a book meant for an adult reader.) How can you achieve this by using the data-filtering mechanism provided by Hibernate?

Solution

For this recipe, every Book class has a rank attribute that specifies the lowest rank that can access a book. Books for adults have a user rank of 3, and books for children have a user rank of 1. We want our filter to allow us to set a user rank so that the books geared toward a "higher rank" (older readers) do not appear for younger readers.

We do this by declaring a reference to a filter along with any parameters for it and then defining the filter. When we want the filter to be applied, it's enabled by name for a specific Session.

How It Works

We can do everything in the Book4 class.[7] The class is very simple; the metadata (the annotations) make it interesting.

```
@Entity
@Data
@NoArgsConstructor
@NamedQueries({
    @NamedQuery(name = "book4.findAll", query = "from Book4 b ")
})
@FilterDefs({
    @FilterDef(name = "rank", parameters = @ParamDef(name = "rank", type = "integer"))
})
@Filters({
    @Filter(name = "rank", condition = "rank <= :rank")
})
public class Book4 {
  @Id
  @GeneratedValue(strategy = GenerationType.AUTO)
```

---

[6]In a perfect world, every bookshop has a lot of children and teenagers as users.
[7]Book4 was chosen for consistency's sake.

```
  public Integer id;
  String title;
  int rank;

  public Book4(String title, int rank) {
    this.title = title;
    this.rank = rank;
  }
}
```

The annotation order doesn't matter, but note that the filters' names need to match, and the filter's condition is expressed in SQL, not HQL or any other general-purpose query-language.[8]

For completeness' sake, here's the Hibernate configuration file that uses this entity:

```xml
<?xml version="1.0" encoding="UTF-8"?>
<!DOCTYPE hibernate-configuration PUBLIC
        "-//Hibernate/Hibernate Configuration DTD 3.0//EN"
        "http://www.hibernate.org/dtd/hibernate-configuration-3.0.dtd">
<hibernate-configuration>
    <session-factory>
        <property name="connection.driver_class">org.h2.Driver</property>
        <property name="connection.url">jdbc:h2:file:./chapter10</property>
        <property name="hibernate.dialect">org.hibernate.dialect.HSQLDialect</property>
        <property name="hibernate.hbm2ddl.auto">create</property>
        <property name="hibernate.show_sql">true</property>
        <property name="hibernate.discriminator.ignore_explicit_for_joined">true</property>
        <property name="connection.username"></property>
        <property name="connection.password"></property>
        <mapping class="com.apress.hibernaterecipes.chapter10.recipe4.Book4" />
    </session-factory>
</hibernate-configuration>
```

Actually using the filter is fairly easy. Once we have a Session, we get a Filter reference through Session.enableFilter(); we can then call Filter.setParameter() to change the data set returned from any queries associated with the filter. Here's a test that builds some data and then queries both with and without an active filter:

```
@Test
public void testFilter() {
  Session session = SessionManager.openSession();
  Transaction tx = session.beginTransaction();
  Book4 book4 = new Book4("The Fog in the Dog", 1);
  session.save(book4);
  book4 = new Book4("Angsty Dead People", 2);
  session.save(book4);
  tx.commit();
  session.close();
```

---

[8]Yes, SQL is a general-purpose query language, but it tends to be specific for each database, whereas HQL and JPAQL try to isolate you from the database-specific SQL extensions.

```
session = SessionManager.openSession();
tx = session.beginTransaction();
Query query = session.getNamedQuery("book4.findAll");
List<Book4> books = (List<Book4>) query.list();
assertEquals(books.size(), 2);
tx.commit();
session.close();

session = SessionManager.openSession();
tx = session.beginTransaction();

// we don't want Angsty Dead People shown to a young child.
session.enableFilter("rank").setParameter("rank", 1);
query = session.getNamedQuery("book4.findAll");
books = (List<Book4>) query.list();
assertEquals(books.size(), 1);
tx.commit();
session.close();
}
```

You can find a slightly more complete example and explanation of filters in *Beginning Hibernate*, 3rd edition, published by Apress.[9]

10-5. Using Interceptors
Problem

Suppose you want to save the date on any insert made into the BookShop database. For example, if a new publisher is inserted, you want to save the created date. The same is true for books: if a new book is entered into the database, you want to know when it was created by referring to the created date. How can you do this by using interceptors provided by Hibernate?

Solution

Because the created date is a property that is used in many classes, you can create an Auditable class and have all classes that need to have a created date extend that class. You create an interceptor that extends Hibernate's EmptyInterceptor and override the onSave() method. In the onSave() method, you assign the date if the object is an instance of Auditable (and return true if the object was modified). Because interceptors are session scoped, every time you request a session from sessionFactory, you need to assign the interceptor to the session when you open the session.

How It Works

You first create a simple Auditable class with one property: createDate. The entity classes that need a created date to be persisted in the database extend this class:

```java
@MappedSuperclass
public class Auditable {
  @Getter
  @Setter
  @Temporal(TemporalType.TIMESTAMP)
  Date createDate;
}
```

In this case, let's create a Book5 class.

```java
@Entity
@Data
@EqualsAndHashCode(callSuper=true)
@NoArgsConstructor
public class Book5 extends Auditable {
  @Id
  @GeneratedValue(strategy = GenerationType.AUTO)
  public Integer id;
  String title;
  int rank;

  public Book5(String title, int rank) {
    this.title = title;
    this.rank = rank;
  }
}
```

Now we create the interceptor class. In this case, we'll call it AuditableInterceptor, and it extends the Hibernate EmptyInterceptor class. EmptyInterceptor doesn't do anything—it is provided by Hibernate for use as a base class for application-defined custom interceptors. In the AuditableInterceptor implementation, you need to override the onSave() method. In this method, you set createDate if the object is of type Auditable, and return true because we've changed the state of the object:

```java
public class AuditableInterceptor extends EmptyInterceptor {
  @Override
  public boolean onSave(Object entity, Serializable id,
                        Object[] state, String[] propertyNames,
                        Type[] types) {
    if (entity instanceof Auditable) {
      for(int i=0;i<propertyNames.length;i++) {
        if("createDate".equals(propertyNames[i])) {
          state[i]=new Date();
          return true;
        }
      }
    }
```

```
      return false;
  }
}
```

You need to assign the interceptor to a Hibernate session when you open the session, so the test has to use the SessionFactory:

```
@Test
  public void testInterceptorOnSave() {
    Session session = SessionManager.getSessionFactory()
        .withOptions().interceptor(new AuditableInterceptor())
        .openSession();
    Transaction tx = session.beginTransaction();
    Book5 book5 = new Book5("Angsty Dead People", 1);
    assertNull(book5.getCreateDate());
    session.save(book5);
    tx.commit();
    session.close();

    assertNotNull(book5.getCreateDate());
  }
```

You can also assign the interceptor at the global level. If you choose to do that, all sessions are assigned the interceptor:

```
Configuration configuration = new Configuration().configure();
config.setInterceptor(new AuditableInterceptor());
ServiceRegistry serviceRegistry = new StandardServiceRegistryBuilder()
        .applySettings(configuration.getProperties())
        .build();
sessionFactory=configuration.buildSessionFactory(serviceRegistry);
Session session=sessionFactory.openSession();
```

Interceptors can also be used in audit logging.

Summary

Now you have a good understanding of the persistence life cycle and the states an object can have during its life cycle. When you're working with a detached object, you can either reattach or merge the object. You should be able to use dynamic data filtering to provide security or access temporal/regional data.

You also learned to use interceptors to persist common properties such as created date and created by.

CHAPTER 11

■ ■ ■

Batch Processing and Native SQL

Batch processing is the processing of groups of elements. From an application standpoint, batch processing means reading data from a persistent store, doing something with the data, and then possibly storing the processed data in the persistent store as a single conceptual operation. Batch processing, which allows for the automation and sharing of computer resources, is usually run when computer resources are less busy.

Let's say that for a bookshop application, you want to increase sales by putting all books in the shop on sale on the 27th and 28th of the month. This is a classic case for implementing batch processing. The night before the 27th, you list all the books that are in stock and implement the required discount. And on the night of the 28th, the discount is removed.[1]

During batch processing, you generally need to insert, update, and delete a lot of database records as single units of work. This chapter discusses Hibernate's batch-update and batch-delete features. For example, the following code snippet tries to insert a million books in a single transaction. This isn't a good approach; it may lead to OutOfMemory issues because Hibernate caches the instances in its cache:

```
Session session = SessionManager.openSession();
Transaction tx = session.beginTransaction();

for(int i=0;i<100000;i++) {
    Book book = new Book();
    book.setName("Book Name "+(i+1));
    book.setPrice(79);
    book.setPublishDate(new Date());
    session.save(book);
}

tx.commit();
session.close();
```

If you're processing one million books in one session, you should call the flush() and clear() methods of the session after every 100 or 200 books;[2] flush() and clear() clear the first-level cache. If the second-level cache is enabled at the entity level, and if you want it to be disabled for the batch-insert method, you need to call Session.setCacheMode (CacheMode.IGNORE). By setting the session's cacheMode to IGNORE, you tell Hibernate not to interact with the second-level cache for that particular session.

---

[1]To be sure, this is not the only way to accomplish the application of discounts based on specific circumstances; a rules engine would work as well, and would *probably* be more appropriate than altering your actual data.

[2]This number is pulled out of a hat. It's a good number and an excellent starting point, but if you really want to know what the best number of operations in a single transaction would be, you have to roll up your sleeves and test. Unfortunately, "best number of operations" is difficult to define in a general sense (outside of "does it work?"), so there's no good way to demonstrate such a test.

On a global level, you can enable the JDBC batch size by setting the `jdbc.batch_size` attribute (recommended values are 5 to 30).[3] You can also disable the second-level caching on the global level in the mapping file by setting the `cache.use_second_level_cache` attribute to `false`:

```
<property name="hibernate.jdbc.batch_size">25</property>
<property name="hibernate.cache.use_second_level_cache">false</property>
```

This chapter also looks into using native SQL to query databases. Native SQL is useful when you want to use database-specific features or tuning. Native SQL queries can be named just like Hibernate and JPA queries can be, and are used in the same fashion.

11-1. Performing Batch Inserts

Problem

How can you perform batch inserts within a single transaction?

Solution

To do a batch insert in a single transaction,[4] use the `flush()` and `clear()` methods of the Session API. These methods are called regularly to control the size of the first-level cache. To have Hibernate not interact with the second-level cache, you need to call `session.setCacheMode.(CacheMode.IGNORE)`.

How It Works

The code for a batch insert is as follows. An additional `if` condition is added to call the `flush()` and `clear()` methods when the iteration reaches the size of the JDBC batch. We want to flush fairly regularly because Hibernate will cache all the new BookCh2 references in the `Session` as they're created, which will give us a rather inconvenient `OutOfMemoryException`.

```
Session session = SessionManager.openSession();
Transaction tx = session.beginTransaction();
session.setCacheMode(CacheMode.IGNORE);
for(int i=0;i<100;i++) {
  BookCh2 book = new BookCh2();
  book.setName("Book Name "+(i+1));
  book.setPrice(79);
  book.setPublishDate(new Date());
  session.save(book);
  if(i % 25 == 0) {
    System.out.println("Flushing in batches");
    session.flush();
```

---

[3]Hey, there's that Hat of Generally Useful Numbers again!

[4]You can `commit` a transaction and start a new one to do a "batch operation" as well, but that would invalidate our (somewhat artificial) requirement to maintain a single transaction. In general, we've been closing the `Session` when committing transactions, mostly to explicitly clear the `Session`'s first-level cache.

```
    session.clear();
    System.out.println("get isbn "+book.getIsbn());
  }
}
tx.commit();
session.close();
```

By setting CacheMode to Ignore, you tell Hibernate not to interact with the second-level cache. You need to do this only if the second-level cache is enabled at the global or entity level.

11-2. Performing Batch Updates and Deletes
Problem

How do you perform batch updates and deletes?

Solution

You can accomplish batch updates in two ways. One way is to use the flush() and clear() methods to free the first-level cache and save in batches. The second way is to use the update statement with a where clause.

How It Works

Suppose that you're planning a promotion for the Hibernate books in our bookshop application. All books with the word *Hibernate* in the name will have a $10 discount.[5] You can do this by querying the matched books first and then updating them one by one:

```
@Test
public void testNoBatchUpdate() {
  Session session = SessionManager.openSession();
  Transaction tx = session.beginTransaction();
  Query query = session.getNamedQuery("Book2.findLikeTitle");
  query.setParameter("title", "%Hibernate%");
  List<Book2> books = query.list();
  for (Book2 book : books) {
    book.setPrice(book.getPrice() - 10.0);
  }
  tx.commit();
  session.close();

  session = SessionManager.openSession();
  tx = session.beginTransaction();
  query = session.getNamedQuery("Book2.findLikeTitle");
  query.setParameter("title", "%Hibernate%");
  books = query.list();
```

---

[5]What we'd *prefer* is that books with *Hibernate* in their titles get a $10 premium. But "discount" it is!

```
  for (Book2 book : books) {
    assertEquals(book.getPrice(), 29.99, 0.001);
  }
  tx.commit();
  session.close();
}
```

The disadvantage of this technique is that you load the complete result set returned by query.list() into memory and then save the records one at a time. Instead, you can use the session.flush() and session.clear() methods to update in batches. You can also use scroll to get a JDBC ResultSet, which is a table of data representing a database result set that is usually generated by executing a statement that queries the database. A default ResultSet maintains a cursor that is navigated from the first row to the last row. Setting CacheMode.IGNORE makes Hibernate not interact with the second-level cache for that particular session:

```
@Test
public void testBatchUpdate() {
  Session session = SessionManager.openSession();
  Transaction tx = session.beginTransaction();
  Query query = session.getNamedQuery("Book2.findLikeTitle")
      .setCacheMode(CacheMode.IGNORE);

  query.setParameter("title", "%Hibernate%");
  ScrollableResults results=query.scroll(ScrollMode.FORWARD_ONLY);
  int counter=0;
  while(results.next()) {
    Book2 book= (Book2) results.get(0);
    book.setPrice(book.getPrice() - 10.0);
    counter++;
    if(counter==25) {
      session.flush();
      session.clear();
      counter=0;
    }
  }
  tx.commit();
  session.close();

  session = SessionManager.openSession();
  tx = session.beginTransaction();
  query = session.getNamedQuery("Book2.findLikeTitle");
  query.setParameter("title", "%Hibernate%");
  List<Book2> books = query.list();
  for (Book2 book : books) {
    assertEquals(book.getPrice(), 29.99, 0.001, book.toString());
  }
  tx.commit();
  session.close();
}
```

You can also accomplish batch updates by using the UPDATE query. The execution of the query is at the SQL level and doesn't involve changing the object state in memory. HQL supports parameter binding. The syntax for an UPDATE or DELETE query is as follows:

```
( UPDATE | DELETE ) FROM? EntityName (WHERE where_conditions)?.
```

The following rules apply to this query:

- The FROM clause is optional.

- The WHERE clause is optional.

- No joins, either implicit or explicit, can be specified in a bulk HQL query.

- Only a single entity can be named in the FROM clause.

So here is an example of UPDATE in action:

```
@Test
public void testSQLUpdate() {
  Session session = SessionManager.openSession();
  Transaction tx = session.beginTransaction();
  Query query = session.createQuery(
      "update Book2 b set b.price=b.price-:discount where b.title like :title");
  query.setParameter("discount", 10.0);
  query.setParameter("title", "%Hibernate%");
  int count=query.executeUpdate();
  assertEquals(count, 1000);
  tx.commit();
  session.close();

  session = SessionManager.openSession();
  tx = session.beginTransaction();
  query = session.getNamedQuery("Book2.findLikeTitle");
  query.setParameter("title", "%Hibernate%");
  List<Book2> books = query.list();
  for (Book2 book : books) {
    assertEquals(book.getPrice(), 29.99, 0.001, book.toString());
  }
  tx.commit();
  session.close();
}
```

11-3. Using Native SQL
Problem

Hibernate provides HQL, and it supports JPAQL criteria and Query by Example mechanisms to execute most queries. But what if you need to use database-specific features such as query hints or keywords? In such scenarios, you need to use Hibernate's support for native SQL. How do you query using native SQL?

Solution

The Session API provides the createSQLQuery() method, which returns the SQLQuery interface. This interface provides methods you can use to query databases using native SQL.

How It Works

Let's say you need to compile some statistics for your top-selling books. This process is very complicated and requires some native features provided by the database. HQL isn't much help in this case, but Hibernate supports using native SQL to query for objects. For demonstration purposes, this recipe doesn't implement complicated statistics—you just create a view to emulate the result of the query. You create the view TOP_SELLING_BOOK by joining the BOOK and PUBLISHER tables:

```
CREATE VIEW TOP_SELLING_BOOK (
ID, ISBN, BOOK_NAME, PUBLISH_DATE, PRICE,
PUBLISHER_ID, PUBLISHER_CODE, PUBLISHER_NAME, PUBLISHER_ADDRESS
) AS
SELECT book.ID, book.ISBN, book.BOOK_NAME, book.PUBLISH_DATE, book.PRICE,
book.PUBLISHER_ID, pub.CODE, pub.PUBLISHER_NAME, pub.ADDRESS
FROM BOOK book LEFT OUTER JOIN PUBLISHER pub ON book.PUBLISHER_ID = pub.ID
```

First, you retrieve the book objects from that view only and ignore the associated publishers. You use native SQL to select all the columns related to a book. The addEntity() method specifies the type of resulting persistent objects:

```
String sql = "SELECT ID, ISBN, BOOK_NAME, PUBLISH_DATE, PRICE, PUBLISHER_ID "+
  "FROM TOP_SELLING_BOOK WHERE BOOK_NAME LIKE ?";
Query query = session.createSQLQuery(sql)
  .addEntity(Book.class)
  .setString(0, "%Hibernate%");
List books = query.list();
```

Because all the columns in the result have the same names as in the mapping definition of Book, you can specify {book.*} in the SELECT clause. Hibernate replaces {book.*} with all the column names in your mapping definition:

```
String sql = "SELECT {book.*}
FROM TOP_SELLING_BOOK book
WHERE BOOK_NAME LIKE ?";
Query query = session.createSQLQuery(sql)
.addEntity("book", Book.class)
.setString(0, "%Hibernate%");
List books = query.list();
```

Next, let's consider the associated publishers. Because not all the column names are identical to those in the mapping definition of Publisher, you need to map them manually in the SQL SELECT clause. The addjoin() method specifies the joined associations:

```
String sql = "SELECT {book.*}, book.PUBLISHER_ID as {publisher.id},"+
  "book.PUBLISHER_CODE as {publisher.code}, book.PUBLISHER_NAME as {publisher.name},"+
  "book.PUBLISHER_ADDRESS as {publisher.address} "+
  "FROM TOP_SELLING_BOOK book WHERE BOOK_NAME LIKE ?";
```

```
Query query = session.createSQLQuery(sql)
    .addEntity("book", Book.class)
    .addJoin("publisher", "book.publisher")
    .setString(0, "%Hibernate%");
List books = query.list();
```

If you want to query for simple values only, you can use the addScalar() method:

```
String sql = "SELECT max(book.PRICE) as maxPrice "+
    "FROM TOP_SELLING_BOOK book "+
    "WHERE BOOK_NAME LIKE ?";
Query query = session.createSQLQuery(sql)
    .addScalar("maxPrice", Hibernate.INTEGER)
    .setString(0, "%Hibernate%");
Integer maxPrice = (Integer) query.uniqueResult();
```

11-4. Using Named SQL Queries

Problem

How do you use named queries?

Solution

You can define named SQL queries in the mapping document (or via annotations) and call them exactly like named HQL queries.

How It Works

Native SQL statements can also be put in a mapping definition and referred to by name in the Java code. You can use <return> and <return-join> to describe the resulting objects. The return-join element is used to join associations. Note that Hibernate doesn't support return-join on stored procedures. In the following query, the publisher of a book is retrieved with the book:

```
<hibernate-mapping package="com.hibernaterecipes.bookstore">
  <sql-query name="TopSellingBook.by.name">
    <return alias="book" class="Book" />
    <return-join alias="publisher" property="book.publisher"/>
    <![CDATA[
SELECT {book.*},
book.PUBLISHER_ID as {publisher.id},
book.PUBLISHER_CODE as {publisher.code},
book.PUBLISHER_NAME as {publisher.name},
book.PUBLISHER_ADDRESS as {publisher.address}
FROM TOP_SELLING_BOOK book
WHERE BOOK_NAME LIKE ?
]]>
  </sql-query>
</hibernate-mapping>
```

```
Query query = session.getNamedQuery("TopSellingBook.by.name")
.setString(0, "%Hibernate%");
List books = query.list();
```

You can also wrap a query for simple values as a named query. In this case, you use <return-scalar> instead:

```
<hibernate-mapping package="com.hibernaterecipes.bookstore">
...
  <sql-query name="TopSellingBook.maxPrice.by.name">
    <return-scalar column="maxPrice" type="int" />
    <![CDATA[
SELECT max(book.PRICE) as maxPrice
FROM TOP_SELLING_BOOK book
WHERE BOOK_NAME LIKE ?
]]>
  </sql-query>
</hibernate-mapping>
```

```
Query query = session.getNamedQuery("TopSellingBook.maxPrice.by.name")
  .setString(0, "%Hibernate%");
Integer maxPrice = (Integer) query.uniqueResult();
```

For a named SQL query, you can group <return> and <return-join> in a *result set mapping* and reference them in <sql-query>. The advantage of a result set mapping is that it can be reused for multiple queries:

```
<hibernate-mapping package=" com.hibernaterecipes.bookstore ">
  <resultset name="bookPublisher">
    <return alias="book" class="Book" />
    <return-join alias="publisher" property="book.publisher" />
  </resultset>
  <sql-query name="TopSellingBook.by.name" resultset-ref="bookPublisher">
    <![CDATA[
SELECT {book.*},
book.PUBLISHER_ID as {publisher.id},
book.PUBLISHER_CODE as {publisher.code},
book.PUBLISHER_NAME as {publisher.name},
book.PUBLISHER_ADDRESS as {publisher.address}
FROM TOP_SELLING_BOOK book
WHERE BOOK_NAME LIKE ?
]]>
  </sql-query>
</hibernate-mapping>
```

In the result set mapping, you can further map each database column to an object property. Doing so can simplify your SQL statements by removing the mapping from the SELECT clause:

```
<hibernate-mapping package=" com.hibernaterecipes.bookstore ">
  <resultset name="bookPublisher">
    <return alias="book" class="Book" />
    <return-join alias="publisher" property="book.publisher">
      <return-property name="id" column="PUBLISHER_ID" />
```

```
        <return-property name="code" column="PUBLISHER_CODE" />
        <return-property name="name" column="PUBLISHER_NAME" />
        <return-property name="address" column="PUBLISHER_ADDRESS" />
      </return-join>
    </resultset>
    <sql-query name="TopSellingBook.by.name" resultset-ref="bookPublisher">
      <![CDATA[
SELECT {book.*},
book.PUBLISHER_ID as {publisher.id},
book.PUBLISHER_CODE as {publisher.code},
book.PUBLISHER_NAME as {publisher.name},
book.PUBLISHER_ADDRESS as {publisher.address}
FROM TOP_SELLING_BOOK book
WHERE BOOK_NAME LIKE ?
]]>
    </sql-query>
</hibernate-mapping>
```

After you move the column mappings to the result set mapping, you can simplify the SELECT clause to a "select all":

```
<hibernate-mapping package=" com.hibernaterecipes.bookstore ">
...
    <sql-query name="TopSellingBook.by.name" resultset-ref="bookPublisher">
      <![CDATA[
SELECT *
FROM TOP_SELLING_BOOK book
WHERE BOOK_NAME LIKE ?
]]>
    </sql-query>
</hibernate-mapping>
```

Summary

This chapter showed you when to use batch processing. You learned how to perform batch inserts, updates, and deletes. You also learned how to manage the first-level and second-level cache during batch processing. And you can now use native SQL and named queries with other Hibernate HQL and criteria queries.

CHAPTER 12

■ ■ ■

Caching in Hibernate

Caching is one of the important features implemented by an application for better performance. From an ORM perspective, data retrieved from a database is cached in memory or to disk, so there is no need to make a call to the database for every request. A *cache* is a local copy of the information from the database that can be used to avoid a database call whenever the following situations occur:

- The application performs a lookup by identifier

- The persistence layer resolves an association or collection lazily

In Figure 12-1, when an application queries for data the first time, Hibernate fetches it from the database; from then on, it fetches data from the cache if the same data is requested.

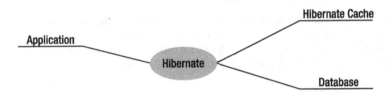

Figure 12-1. How Hibernate caches

Hibernate provides a way to configure caching at the class level, at the collection level, and also at the query result-set level. Cached data is available at three different scopes in an application:

- *Transaction scope*: As you saw in earlier chapters, a transaction is defined as a unit of work. How does caching affect data in a transaction? If data is fetched in one session, and the same query is executed again in that same session before that unit of work is completed, is that data stored in memory/disk? Does this avoid a call to the database? Yes. This data is stored in memory/disk by default, so the call to the database for the second query is avoided. Because a unit of work is for one request, this data isn't shared or accessed concurrently.

- *Process scope*: Data is cached across sessions or across units of work. If a query is executed in one session, and the same query is executed in a second session after closing the first, this data is cached so that the second call to the database is avoided. Because two requests can access the same data in these two sessions, this data is accessed concurrently. You should use this scope with caution.

- *Cluster scope*: Data is shared between multiple processes on the same machine or on different machines in a cluster.

A process-scoped cache makes data retrieved from the database in one unit of work visible to another unit of work, which may have some unwanted consequences that you need to avoid. If an application has non-exclusive access to the database, you shouldn't use process scope because the application has concurrent access to the database, and one request can share data with another request. In this case, process scope should be used when data doesn't change often and if it can be refreshed safely when the local cache expires.

Any application that is designed to be scalable should support caching at the cluster level. Process scope doesn't maintain consistency of data between machines, so you should use cluster-level caching.

Hibernate has a two-level cache architecture:

- The first-level cache is the *persistence context cache*, which is at the unit-of-work level. It corresponds to one session in Hibernate for a single request and is enabled by default for the Hibernate session.

- The second-level cache, which is either at the *process scope* or the *cluster scope*, is the cache of the state of the persistence entities. A cache-concurrency strategy defines the transaction isolation details for a particular item of data, and the cache provider represents the physical cache implementation.

Hibernate also implements caching for query result sets, which requires two additional physical cache regions that hold the cached query result sets and the timestamp when a table was last updated.

This chapter first shows you how to use and configure the second-level cache and then looks at the query-level cache in Hibernate.

Using the Second-Level Cache in Hibernate

At the second-level cache, all persistence contexts that started from the same `SessionFactory` share the same cached data. Different kinds of data require different cache policies: for example, how long the cache should be maintained before evicting data, at what scope the data should be cached, whether the data should be cached in memory, and so on. The cache policy involves setting the following:

- Whether the second-level cache is enabled

- The Hibernate concurrency strategy

- Cache expiration policies (such as timeout, least recently used, and memory sensitive)

- The physical format of the cache (memory, indexed files, or cluster-replicated)

To reiterate, the second-level cache is more useful when there is less data that is often updated. In other words, it is useful when there is more read-only data.

You set up the second-level cache in two steps. First, you have to decide on the concurrency strategy; then you configure the cache expiration and physical cache attributes using the cache provider.

Concurrency Strategies

There are four built-in concurrency strategies:

- *Transactional*: This strategy should be used when there is more data to read. It prevents stale data in concurrency strategies and is equivalent to isolation level: repeatable read.

- *Read-write*: This strategy maintains a read-committed isolation level.

- *Non-strict read-write*: This strategy doesn't guarantee that you won't read stale data. It also doesn't guarantee consistency between cache and database.

- *Read-only*: This strategy is appropriate for data that never changes.

Cache Providers

Hibernate uses the concept of a *cache provider* to offer second-level cache capabilities. Three are provided as open-source alternatives, but there are many others, commercial and otherwise.[1] One is built on ConcurrentHashMap, meant for testing only; another is EHCache;[2] and yet another is Infinispan.[3] Both EHCache and Infinispan provide clustered cache.

You can develop an adapter for your application by implementing org.hibernate.cache. CacheProvider.

Not every cache provider is compatible with every concurrency strategy. Check the documentation for details.

You can configure the cache for a specific class or a collection. The <cache> element is used to configure cache in the hibernate.cfg.xml file. The <cache> element is defined as follows:

```
<cache  usage="transactional|read-write|nonstrict-read-write|read-only"
        region="RegionName" include="all|lazy"/>
```

Table 12-1 defines the <cache> element attributes.

Table 12-1. *<cache> Element Attributes*

Attribute	Description
usage	The caching strategy.
region	The region name. Region names are references to actual cached data.
include	Specifies that properties of the entity mapped with lazy=true can't be cached when the attribute level lazy fetching is enabled.

Cache Regions

Cache regions are handles by which you can reference classes and collections in the cache provider configuration and set the expiration policies applicable to that region. Regions are buckets of data of two types: one type contains disassembled data of entity instances, and the other contains only identifiers of entities that are linked through a collection.

---

[1]Some examples of cache providers available for Hibernate include Coherence (http://docs.oracle.com/cd/ E15357_01/coh.360/e15830/usehibernateascoh.htm), Hazelcast (http://hazelcast.com/use-cases/hibernate-2nd-level/), GigaSpaces (http://wiki.gigaspaces.com/wiki/display/XAP9/GigaSpaces+for+Hibernate+ORM+ Users), GridGain (http://atlassian.gridgain.com/wiki/display/GG60/Hibernate+L2+Cache), plus a host of others that don't immediately come to mind.
[2]See http://ehcache.org/generated/2.9.0/html/ehc-all/#page/Ehcache_Documentation_Set/to-hib_using _ehcache_with_hibernate.html#.
[3]See http://infinispan.org/docs/5.3.x/user_guide/user_guide.html#_using_infinispan_as_jpa_hibernate_ second_level_cache_provider.

The name of the region is the class name in the case of a class cache or the class name together with the property name in the case of a collection cache.

Caching Query Results

A query's result set can be configured to be cached. By default, caching is disabled; and every HQL, JPA QL, and Criteria query hits the database. You enable the query cache as follows:

```
hibernate.cache.use_query_cache = true
```

In addition to setting this configuration property, you should use the org.hibernate.Query interface:

```
Query bookQuery = session.createQuery("from Book book where book.name < ?");
bookQuery.setString("name","HibernateRecipes");
bookQuery.setCacheable(true);
```

The setCacheable() method enables the result to be cached.

12-1. Using the First-Level Cache

Problem

What is the first-level cache, and how is it used in Hibernate?

Solution

The first-level cache is at the transaction level or the unit of work. It is enabled by default in Hibernate. Caching at the first level is associated with a session. If the same query is executed multiple times in the same session, the data associated with the query is cached.

How It Works

The general concept of caching persistent objects is that when an object is first read from external storage, a copy of it is stored in the cache. Subsequent readings of the same object can be retrieved from the cache directly. Because caches are typically stored in memory or on local disk, it is faster to read an object from cache than from external storage.[4] If you use it properly, caching can greatly improve the performance of your application.

---

[4]There are three kinds of storage. *Primary* storage is in-memory, ready for direct access. *Secondary* storage is on disk or an equivalent, something ready for random access and generally available for both read and write operations. *Tertiary* storage is passive and primarily read-only—think tape or DVD backups. (As usual, this explanation skips a lot of details, and there are different types of storage even in each level: CPU cache against RAM, for example, for primary storage). Caches move objects from secondary storage to primary storage without making the program keep track of the objects. If you want all the gory details about memory, see http://en.wikipedia.org/wiki/Computer_data_storage.

As a high-performance ORM framework, Hibernate supports the caching of persistent objects at different levels. Suppose you retrieve an object more than once within a session. Does Hibernate query the database as many times as the query is invoked?

```
Session session = factory.openSession();
try {
        Book book1 = (Book) session.get(Book.class, id);
        Book book2 = (Book) session.get(Book.class, id);
} finally {
        session.close();
}
```

If you inspect the SQL statements executed by Hibernate, you find that only one database query is made. That means Hibernate is caching your objects in the same session. This kind of caching is called *first-level caching*, and its caching scope is a session.

But how about getting an object with same identifier more than once in two different sessions?

```
Session session1 = factory.openSession();
try {
        Book book1 = (Book) session1.get(Book.class, id);
} finally {
        session1.close();
}
Session session2 = factory.openSession();
try {
        Book book2 = (Book) session2.get(Book.class, id);
} finally {
        session2.close();
}
```

Two database queries are made, which means that Hibernate isn't caching the persistent objects across different sessions by default. You need to turn on this *second-level caching*, whose caching scope is a *session factory*.

12-2. Configuring the Second-Level Cache

Problem

What is the second-level cache, and how is it configured and used in Hibernate?

Solution

Second-level cache is configured at the process level or the cluster level. In Hibernate, you can configure it for a particular class or for a collection to improve performance. You can use the second-level cache with large and complex object graphs that may be loaded often. It is associated with one SessionFactory and can be reused in more than one Session created from the same SessionFactory.

How It Works

To turn on the second-level cache, the first step is to choose a cache provider in the Hibernate configuration file hibernate.cfg.xml. Hibernate supports several cache implementations, including EHCache, OSCache, HazelCast, and Infinispan (as discussed earlier). In a nondistributed environment, you can choose EHCache, which is Hibernate's default cache provider.

Let's look at an example to show the second-level cache in operation. First, you have to add EHCache as a dependency so that the compilation and runtime units can see it. Add the following to the pom.xml file:

```
<dependencies>
    <!-- other dependencies -->
    <dependency>
        <groupId>net.sf.ehcache</groupId>
        <artifactId>ehcache-core</artifactId>
        <version>2.6.9</version>
    </dependency>
    <dependency>
        <groupId>org.hibernate</groupId>
        <artifactId>hibernate-ehcache</artifactId>
        <version>[4.3.6.Final,)</version>
    </dependency>
</dependencies>
```

You can configure EHCache through the configuration file ehcache.xml, which is located in the root folder of the classpath. Objects are stored in *regions* that store different kinds of objects. You can specify different settings for different cache regions, such as object expiration (when things disappear from the cache), but these settings are generally cache-specific.[5] These examples rely on the default configuration, which is workable in the general sense.

Now you need to enable caching for a particular persistent class. Let's look at what goes on behind the scenes when caching is enabled in Hibernate.

When you enable a class with the second-level cache, Hibernate doesn't store the actual instances in cache; it caches the individual properties of that object. In this example, the instance of Book isn't cached; the properties in the book object such as title are cached. The cached objects are stored in a region that has the same name as the persistent class, such as com.apress.hibernaterecipes.chapter12.recipe2.Book2.

You can choose several cache usages for a persistent class. If the persistent objects are read-only and never modified, the most efficient usage is read-only, but there are implications for using a read-only cache: namely, that inadvertent modifications will throw an exception. This is proper behavior (you'd want to know!) but it is not part of a normal update path to look for an exception.[6]

Let's look at the Hibernate configuration for two simple tests that demonstrate (and validate) the second-level cache:

```
<?xml version="1.0" encoding="UTF-8"?>
<!DOCTYPE hibernate-configuration PUBLIC
        "-//Hibernate/Hibernate Configuration DTD 3.0//EN"
        "http://www.hibernate.org/dtd/hibernate-configuration-3.0.dtd">
<hibernate-configuration>
```

---

[5]That is to say, the actual configuration is cache-specific. Most caches provide similar capabilities, just in different ways.
[6]This rather mild warning is brought to you by the letter "organic ink."

```
    <session-factory>
        <property name="connection.driver_class">org.h2.Driver</property>
        <property name="connection.url">jdbc:h2:file:./chapter12</property>
        <property name="hibernate.dialect">org.hibernate.dialect.HSQLDialect</property>
        <property name="hibernate.hbm2ddl.auto">create</property>
        <property name="hibernate.show_sql">true</property>
        <property name="hibernate.discriminator.ignore_explicit_for_joined">true</property>
        <property name="hibernate.generate_statistics">true</property>
        <property name="connection.username"></property>
        <property name="connection.password"></property>
        <property name="hibernate.cache.region.factory_class">
            org.hibernate.cache.ehcache.EhCacheRegionFactory
        </property>
        <mapping class="com.apress.hibernaterecipes.chapter12.recipe2.Book2"/>
    </session-factory>
</hibernate-configuration>
```

Now let's take a look at the Book2 class, which serves as the data model:

```
@Entity
@Data
@Cacheable
@org.hibernate.annotations.Cache(usage = CacheConcurrencyStrategy.READ_ONLY)
public class Book2 {
  @Id
  @GeneratedValue(strategy = GenerationType.AUTO)
  int id;
  String title;
}
```

Note that we mark the object as @Cacheable and that we use a Hibernate-specific annotation to note that it is a read-only cache. Let's take a look at the tests, so we can validate what happens when the entity is used. There are two tests: one shows the second-level cache in action, and the other validates that the objects in the cache are read-only:

```
@BeforeMethod
public void clearData() {
  SessionManager.deleteAll("Book2");
}

@Test
public void test2LCache() {
  SessionFactory sessionFactory = SessionManager.getSessionFactory();
  Statistics stats = sessionFactory.getStatistics();

  Session session = sessionFactory.openSession();
  Transaction tx = session.beginTransaction();

  Book2 book2 = new Book2();
  book2.setTitle("My Title");

  session.persist(book2);
```

```
    tx.commit();
    session.close();

    sessionFactory.getCache().evictAllRegions();

    session = sessionFactory.openSession();
    tx = session.beginTransaction();

    Book2 b = (Book2) session.byId(Book2.class).load(book2.getId());
    Book2 b2 = (Book2) session.byId(Book2.class).load(book2.getId());

    assertEquals(book2, b);
    assertEquals(book2, b2);

    tx.commit();
    session.close();

    // this is the initial select
    assertEquals(stats.getSecondLevelCacheMissCount(), 1);
    // we put one element in the cache from the miss
    assertEquals(stats.getSecondLevelCachePutCount(), 1);
    // we still didn't hit the cache, because of 1L cache
    assertEquals(stats.getSecondLevelCacheHitCount(), 0);

    session = sessionFactory.openSession();
    tx = session.beginTransaction();

    b = (Book2) session.byId(Book2.class).load(book2.getId());
    assertEquals(book2, b);
    tx.commit();
    session.close();

    // same miss count (we should hit now)
    assertEquals(stats.getSecondLevelCacheMissCount(), 1);
    // same put count (we didn't put anything new)
    assertEquals(stats.getSecondLevelCachePutCount(), 1);
    // now we hit the 2L cache for load
    assertEquals(stats.getSecondLevelCacheHitCount(), 1);
}

@Test(expectedExceptions = {UnsupportedOperationException.class})
public void updateReadOnly() {
  Session session = SessionManager.openSession();
  Transaction tx = session.beginTransaction();
  Book2 book2 = new Book2();
  book2.setTitle("My Title");

  session.persist(book2);

  tx.commit();
  session.close();
```

```
session = SessionManager.openSession();
try {
  tx = session.beginTransaction();

  Book2 b = (Book2) session.byId(Book2.class).load(book2.getId());
  b.setTitle("The Revised Title");
  session.flush();
} catch (UnsupportedOperationException e) {
  tx.rollback();
  session.close();
  throw e;
}
tx.commit();
session.close();
fail("Should have gotten an exception");
}
```

This test first validates the first-level cache, the cache in a given Session. When we first load a Book2, we should have a cache miss as well as a cache put, with only one SQL SELECT. Hibernate runs the SELECT once to retrieve the object from the database and then stores the object's data in the second-level cache, and the second query uses the first-level cache. Because the object is available in the first-level cache, the second-level cache doesn't get used for the second retrieval.

The second part of the first test uses a new Session, so the object is no longer available in the first-level cache. When we try to load it, Hibernate finds it in the second-level cache and uses that information.

The second test attempts to update a Book2 instance, and the test therefore expects to handle an exception.[7]

In some cases, such as when the database is updated by other applications, you may want to invalidate the cached objects manually. You can do it through the methods provided by the session factory. You can invalidate either one instance or all instances of a persistent class:

```
factory.evict(Book.class);
factory.evict(Book2.class, id);
factory.evictEntity("com.apress.hibernaterecipes.chapter12.recipe2.Book2");
factory.evictEntity("com.apress.hibernaterecipes.chapter12.recipe2.Book2", id);
```

After the cached object is evicted from cache, and you want to fetch data from the database, the query is executed, and the updated data is retrieved. This avoids having stale data in cache. Note that the eviction from the second-level cache is nontransactional, meaning that the cache region isn't locked during the eviction process.

---

[7]Astute readers will notice that the resource management in this test is *terrible*. When an exception occurs, Session.close() is skipped, and the Transaction is abandoned; no cleanup is attempted. This is done for brevity, as it is through the rest of this book; it's a lot of code to wade through when what you're *interested* in is whether the exception is thrown. Let's just leave with this warning: *Don't leave resources dangling like this*. Clean up everything before exiting a method for *any* reason, including exceptional conditions; don't copy the testing code's methodology in production code.

CacheMode options are provided to control the interaction of Hibernate with the second-level cache:

```
Session session1 = factory.openSession();
Session.setCacheMode(CacheMode.IGNORE);
try {
  Book2 book2 = new Book();
  book2.setTitle("New Book");
  session1.save(book2);
  session1.flush();
} finally {
  session1.close();
}
```

CacheMode.IGNORE tells Hibernate not to interact with second-level cache for that session. Options available in CacheMode are as follows:

- CacheMode.NORMAL: The default behavior.

- CacheMode.IGNORE: Hibernate doesn't interact with the second-level cache. When entities cached in the second-level cache are updated, Hibernate invalidates them.

- CacheMode.GET: Hibernate only reads and doesn't add items to the second-level cache. When entities cached in the second-level cache are updated, Hibernate invalidates them.

- CacheMode.PUT: Hibernate only adds and doesn't add read from the second-level cache. When entities cached in the second-level cache are updated, Hibernate invalidates them.

- CacheMode.REFRESH: Hibernate only adds and doesn't read from the second-level cache. In this mode, the setting of hibernate.cache.use_minimal_puts is bypassed as the refresh is forced.

12-3. Caching Associations

Problem

Can associated objects be cached? How do you configure them?

Solution

Associated objects have a parent-child relationship in the database. How does caching work in this case? If the parent object is cached, is the child object also cached? By default, associated objects aren't cached. If you need to cache these objects, you can configure them explicitly. The primary reason to cache associations is to avoid additional calls to the database.

How It Works

Associations are cached just as entities are: when they're marked as being cacheable, they're cached.[8] We can test with a simple association, of course. First, let's look at the entity model, which is made of a Book3 class and a Publisher3 class:

```
@Entity
@Data
@Cacheable
@org.hibernate.annotations.Cache(usage = CacheConcurrencyStrategy.READ_ONLY)
public class Book3 {
  @Id
  @GeneratedValue(strategy = GenerationType.AUTO)
  int id;
  String title;
  @ManyToOne
  Publisher3 publisher;
}

@Entity
@Data
@Cacheable
@org.hibernate.annotations.Cache(usage = CacheConcurrencyStrategy.READ_ONLY)
public class Publisher3 {
  @Id
  @GeneratedValue(strategy = GenerationType.AUTO)
  int id;
  String name;
}
```

Now let's take a look at the test, which follows the same methodology as the previous recipe in this chapter: it creates data and then loads it to see whether a cache was used, and then which cache was used:

```
@BeforeMethod
public void clearData() {
  SessionManager.deleteAll("Book3");
  SessionManager.deleteAll("Publisher3");
}

@Test
public void testAssociationCache() {
  SessionFactory sessionFactory = SessionManager.getSessionFactory();
  Statistics stats = sessionFactory.getStatistics();

  Session session = sessionFactory.openSession();
  Transaction tx = session.beginTransaction();
  Publisher3 publisher3 = new Publisher3();
  publisher3.setName("My Publisher");
  session.persist(publisher3);
```

---

[8]This makes a certain kind of sense: "When something is painted purple, it becomes purple." This is a *tautology*, a thing described in terms of itself. Back to Hibernate!

```
    Book3 book3 = new Book3();
    book3.setTitle("My Title");
    book3.setPublisher(publisher3);

    session.persist(book3);

    tx.commit();
    session.close();

    sessionFactory.getCache().evictAllRegions();

    session = sessionFactory.openSession();
    tx = session.beginTransaction();

    Book3 b = (Book3) session.byId(Book3.class).load(book3.getId());
    Book3 b2 = (Book3) session.byId(Book3.class).load(book3.getId());
    Publisher3 p = b.getPublisher();

    assertEquals(b, b2);
    assertEquals(b, book3);
    assertEquals(p, publisher3);

    tx.commit();
    session.close();

    assertEquals(stats.getSecondLevelCacheHitCount(), 0);
    assertEquals(stats.getSecondLevelCacheMissCount(), 1);
    assertEquals(stats.getSecondLevelCachePutCount(), 2);

    session = sessionFactory.openSession();
    tx = session.beginTransaction();

    b = (Book3) session.byId(Book3.class).load(book3.getId());
    b2 = (Book3) session.byId(Book3.class).load(book3.getId());
    p = b.getPublisher();

    assertEquals(b, b2);
    assertEquals(b, book3);
    assertEquals(p, publisher3);

    tx.commit();
    session.close();

    // our values accumulate, because it's the same session factory
    assertEquals(stats.getSecondLevelCacheHitCount(), 2);
    assertEquals(stats.getSecondLevelCacheMissCount(), 1);
    assertEquals(stats.getSecondLevelCachePutCount(), 2);
}
```

12-4. Caching Collections

Problem

How do you cache collections?

Solution

Collections also can be cached explicitly in Hibernate. If a persistent object contains associated objects in a collection, the collection can also be cached explicitly. If the collection contains value types, they are stored by their values. If the collection contains objects, the object's identifiers are cached.

How It Works

For the associated chapters of a book to be cached, you enable caching for the Chapter4 collection in the same way you enable caching for an entity. Here's a Book4 and Chapter4 model, in which the set of Chapter4 objects is cached, using a region whose name is based on the fully qualified class name (the package and class name):

```
@Entity
@Data
@Cacheable
@org.hibernate.annotations.Cache(usage = CacheConcurrencyStrategy.NONSTRICT_READ_WRITE)
public class Book4 {
    @Id
    @GeneratedValue(strategy = GenerationType.AUTO)
    int id;
    String title;
    @OneToMany
    @Cascade(CascadeType.ALL)
    @org.hibernate.annotations.Cache(usage = CacheConcurrencyStrategy.NONSTRICT_READ_WRITE)
    Set<Chapter4> chapters=new HashSet<>();
}

@Entity
@Data
@NoArgsConstructor
@org.hibernate.annotations.Cache(usage = CacheConcurrencyStrategy.NONSTRICT_READ_WRITE)
public class Chapter4 {
    @Id
    @GeneratedValue(strategy = GenerationType.AUTO)
    int id;
    String name;
    public Chapter4(String name) {
        setName(name);
    }
}
```

Now let's look at a test that demonstrates that the caching has been effective:

```java
public class Test4 {
  Book4 book4;

  @BeforeMethod
  public void clear() {
    SessionManager.deleteAll("Chapter4");
    SessionManager.deleteAll("Book4");

    Session session = SessionManager.openSession();
    Transaction tx = session.beginTransaction();
    book4 = new Book4();
    book4.setTitle("sample book");
    book4.getChapters().add(new Chapter4("chapter one"));
    book4.getChapters().add(new Chapter4("chapter two"));
    session.persist(book4);
    tx.commit();
    session.close();
  }

  @Test
  public void testCollectionCache() {
    SessionFactory sessionFactory = SessionManager.getSessionFactory();
    Statistics stats = sessionFactory.getStatistics();

    Session session = SessionManager.openSession();
    Transaction tx = session.beginTransaction();
    Book4 book = (Book4) session.byId(Book4.class).load(book4.getId());
    assertEquals(book.getTitle(), book4.getTitle());
    assertEquals(book.getChapters().size(), 2);
    tx.commit();
    session.close();
    assertEquals(stats.getSecondLevelCacheHitCount(), 0);
    assertEquals(stats.getSecondLevelCacheMissCount(), 2);
    // one book, two chapters, one collection
    assertEquals(stats.getSecondLevelCachePutCount(), 4);

    session = SessionManager.openSession();
    tx = session.beginTransaction();
    book = (Book4) session.byId(Book4.class).load(book4.getId());
    assertEquals(book.getTitle(), book4.getTitle());
    assertEquals(book.getChapters().size(), 2);
    tx.commit();
    session.close();

    // should hit the book, chapters, collection now
    assertEquals(stats.getSecondLevelCacheHitCount(), 4);
    assertEquals(stats.getSecondLevelCacheMissCount(), 2);
    // one book, two chapters, one collection
    assertEquals(stats.getSecondLevelCachePutCount(), 4);
  }
}
```

If the collection stores simple values, the values are cached. If the collection stores persistent objects, the identifiers of the objects are cached in the collection region, and the persistent objects are cached in their own region.

To invalidate a particular collection or all the collections in a region, you can use the following methods provided by the session factory:

```
factory.getCache().evictCollection("your.packagedeclaration.Book4.chapters");
factory.getCache().evictCollection("your.packagedeclaration.Book4.chapters", bookId);
```

12-5. Caching Queries

Problem

Can queries be cached? How is this achieved in Hibernate?

Solution

Query result sets can be cached, which is useful when you run a particular query often with the same parameters.

How It Works

In addition to caching objects loaded by a session, a query with HQL can be cached. Suppose that you're running the same query in two different sessions:

```
Session session1 = SessionManager.openSession();
try {
        Query query = session1.createQuery("from Book5 b where b.name like ?");
        query.setString(0, "%Hibernate%");
        List books = query.list();
} finally {
        session1.close();
}
Session session2 = SessionManager.openSession();
try {
        Query query = session2.createQuery("from Book5 b where b.name like ?");
        query.setString(0, "%Hibernate%");
        List books = query.list();
} finally {
        session2.close();
}
```

By default, the HQL queries aren't cached. You must first enable the query cache in the Hibernate configuration file:

```
<hibernate-configuration>
      <session-factory>
      ...
      <property name="hibernate.cache.use_query_cache">true</property>
      ...
      </session-factory>
</hibernate-configuration>
```

The setting cache.use_query_cache creates two cache regions: one holds the cached query result sets, and the other holds timestamps of the more recent updates to queryable tables.

By default, the queries aren't cached. In addition to using the previous setting, to enable caching, you need to call Query.setCacheable(true), which enables the query to look for existing cache results or add the results of the query to the cache.

You have to set the query to be cacheable before execution. The query result is cached in a region named org.hibernate.cache.QueryCache by default.

How can a query be cached by Hibernate? If the query returns simple values, the values are cached. If the query returns persistent objects, the identifiers of the objects are cached in the query region, and the persistent objects are cached in their own region. Let's take a look:

```
@Entity
@Data
@Cacheable
@org.hibernate.annotations.Cache(usage = CacheConcurrencyStrategy.READ_ONLY)
public class Book5 {
  @Id
  @GeneratedValue(strategy = GenerationType.AUTO)
  int id;
  String title;
}
```

The test that shows the cache in action uses a method to execute the queries to reduce code duplication:

```
public class Test5 {
  @BeforeMethod
  public void clear() {
    SessionManager.deleteAll("Book5");
    Session session = SessionManager.openSession();
    Transaction tx = session.beginTransaction();
    Book5 book5 = new Book5();
    book5.setTitle("My Book");
    session.persist(book5);
    tx.commit();
    session.close();
  }
```

```java
public List<Book5> runQuery(boolean cacheStatus) {
  Session session = SessionManager.openSession();
  Transaction tx = session.beginTransaction();
  Query query = session.createQuery("from Book5 b where b.title like :title");
  query.setString("title", "My%");
  query.setCacheable(cacheStatus);
  List<Book5> books = (List<Book5>)query.list();
  tx.commit();
  session.close();
  return books;
}

@Test
public void testNoQueryCache() {
  SessionFactory factory=SessionManager.getSessionFactory();
  Statistics stats = factory.getStatistics();
  assertEquals(runQuery(false).size(), 1);
  assertEquals(runQuery(false).size(), 1);
  assertEquals(stats.getQueryCacheHitCount(),0);
  assertEquals(stats.getSecondLevelCacheHitCount(), 0);
}

@Test
public void testQueryCache() {
  SessionFactory factory=SessionManager.getSessionFactory();
  Statistics stats = factory.getStatistics();
  assertEquals(runQuery(true).size(), 1);
  assertEquals(runQuery(true).size(), 1);
  assertEquals(stats.getQueryCacheHitCount(),1);
  assertEquals(stats.getSecondLevelCacheHitCount(), 1);
}
}
```

You can also specify the cache region for a query. Doing so lets you separate query caches in different regions and reduces the number of caches in one particular region:

```java
query.setCacheable(true);
query.setCacheRegion("custom.region.Here");
```

Summary

This chapter described what caching is and the different levels of caching in Hibernate. Caching can be enabled at the transaction level, in which data is cached for one unit of work; this is the default behavior in Hibernate. Multiple queries in a particular session share the cached data.

You learned that at the second level, caching is enabled for a process, and the cache is associated with a SessionFactory. Multiple sessions within a SessionFactory share the same data. Configuring the second-level cache is a two-step process: first, you decide on the concurrent strategy and then you choose the provider that implements the caching strategy.

You also learned that you can use four concurrent strategies: read-only, read-write, transactional, and not-strict read-write. There are many open source cache providers, including OSCache, EHCache, SwarmCache, and JBoss Cache. Each of these providers provides different concurrent strategies.

Query result sets also can be cached. You do so through configuration and by invoking setCacheable(true). Associated objects and collections can also be cached explicitly.

The next chapter takes a look at transactions and concurrency.

CHAPTER 13

▪ ▪ ▪

Transactions and Concurrency

Let's say that a buyer logs in to the bookshop application and purchases a book. The following actions should take place in the event of a purchase:

- Charge the buyer the cost of the book

- Reduce the stock of the book

If the charge on the credit card fails, the stock shouldn't be reduced. Also, when the book is out of stock, the buyer shouldn't be charged. So both actions should be successfully completed or else they should have no effect. These actions collectively are called *transactions* or *units of work*. In essence, transactions provide an all-or-nothing proposition.

The concept of transactions is inherited from database management systems. By definition, a transaction must be **a**tomic, **c**onsistent, **i**solated, and **d**urable (ACID):

- *Atomicity* means that if one step fails, the whole unit of work fails.

- *Consistency* means that the transaction works on a set of data that is consistent before and after the transaction. The data must be clean after the transaction. From a database perspective, the clean and consistent state is maintained by integrity constraints. From an application's perspective, the consistent state is maintained by the business rules.

- *Isolation* means that one transaction isn't visible to other transactions. Isolation makes sure that the execution of a transaction doesn't affect other transactions.

- *Durability* means that when data has been persisted, it isn't lost.

In an application, you need to identify when a transaction begins and when it ends. The starting and ending points of a transaction are called *transaction boundaries*, and the technique of identifying them in an application is called *transaction demarcation*.[1] You can set the transaction boundaries either programmatically or declaratively. This chapter shows you how.

Multiuser systems such as databases need to implement concurrency control to maintain data integrity. There are two main approaches to concurrency control:

- *Optimistic:* Involves some kind of versioning to achieve control

- *Pessimistic:* Uses a locking mechanism to obtain control

---

[1]Pay attention to this term—it shows up a lot.

Some of the methods that are used in concurrency control are as follows:

- *Two-phase locking*: This is a locking mechanism that uses two distinct phases to achieve concurrency. In the first phase of transaction execution, called the *expanding phase*, locks are acquired, and no locks are released. In the second phase, called the *shrinking phase*, locks are released, and no new locks are acquired, which guarantees serializability. The transactions are serialized in the order in which the locks are acquired. *Strict two-phase locking* is a subset of two-phase locking. All the write locks are released only at the end (after committing or aborting), and read locks are released regularly during phase 2. With both these locking mechanisms, a deadlock is possible but can be avoided if you maintain a canonical order for obtaining locks. So if two processes need locks on A and B, they both request first A and then B.

- *Serialization*: A *transaction schedule* is a sequential representation of two or more concurrent transactions. The transaction schedules have a property called *serializability*. Two transactions that are updating the same record are executed one after the other; they don't overlap in time.

- *Timestamp-based control*: This is a nonlocking mechanism for concurrency control. Every transaction is given a timestamp when it starts. Every object or record in the database also has a read timestamp and a write timestamp. These three timestamps are used to define the isolation rules that are used in this type of concurrency control.

- *Multiversion concurrency control*: When a transaction does a read on a database, a snapshot is created, and the data is read from that snapshot. This process isolates the data from other concurrent transactions. When the transaction modifies a record, the database creates a new record version instead of overwriting the old record. This mechanism gives good performance because lock contention between concurrent transactions is minimized. In fact, lock contention is eliminated between read locks and write locks, which means that read locks never block a write lock. Most current databases—such as Oracle, MySQL, SQL Server, and PostgreSQL—implement the multiversion concurrent control for concurrency.

This chapter shows how Hibernate implements the optimistic and pessimistic concurrency approaches.

13-1. Using Programmatic Transactions in a Stand-alone Java Application

Problem

If you're working on a stand-alone Java application, how do you achieve transaction demarcation?

Solution

In a multiuser application, you need more than one connection to support multiple concurrent users. It is also expensive to create new connections when you need to interact with the database. For this, you need to have a connection pool that creates and manages database connections. Every thread that needs to interact with the database requests a connection from the pool and executes its queries. After it is done, the connection is returned to the pool. Then, if another thread requests a connection, the connection pool may provide it with same connection.

An application server usually provides a connection pool. When you're working in a stand-alone Java application, you need to use a third-party solution that provides connection pools. Hibernate comes with an open source third-party connection pooling framework called C3P0. Apache also provides a connection-pooling framework called Commons DBCP. You have to configure Hibernate to use one of these frameworks. After the connection pool is configured, you can use the Hibernate Transaction API for transaction demarcation and use connections from the connection pool.

How It Works

We use c3p0 for connection pooling because it is well-known, robust, and well-supported.[2] We need to add c3p0 to our Maven build and then configure it in `hibernate.cfg.xml`. Let's look at the `pom.xml` file for this chapter.

You need to add the `c3p0-0.9.1.jar` file that comes with Hibernate to the build path. In the Eclipse IDE, select your Java project and right-click to edit the build path. (See the explanation in Chapter 1 if you have trouble adding the JAR to the build path.) In the `hibernate.cfg.xml` file, add the following configuration:

```
<property name="hibernate.c3p0.min_size">5</property>
<property name="hibernate.c3p0.max_size">10</property>
<property name="hibernate.c3p0.timeout">300</property>
<property name="hibernate.c3p0.max_statements">50</property>
<property name="hibernate.c3p0.acquire_increment">1</property>
<property name="hibernate.c3p0.idle_test_period">3000</property>
```

Here's an explanation for each of the parameters you set:

- `min_size` is the minimum number of connections that are ready at all times.

- `max_size` is the maximum number of connections in the pool. This is the only property that is required for c3p0 to be enabled.

- `timeout` is the maximum idle time for a connection, after which the connection is removed from the pool.

- `max_statements` is the maximum number of prepared statements that can be cached.

- `idle_test_period` is the time in seconds before which a connection is automatically validated.

- `acquire_increment` is the number of connections acquired when the pool is exhausted.

These are all the settings required in the configuration file. Hibernate uses c3p0 if any parameters specific to c3p0 are used (so any of those properties will cause Hibernate to use c3p0.) Hibernate also provides a property called `hibernate.transaction.factory_class` that you can set in the configuration file. It provides the factory to use to instantiate transactions, and it defaults to `JDBCTransactionFactory`.

---

[2]This is not to imply that the Apache Commons-DBCP is not well-known, robust, or well-supported; it's just that to Your Author, c3p0 is well-knownier, robuster, and well-supporteder. In other words, it is purely personal preference, and either library would work, although they're configured differently.

We need to start considering better transaction management. For most of the book, transactions have been very much simplified, so the pattern has been something like this:

```java
@Test
public void testConnection() {
  Session session= SessionManager.openSession();
  Transaction tx=session.beginTransaction();
  Book1 book1=new Book1();
  book1.setTitle("The Dog Barker");
  session.persist(book1);
  tx.commit();
  session.close();
}
```

We need to be more rigorous in real life; exceptions happen, and methods are rarely this simple. We start by using a better transaction model, one that looks more like this:

```java
@Test
public void testTransactionWithExceptionHandling() {
  Session session = SessionManager.openSession();
  Transaction tx = session.beginTransaction();
  try {
    Book1 book1 = new Book1();
    book1.setTitle("The Dog Barker");
    session.persist(book1);
    tx.commit();
  } catch (Exception e) {
    tx.rollback();
  } finally {
    session.close();
  }
}
```

Note that not every method will look like this; transaction demarcation[3] is a tricky issue, and general solutions may not always apply. You may see some variations on this model as we progress through the chapter.

The session is provided by the same SessionManager.openSession() call we've used all along; the only difference is that Hibernate uses the connection pool (as implemented by c3p0 in this case) to find a valid JDBC connection. When using a pool, a database connection isn't opened when the session is created, which keeps the session creation a non-expensive task. The database connection is retrieved from the connection pool when the call session.beginTransaction() is made, and all queries are executed using this connection. The entities to be persisted are cached in the persistent context of the session. The commit() on the Transaction flushes the persistent context and completes the save of the entities. Another Transaction can be opened after the current Transaction is committed. A new connection is then provided by the connection pool. All resources and connections are released when close() is called on the Session.

---

[3]We told you that you'd see the term "transaction demarcation" again!

The exceptions thrown by Hibernate are RuntimeExceptions and subtypes of RuntimeExceptions. These exceptions are fatal, so you have to roll back your transactions. Because rolling back a transaction can also throw an exception, you may want to call the rollback method within a try/catch block.[4]

With the Java Persistence Architecture, you have to define the same configurations as for Hibernate, and the EntityTransaction API is used to manage transactions:

```
EntityManagerFactory managerFactory = Persistence.createEntityManagerFactory("book");
manager = managerFactory.createEntityManager();
tx = manager.getTransaction();
tx.begin();
try {
  Book1 book1 = new Book1();
  book1.setTitle("The Dog Barker");
  session.persist(book1);
  tx.commit();
} catch (Exception e) {
  tx.rollback();
} finally {
  manager.close();
}
```

getTransaction() is called on the EntityManager class to get a transaction. The actual connection is requested from the pool with the transaction's begin() method. The commit() method on the transaction flushes the persistent context and completes the save of the entities. The EntityManager's close() method is called in the finally block to make sure that the session is closed, even in the case of an exception.

13-2. Using Programmatic Transactions with JTA

Problem

Suppose that you're using an application server that provides support to manage resources. Application servers such as WebLogic, WebSphere, and JBoss can provide connections from a connection pool and manage transactions. How do you achieve programmatic transaction demarcation using the Java Transaction API (JTA)?[5]

Solution

You have to configure a Java enterprise application with Hibernate as the persistent framework. You also need to configure Hibernate to use JTATransactionFactory to provide JTATransaction objects. You then need to use the UserTransaction interface to manage transactions programmatically.

---

[4]Then again, you may not feel the need to execute rollback() in a try/catch block. There's not much you can do if a rollback fails; it is probably one of those cases where you want to see a catastrophic failure so you can find out what went horribly, horribly wrong, as opposed to trying to recover. You see the same philosophy in motion when the openSession() call is not in a try/catch block; if I can't open a Session, there's no point in recovery. I want to fix that problem.

[5]The technical reviewer (correctly) pointed out that JTA is an API, not an implementation, and it doesn't actually provide transactions—only a way to manage them. If you use JTA in an environment outside of an application server, for example, you have to provide a JTA implementation as well.

How It Works

WebLogic (version 9.2) is used as the application server to demonstrate using JTA for programmatic transaction demarcation. The assumption is that you're well-versed in building and deploying your application.

To begin, configure the data source on the application server. To do so, start the WebLogic server, log in to the console, and configure the data source. You must also add the database driver to the server library. For Derby, you add derbyClient.jar to the server library. Make sure that you test connectivity from the console!

You need to provide the following information (with your values):

- *JNDI Name*: local_derby. The application uses this to obtain database connections.

- *Database Name*: BookShopDB

- *Host Name*: localhost. If you're pointing to a remote database, this value is something like the IP of that machine.

- *Port*: 1527

- *User*: book

- *Password*: book

After you successfully configure the data source on the application server, you have to configure Hibernate. The key properties you're required to provide are as follows:

- Hibernate.connection.datasource: The value of this property must be the same as the JNDI name of the data source you configured on the application server.

- Hibernate.transaction.factory_class: The default value for this is JDBCTransactionFactory, but because you want to use a JTA transaction for transaction demarcation, you need to define this as JTATransactionFactory.

- Hibernate.transaction.manager_lookup_class: The value of this transaction manager is dependent on the application server. Each application server has a different JTA implementation, so you have to tell Hibernate which JTA implementation to use. Hibernate supports most major application server implementation; use org.hibernate.transaction. WeblogicTransactionManagerLookup for WebLogic.

The following is the Hibernate configuration:

```
<?xml version="1.0" encoding="UTF-8"?>
<!DOCTYPE hibernate-configuration PUBLIC
            "-//Hibernate/Hibernate Configuration DTD 3.0//EN"
            "http://hibernate.sourceforge.net/hibernate-configuration-3.0.dtd">
<hibernate-configuration>
    <session-factory name="book">
            <property name="hibernate.connection.datasource">local_derby</property>
        <property name="hibernate.transaction.factory_class">org.hibernate.transaction.
JTATransactionFactory</property>
            <property name="hibernate.transaction.manager_lookup_class">org.hibernate.
```

```
transaction.WeblogicTransactionManagerLookup</property>
        <property name="hibernate.dialect">org.hibernate.dialect.DerbyDialect</property>
        <property name="hibernate.show_sql">true</property>
        <property name="hibernate.cache.use_second_level_cache">false</property>
        <mapping resource="book.xml" />

    </session-factory>
 </hibernate-configuration>
```

You now need to write a class that provides SessionFactory for the complete application. To do so, a utility class was defined that has a static method to return the SessionFactory. Here's the code implementation:

```java
import org.hibernate.SessionFactory;
import org.hibernate.cfg.Configuration;

public class HibernateUtil {

        private HibernateUtil(){}

        public static SessionFactory getSessionFactory()
        {
                SessionFactory factory = null;;
                try {

                        factory = new Configuration().configure().buildSessionFactory();

                } catch (Exception e) {

                        e.printStackTrace();
                }
                return factory;
        }
}
```

Now you're ready to use JTA for transaction demarcation. You get the UserTransaction by looking up the JNDI registry:

```java
public void saveBook(Book book)
  throws NotSupportedException, SystemException, NamingException, Exception {
  System.out.println("Enter DAO Impl");
  Session session = null;
  UserTransaction tx = (UserTransaction)new InitialContext()
    .lookup("java:comp/UserTransaction");
  try {
    SessionFactory factory = HibernateUtil.getSessionFactory();
    tx.begin();
    session = factory.openSession();
    session.saveOrUpdate(book);
```

```
        session.flush();
        tx.commit();
    }catch (Exception e) {
        tx.rollback();
    } finally {
        session.close();
    }
}
```

Note that you explicitly call session.flush(). You need to do an explicit flush because Hibernate's default implementation doesn't flush the session. You can, however, override the default implementation by configuring the hibernate.transaction.flush_before_completion property. You can also configure the hibernate.transaction.auto_close_session property to avoid calling session.close() explicitly in every method. The Hibernate configuration file is as follows:

```
<session-factory name="book">
            <property name="hibernate.connection.datasource">local_derby</property>
        <property name="hibernate.transaction.factory_class">org.hibernate.transaction.
JTATransactionFactory</property>
        <property name="hibernate.transaction.manager_lookup_class">org.hibernate.
transaction.WeblogicTransactionManagerLookup</property>
        <property name="hibernate.transaction.flush_before_completion">true</property>
        <property name="hibernate.transaction.auto_close_session">true</property>
        <property name="hibernate.dialect">org.hibernate.dialect.DerbyDialect</property>
        <property name="hibernate.show_sql">true</property>
        <property name="hibernate.cache.use_second_level_cache">false</property>

        <!--<property name="hbm2ddl.auto">create</property>-->

            <mapping resource="book.xml" />

    </session-factory>
```

And the code looks a little simpler, as shown here:

```
public void saveBook(Book book)
    throws NotSupportedException, SystemException, NamingException, Exception {
    System.out.println("Enter DAO Impl");
    Session session = null;
    UserTransaction tx = (UserTransaction)new InitialContext()
        .lookup("java:comp/UserTransaction");
    try {
        SessionFactory factory = HibernateUtil.getSessionFactory();
        tx.begin();
        session = factory.openSession();
        session.saveOrUpdate(book);
        session.flush();
        tx.commit();
    }catch (Exception e) {
        tx.rollback();
    }
}
```

In JPA, the implementation is very similar to Hibernate:

```
EntityManager manager = null;
UserTransaction tx = (UserTransaction)new InitialContext()
.lookup("java:comp/UserTransaction");
EntityManagerFactory managerFactory = HibernateUtil.getFactory();
manager = managerFactory.createEntityManager();
tx.begin();

try {
  manager.persist(book);
  tx.commit();
} catch (RuntimeException e) {
  if(tx != null) {
    tx.rollback();
  } finally {
    manager.close();
  }
}
```

13-3. Enabling Optimistic Concurrency Control
Problem

Suppose that two transactions are trying to update a record in the database. The first transaction updates and commits successfully, but the second transaction tries to update and fails. So the transaction is rolled back. The problem is that the first update is lost. Or what if the second transaction successfully updates, as illustrated in Table 13-1? The changes made by the first transaction are overwritten.

Table 13-1. *Lost Updates: Transaction 1 Updates Are Lost*

Time	Transaction Account
T1	Transaction 1 begins.
T2	Transaction 2 begins.
T3	Transaction 1 updates record R1.
T4	Transaction 2 updates record R1.
T5	Transaction 1 commits.
T6	Transaction 2 commits.

How do you handle such cases of lost updates? And how do you enable versioning in Hibernate?

Solution

You have to understand isolation levels to choose a concurrency control mechanism. Access to database records is classified as reads and writes. The concurrency control mechanisms define the rules that dictate when to allow reads and writes.

A *dirty read* occurs when one transaction reads changes made by another transaction that haven't yet been committed (see Table 13-2). Basically, a dirty read means reading uncommitted data.

Table 13-2. *Dirty Read: A Transaction Reading Uncommitted Data*

Time	Transaction Account
T1	Transaction 1 begins.
T2	Transaction 2 begins.
T3	Transaction 1 updates record R1.
T4	Transaction 2 reads uncommitted record R1.
T5	Transaction 1 rolls back its update.
T6	Transaction 2 commits.

An *unrepeatable read* occurs when a transaction reads a record twice, and the record state is different between the first and the second read. This happens when another transaction updates the state of the record between the two reads (see Table 13-3).

Table 13-3. *Unrepeatable Read: A Transaction Reading a Record Twice*

Time	Transaction Account
T1	Transaction 1 begins.
T2	Transaction 1 reads record R1.
T3	Transaction 2 begins.
T4	Transaction 2 updates record R1.
T5	Transaction 2 commits.
T6	Transaction 1 reads record R1 (the record R1 read at time T2 is in a different state than at time T6).
T7	Transaction 1 commits.

A *phantom read* occurs when a transaction executes two identical queries, and the collection of rows returned by the second query is different from the first. It also happens when another transaction inserts records into or deletes records from the table between the two reads.

Table 13-4. Phantom Read: Reading a Range of Data That Changes in Size During a Transaction

Time	Transaction Account
T1	Transaction 1 begins.
T2	Transaction 1 reads a range of records RG1.
T3	Transaction 2 begins.
T4	Transaction 2 inserts records.
T5	Transaction 2 commits.
T6	Transaction 1 reads the range of records RG1 (RG1's size has changed from time T2 to T6).
T7	Transaction 1 commits.

Isolation, which is one of the ACID properties, defines how and when changes made by one transaction are made visible to other transactions. For better performance and concurrency control, isolation is divided by the ANSI SQL standard into levels that define the degree of locking when you select data. The four isolation levels are as follows (see also Table 13-5):

- *Serializable*: Transactions are executed serially, one after the other. This isolation level allows a transaction to acquire read locks or write locks for the entire range of data that it affects. The Serializable isolation level prevents dirty reads, unrepeatable reads, and phantom reads, but it can cause scalability issues for an application.

- *Repeatable Read*: Read locks and write locks are acquired. This isolation level doesn't permit dirty reads or unrepeatable reads. It also doesn't acquire a range lock, which means it permits phantom reads. A read lock prevents any write locks from being acquired by other concurrent transaction. This level can still have some scalability issues.

- *Read Committed*: Read locks are sacquired and released immediately, and write locks are acquired and released at the end of the transaction. Dirty reads aren't allowed in this isolation level, but unrepeatable reads and phantom reads are permitted. By using the combination of persistent context and versioning, you can achieve the Repeatable Read isolation level.

- *Read Uncommitted*: Changes made by one transaction are made visible to other transactions before they're committed. All types of reads, including dirty reads, are permitted. This isolation level isn't recommended for use. If a transaction's uncommitted changes are rolled back, other concurrent transactions may be seriously affected.

Table 13-5. Summarizing the Reads That Are Permitted for Various Isolation Levels

Isolation Level	Dirty Read	Unrepeated Read	Phantom Read
Serializable	-	-	-
Repeatable Read	-	-	Permitted
Read Committed	-	Permitted	Permitted
Read Uncommitted	Permitted	Permitted	Permitted

Every database management system has a default setting for the isolation level. You can change the default isolation level in the DBMS configuration. On JDBC, you can set the isolation level by using a property called `hibernate.connection.isolation`. Hibernate uses the following values to set a particular isolation level:

- 8: Serializable isolation

- 4: Repeatable Read isolation

- 2: Read Committed isolation

- 1: Read Uncommitted isolation

This setting is applicable only when the connection isn't obtained from an application server. In this scenario, you need to change the isolation level in the application server configuration.

Now, let's come back to the case of lost updates described at the beginning of this recipe (also in Table 13-1). You saw a case in which an update made by transaction 1 is lost when transaction 2 commits. Most applications are database connections with Read Committed isolation and use the optimistic concurrency control. One way of implementing optimistic control is to use versioning.

How It Works

Hibernate provides automatic versioning. Each entity can have a version, which can be a number or a timestamp. Hibernate increments the number when the entity is modified. If you're saving with an older version (which is the case for transaction 2 in the lost-update problem), Hibernate compares the versions automatically and throws an exception.

To add a version number to an entity, add a property called `version` of type `int` or `Integer`:

```
public class BookCh2 {
        private long isbn;
        private String name;
        private Date publishDate;
        private int price;
        private int version;
}
```

In the `book.xml` configuration file, add the `version` element. Note that the `version` element must be placed immediately after the `id` element:

```
<hibernate-mapping package="com.hibernaterecipes.chapter2" auto-import="false" >
        <import class="BookCh2" rename="bkch2"/>
        <class name="BookCh2" table="BOOK" dynamic-insert="true" dynamic-update="true"
schema="BOOK">
                <id name="isbn"  column="isbn" type="long">
                        <generator class="hilo">
                        </generator>
                </id>
                <version name="version" access="field" column="version"></version>
                <property name="name" type="string" column="BOOK_NAME" />
                <property name="publishDate" type="date" column="PUBLISH_DATE" />
                <property name="price" type="int" column="PRICE" />
        </class>
</hibernate-mapping>
```

A new column called version is created in the BOOK table. Using JPA, add the version variable to the Book class and annotate it with the Version element:

```
@Entity (name="bkch2")
@org.hibernate.annotations.Entity(dynamicInsert = true, dynamicUpdate = true)
@Table        (name="BOOK")
public class BookCh2 {

        @Id
        @GeneratedValue (strategy=GenerationType.TABLE)
        @Column (name="ISBN")
        private long isbn;

        @Version
        @Column (name="version")
        private Integer version;

        @Column (name="book_Name")
        private String bookName;

        /*@Column (name="publisher_code")
        String publisherCode;*/

        @Column (name="publish_date")
        private Date publishDate;

        @Column (name="price")
        private Long price;
        // getters and setters
}
```

You can also use timestamps to version by adding a variable of type Date:

```
public class BookCh2 implements Serializable{
        private long isbn;
        private String name;
        private Date publishDate;
        private int price;
        private Date timestamp;
        // getters and setters
}
```

The XML mapping file has a timestamp element, as shown here:

```
<hibernate-mapping package="com.hibernaterecipes.chapter2" auto-import="false" >
        <import class="BookCh2" rename="bkch2"/>
        <class name="BookCh2" table="BOOK" dynamic-insert="true" dynamic-update="true"
schema="BOOK">
                <id name="isbn"  column="isbn" type="long">
                        <generator class="hilo">
                        </generator>
                </id>
```

```
                    <timestamp name="timestamp" access="field" column="timestamp"></timestamp>
                    <property name="name" type="string" column="BOOK_NAME" />
                    <property name="publishDate" type="date" column="PUBLISH_DATE" />
                    <property name="price" type="int" column="PRICE" />
        </class>
</hibernate-mapping>
```

You can also implement versioning without a version or timestamp by using the attribute optimistic-lock on the class mapping. It works when the entity is retrieved and modified in the same session. It doesn't work with detached objects; if you need to use optimistic concurrency control with detached objects, you must use a version or timestamp:

```
<hibernate-mapping package="com.hibernaterecipes.chapter2" auto-import="false" >
        <import class="BookCh2" rename="bkch2"/>
        <class name="BookCh2" table="BOOK" dynamic-insert="true" dynamic-update="true"
schema="BOOK" optimistic-lock="all">
                <id name="isbn"  column="isbn" type="long">
                        <generator class="hilo">
                        </generator>
                </id>
                <property name="name" type="string" column="BOOK_NAME" />
                <property name="publishDate" type="date" column="PUBLISH_DATE" />
                <property name="price" type="int" column="PRICE" />
        </class>
</hibernate-mapping>
```

This isn't a popular option because it is slower and is complex to implement. In addition, JPA does not standardize this technique. So if you need to use optimistic locking in JPA, you must use Hibernate's annotations, as shown here:

```
@Entity (name="bkch2")
@org.hibernate.annotations.Entity
 (dynamicInsert = true, dynamicUpdate = true,
                 optimisticLock=org.hibernate.annotations.OptimisticLockType.ALL)
@Table        (name="BOOK")
public class BookCh2 {

        @Id
        @GeneratedValue (strategy=GenerationType.TABLE)
        @Column (name="ISBN")
        private long isbn;

        @Version
        @Column (name="version")
        private Integer version;

        @Column (name="book_Name")
        private String bookName;
```

```
/*@Column (name="publisher_code")
String publisherCode;*/

@Column (name="publish_date")
private Date publishDate;

@Column (name="price")
private Long price;
// getters and setters
}
```

13-4. Using Pessimistic Concurrency Control

Problem

How do you implement pessimistic concurrency control in your application to save the book entity?

Solution

Most applications have Read Committed as the isolation level, but it permits unrepeatable reads, which isn't desirable. One way to avoid unrepeatable reads is to implement versioning in the application. This upgrading of the isolation level from Read Committed to Repeatable Read comes with scalability issues. As an application developer, you may not want to make an application-wide upgrade to versioning—you may just want to upgrade the isolation level on a per-unit basis. To do so, Hibernate provides the lock() method in the Hibernate session object.

How It Works

The following code demonstrates how an unrepeatable read can happen. You first get the book using the session.get() method and then you use a query to read the name of the book. If an update happens between these two calls to the book's record in the database by a concurrent transaction, you have a case of unrepeatable reads:

```
Session session = getSession();
Transaction tx = null;
tx = session.beginTransaction();
BookCh2 book = (BookCh2)session.get(BookCh2.class, new Long(32769));
String name = (String) session.createQuery("select b.name from bkch2 b where b.isbn = :isbn")
              .setParameter("isbn", book.getIsbn()).uniqueResult();
System.out.println("BOOk's Name- "+name);
tx.commit();
session.close();
```

You can use session.lock() to upgrade the isolation level. The previous code is updated as follows:

```
Session session = getSession();
Transaction tx = null;
tx = session.beginTransaction();
BookCh2 book = (BookCh2)session.get(BookCh2.class, new Long(32769));
session.lock(book, LockMode.UPGRADE);
String name = (String) session.createQuery("select b.name from bkch2 b where b.isbn = :isbn")
                .setParameter("isbn", book.getIsbn()).uniqueResult();
System.out.println("BOOk's Name- "+name);
tx.commit();
session.close();
```

Or you can directly call the following:

```
BookCh2 book = (BookCh2)session.get(BookCh2.class, new Long(32769),LockMode.UPGRADE);
```

LockMode.UPGRADE creates a lock on the specific book record in the database. Now other concurrent transactions can't modify the book record.

Hibernate supports the following lock modes:

- LockMode.NONE: This is the default lock mode. If an object is requested with this lock mode, a READ lock is obtained if it is necessary to read the state from the database instead of pulling it from a cache.

- LockMode.READ: In this lock mode, an object is read from the database. The object's version is checked, just as in memory.

- LockMode.UPGRADE: Objects loaded in this lock mode are materialized using an SQL select ... for update. It is equivalent to LockModeType.READ in Java Persistence.

- LockMode.UPGRADE_NOWAIT: This lock mode attempts to obtain an upgrade lock using an Oracle-style select for update nowait. Once obtained, the semantics of this lock mode are the same as UPGRADE.

- LockMode.FORCE: This lock mode results in a forced version increment. It is equivalent to LockModeType.Write in Java Persistence.

- LockMode.WRITE: A WRITE lock is obtained when an object is updated or inserted. This lock mode is for internal use only and isn't a valid mode for load() or lock().

Summary

In this chapter, you saw how to manage transactions programmatically. You also learned to use the Hibernate Transaction API and the Java Transaction API for transaction demarcation.

Optimistic concurrency control and pessimistic concurrency control are the two approaches used to achieve concurrency control. Optimistic concurrency control involves using either a version or a timestamp to maintain the version as a database column. Pessimistic control is used on a per-transaction basis and is achieved by using session.lock() with a lock mode of UPGRADE or UPGRADE_NOWAIT.

The next chapter takes a look at exposing Hibernate services over HTTP, using a RESTful API, which is a common way to expose services for modern applications.

■ ■ ■

CHAPTER 14

Web Applications

So far, you've seen a lot of aspects of working with data, and it's time to look at one way[1] to use Hibernate to access data over the Web, which is (obviously) a very common access method. (If it's not obvious, trust me: it's obvious.)

What you'll see is a simple way to present management of authors and books over the Web so that a front end can easily be written with a JavaScript framework such as AngularJS,[2] with services provided through REST.[3] As an architectural choice, it makes the service layer very easy to write; as luck would have it, if we used any other architectural design (such as JSF, or Struts 2, or almost anything else) our services would look much the same.

What Is REST?

REST is an architectural pattern born from the use of HTTP.[4] The idea behind REST is that data is represented cleanly as a *resource*, and interactions with that resource can take place through the use of HTTP *verbs*.

Let's look at some data as an example. Consider a person: our data model might contain the person's name and address, as well as some kind of unique identifier.

We can assign that person a uniform resource identifier (URI) and potentially expose it to client applications. If a person has an identifier of 62512412, we might say that the URI is `http://imaginarysite.com/people/62512412`. If we want to get the information, we might direct a web browser to get that URL (with GET being one of the HTTP verbs, of course).

Similarly, if we want to indicate that we are creating a person, we might use another verb: POST is most often advocated for the creation of new resources. If we want to modify the person's information, we can use PUT instead; and there's a DELETE verb as well if we want to remove the data.[5]

---

[1]Dear reader, everything in this chapter is merely one option in a sea of choices. Any time you see something being done, you should keep in mind that there are likely to be a hundred other possibilities, each with its own strengths and weaknesses.

[2]AngularJS (`http://angularjs.org`) is a JavaScript application framework.

[3]REST stands for "Representational State Transfer." We'll explain it further as we go through the chapter because it's rather important for our design, but for starters, see `http://en.wikipedia.org/wiki/Representational_state_transfer`

[4]Speaking of options in a sea of choices: another architectural pattern over HTTP is service-oriented architecture, in which actual services are exposed instead of resources. REST is simpler, though, and pushes application definition over to the client layer, which is arguably where it belongs.

[5]The HTTP verbs aren't exactly rocket science.

Just as Java has the Java Persistence API (JPA) specification for persistence (which Hibernate implements, although we've been using the native Hibernate API for most things in this book), Java has the Java API for RESTful[6] Web Services, usually shown as JAX-RS. There are multiple projects that implement this standard (just as there are for the persistence API), but we'll be using the reference implementation, Jersey.[7]

It's worth noting that web applications (and web application frameworks) justify books in and of themselves, and this one won't attempt to walk through every permutation of configuration and deployment. The web application poses some problems that you need to be aware of from the standpoint of using Hibernate, but for general web development, Apress has some excellent resources for your perusal.[8]

14-1. Exposing Persistence Over the Web

We will create a simple application to provide management of books and authors. The data model is very simple: an author can publish multiple books. What we'll need to do is create the data model (which is trivial) and then create a service to expose that data model to a web browser. Finally, we'll look at how we'd use that data from a client application.

First, let's take a look at the Author and Book entities. Author first because authors are really important:[9]

```
import lombok.Data;
import lombok.NoArgsConstructor;

import javax.persistence.*;
import javax.xml.bind.annotation.XmlElement;
import javax.xml.bind.annotation.XmlRootElement;

@Entity
@Data
@NoArgsConstructor
@NamedQueries(
        {@NamedQuery(name = "author.findAll", query = "from Author a")}
)
@XmlRootElement(name = "author")
public class Author {
    @Id
    @GeneratedValue(strategy = GenerationType.AUTO)
    Integer id;
    @Column(unique = true)
    String name;
}
```

---

[6]Another *horribly* short summary of REST: objects (nouns—things) are exposed as locations over HTTP. To interact with them, we use HTTP actions—verbs—such as GET, POST, PUT, and DELETE. Each has normal implications: GET retrieves, POST updates an existing resource, PUT creates a new resource, and DELETE—surprisingly—makes it unavailable.

[7]Jersey's home page is https://jersey.java.net/

[8]In particular, see Adam Freeman's *Pro AngularJS* from Apress; its URL is http://www.apress.com/9781430264484

[9]Your author knows exactly how important authors are, being one; besides, who would write books if there were no authors? This question made my head hurt.

Although authors may be *important,* apparently all they have are names. We need to see the Book entity next. It is more verbose than we're used to seeing with Lombok, largely because we need to exclude the author reference from the equals() and hashCode() methods.

```java
package com.apress.hibernaterecipes.chapter14.model;

import lombok.*;

import javax.persistence.*;
import javax.xml.bind.annotation.XmlRootElement;

@NoArgsConstructor
@Entity
@EqualsAndHashCode(exclude = "author")
@ToString
@Table(uniqueConstraints = {
        @UniqueConstraint(columnNames = {"title", "author"})
})
@NamedQueries(
        {
                @NamedQuery(name = "book.findByIdAndAuthor",
                        query = "from Book b where b.id=:id and b.author.id=:authorId"),
                @NamedQuery(name = "book.findByAuthor",
                        query = "from Book b where b.author.id=:authorId")
        }
)
@XmlRootElement(name = "book")
public class Book {
    @Id
    @GeneratedValue(strategy = GenerationType.AUTO)
    @Getter
    @Setter
    Integer id;
    @Column(unique = true)
    @Getter
    @Setter
    String title;
    @Getter
    @Setter
    int edition;
    @ManyToOne
    @JoinColumn(name = "author")
    @Getter
    @Setter
    Author author;
    @Getter
    @Setter
    int copiesSold;
}
```

Finally (and for completeness' sake), let's take a look at the `hibernate.cfg.xml` file:

```xml
<?xml version="1.0" encoding="UTF-8"?>
<!DOCTYPE hibernate-configuration PUBLIC
        "-//Hibernate/Hibernate Configuration DTD 3.0//EN"
        "http://www.hibernate.org/dtd/hibernate-configuration-3.0.dtd">
<hibernate-configuration>
    <session-factory>
        <property name="connection.driver_class">org.h2.Driver</property>
        <property name="connection.url">jdbc:h2:file:../chapter14</property>
        <property name="hibernate.dialect">org.hibernate.dialect.H2Dialect</property>
        <property name="hibernate.hbm2ddl.auto">create</property>
        <property name="hibernate.show_sql">true</property>
        <property name="hibernate.discriminator.ignore_explicit_for_joined">true</property>
        <property name="connection.username"></property>
        <property name="connection.password"></property>
        <property name="hibernate.c3p0.min_size">5</property>
        <property name="hibernate.c3p0.max_size">10</property>
        <property name="hibernate.c3p0.timeout">300</property>
        <property name="hibernate.c3p0.max_statements">50</property>
        <property name="hibernate.c3p0.acquire_increment">1</property>
        <property name="hibernate.c3p0.idle_test_period">3000</property>
        <mapping class="com.apress.hibernaterecipes.chapter14.model.Book"/>
        <mapping class="com.apress.hibernaterecipes.chapter14.model.Author"/>
    </session-factory>
</hibernate-configuration>
```

So far, we've seen nothing out of the ordinary - but we've also not taken a look at our pom. xml, which needs to have Jersey and some other things added to it in order to work properly.

```xml
<project xmlns="http://maven.apache.org/POM/4.0.0"
        xmlns:xsi="http://www.w3.org/2001/XMLSchema-instance"
        xsi:schemaLocation="http://maven.apache.org/POM/4.0.0 http://maven.apache.org/
maven-v4_0_0.xsd">

    <modelVersion>4.0.0</modelVersion>
    <artifactId>chapter14</artifactId>

    <parent>
        <artifactId>ver2</artifactId>
        <groupId>com.apress.hibernaterecipes</groupId>
        <version>1.0.0</version>
    </parent>

    <properties>
        <version.jetty>9.3.0.M1</version.jetty>
        <servlet.version>3.0.1</servlet.version>
        <jersey.version>2.15</jersey.version>
    </properties>
```

```xml
<packaging>war</packaging>
<dependencyManagement>
    <dependencies>
        <dependency>
            <groupId>org.glassfish.jersey</groupId>
            <artifactId>jersey-bom</artifactId>
            <version>${jersey.version}</version>
            <type>pom</type>
            <scope>import</scope>
        </dependency>
    </dependencies>
</dependencyManagement>
<dependencies>
    <dependency>
        <groupId>org.hibernate</groupId>
        <artifactId>hibernate-c3p0</artifactId>
    </dependency>
    <dependency>
        <groupId>com.h2database</groupId>
        <artifactId>h2</artifactId>
    </dependency>
    <dependency>
        <groupId>org.projectlombok</groupId>
        <artifactId>lombok</artifactId>
    </dependency>

    <dependency>
        <groupId>org.glassfish.jersey.containers</groupId>
        <artifactId>jersey-container-grizzly2-http</artifactId>
    </dependency>
    <dependency>
        <groupId>org.glassfish.jersey.media</groupId>
        <artifactId>jersey-media-moxy</artifactId>
    </dependency>
</dependencies>
<build>
    <plugins>
        <plugin>
            <groupId>org.apache.maven.plugins</groupId>
            <artifactId>maven-war-plugin</artifactId>
            <version>2.3</version>
            <configuration>
                <failOnMissingWebXml>false</failOnMissingWebXml>
            </configuration>
        </plugin>
```

```
            <plugin>
                <groupId>org.codehaus.mojo</groupId>
                <artifactId>exec-maven-plugin</artifactId>
                <version>1.2.1</version>
                <executions>
                    <execution>
                        <goals>
                            <goal>java</goal>
                        </goals>
                    </execution>
                </executions>
                <configuration>
                    <mainClass>com.apress.hibernaterecipes.chapter14.Main</mainClass>
                </configuration>
            </plugin>
        </plugins>
    </build>
</project>
```

This code builds our application and allows us to run it from the command line with the following:

```
mvn -pl chapter14 exec:java
```

Let's build our API. We have two different types of interactions: interactions around authors and around books. We can (and probably should) isolate these behaviors into separate interfaces:

```
public interface AuthorController {
    Author getAuthor(Integer id);
    Author removeAuthor(Integer id);
    Author updateAuthor(Integer id, Author updatedAuthor);
    Author createAuthor(Author model);
    Author[] getAuthors();
}

public interface BookController {
    Book getBook(Integer authorId, Integer id);
    Book removeBook(Integer authorId, Integer id);
    Book updateBook(Integer authorId, Integer id, Book updatedBook);
    Book createBook(Integer authorId, Book model);
    public Book[] getBooks(Integer authorId);
}
```

Now we'll take a look at the REST API. First, let's look at a simple REST call, a simple "Hello, World." We'll use two classes to expose this: one starts an embedded web server (and will remain untouched for the rest of this chapter), and the other is our service implementation and will eventually implement our interfaces.

First[10] is the embedded web server, rather imaginatively called Main:

```
package com.apress.hibernaterecipes.chapter14;

import org.glassfish.grizzly.http.server.HttpServer;
import org.glassfish.grizzly.http.server.StaticHttpHandler;
import org.glassfish.jersey.grizzly2.httpserver.GrizzlyHttpServerFactory;
import org.glassfish.jersey.server.ResourceConfig;

import java.io.IOException;
import java.net.URI;

public class Main {
    public static final String BASE_URI = "http://localhost:8080/app/";

    public static HttpServer startServer() {
        final ResourceConfig rc = new ResourceConfig()
                .packages("com.apress.hibernaterecipes.chapter14.services");

        HttpServer server=GrizzlyHttpServerFactory.createHttpServer(URI.create(BASE_URI), rc);
        server.getServerConfiguration()
            .addHttpHandler(new StaticHttpHandler("./chapter14/src/main/webapp"));

        return server;
    }

    public static void main(String[] args) throws IOException {
        final HttpServer server = startServer();
        System.out.println(String.format("Jersey app started with WADL available at "
                + "%sapplication.wadl\nHit enter to stop it...", BASE_URI));
        System.in.read();
        server.shutdownNow();
    }
}
```

Here's a "Hello, World" service:

```
package com.apress.hibernaterecipes.chapter14.services;

import javax.ws.rs.*;

@Path("library")
public class ServiceImpl {
    @GET
    @Path("/hello")
    @Produces("application/json")
    public String heartbeat() {
        return "Hello, world";
    }
}
```

---

[10]There are a lot of "firsts" in this chapter, sadly. Welcome to enterprise development!

The annotations serve to describe how this service can be located and with what HTTP verb it should be invoked. If the web application root is `http://localhost:8080/app` (as our `Main` specifies), this service can be invoked via GET `http://localhost:8080/app/library/hello`. Thus, after running our build (again, with `"mvn -pl chapter14 exec:java"`), we see the following:

If you look at the code carefully, you'll see that we specify JSON as the output format, but because this data is a simple `String`, our output remains very simple.[11]

Now that you know all there is to creating a RESTful endpoint,[12] let's look at actual services.

When we create services, we need to think of our Hibernate `Session` as something that exists in the context of a request. As a result, we have to build our complete model (and populate it) before allowing the `Session` to close. Otherwise, if we access an element in our data model that Hibernate has not loaded, we'll get a `LazyInitializationException`, which is rarely what we desire.

There are multiple solutions for this, but the one we'll use here is very straightforward: we'll assume that the service knows what it should be returning and will initialize the entire data object while the session is present.

Let's take a look at our author services:

```
@GET
@Path("/authors/")
@Consumes("application/json")
@Produces("application/json")
@Override
public Author[] getAuthors() {
    Session session = SessionManager.openSession();
    Transaction tx = session.beginTransaction();
    try {
        Query query = session.getNamedQuery("author.findAll");
        query.setReadOnly(true);
        @SuppressWarnings("unchecked")
        List<Author> authors = (List<Author>) query.list();
        for (Author author : authors) {
            Hibernate.initialize(author);
        }
```

---

[11]Issuing a request like that through a browser's location bar issues an HTTP GET.

[12]This was a sarcastic statement; not only have we covered very little about REST, I don't think this chapter in its entirety could serve as much more than a cursory overview. Sorry about that—it's a giant topic.

```
        tx.commit();
        return authors.toArray(new Author[0]);
    } finally {
        if (tx.isActive()) {
            tx.rollback();
        }
        session.close();
    }
}
```

The first method here is the getAuthors() service call, which returns our entire list of authors. It's very simple, taking no arguments, and is accessed via GET http://localhost:8080/app/library/authors/, producing a JSON array.

JSON, which stands for JavaScript Object Notation, is a simple way to present data. Basically, it's a way of defining a dictionary that can include other dictionaries (a map of maps) with named elements. It is much like XML, but it's far easier to work with.[13] As an example, in XML our Author might look like this:

```
<?xml version="1.0"?>
272103_1_En
   <id>1</id>
   <name>Joseph B. Ottinger</name>
</author>
```

In JSON, it might look like this instead:

```
{
    "id":"1";
    "name":"Joseph B. Ottinger"
}
```

Back to the actual service itself: the only potentially unexpected element to the call is that it *forcibly* initializes the Author objects. It does this because when the method exits, the library that formats the output as JSON does not have access to the Session object, therefore is susceptible to the LazyInitializationException. Believe it or not, this is *the* primary thing our service calls have to consider, and you'll see it over and over again.

Let's look at how we add an author:

```
@POST
@Path("/authors")
@Consumes("application/json")
@Produces("application/json")
public Author createAuthor(Author model) {
    Session session = SessionManager.openSession();
    Transaction tx = session.beginTransaction();
```

---

[13]XML is great when you need to specify that a structure fits a specific description and that types are specific. It's also very verbose and thus rather noisy. Programmers are lazy; JSON is more common, especially because JavaScript can use the object structures as is, rather than having to unpack XML.

```
    try {
        session.persist(model);
        tx.commit();
        return model;
    } finally {
        if (tx.isActive()) {
            tx.rollback();
        }
        session.close();
    }
}
```

The application supplies an Author object in JSON format ({name:"Joseph Ottinger"} as an example),
which the method uses to create a database record, returning the persisted model (which will now have a
database identifier). This identifier can be used to form a URL through which we can retrieve an author with
the next method.

Our method to look at a specific author is as follows:

```
@GET
@Path("/authors/{id}")
@Consumes("application/json")
@Produces("application/json")
public Author getAuthor(@PathParam("id") Integer id) {
    Session session = SessionManager.openSession();
    Transaction tx = session.beginTransaction();
    try {
        Author author = (Author) session.byId(Author.class)
                .with(LockOptions.NONE)
                .getReference(id);
        Hibernate.initialize(author);
        tx.commit();
        return author;
    } finally {
        if (tx.isActive()) {
            tx.rollback();
        }
        session.close();
    }
}
```

This method accepts the ID for the author in the URL. If the author identifier is 1, our author's URL
is http://localhost:8080/app/library/authors/1. The REST library will convert the URL so that our
method can simply use the identifier to look up an Author and return it after fully initializing it.

This pattern repeats itself for our other Author-related methods:

```
@DELETE
@Path("/authors/{id}")
@Consumes("application/json")
@Produces("application/json")
```

```
public Author removeAuthor(@PathParam("id") Integer id) {
    Session session = SessionManager.openSession();
    Transaction tx = session.beginTransaction();
    try {
        Author author = (Author) session.byId(Author.class)
                .with(LockOptions.NONE)
                .getReference(id);
        session.delete(author);
        tx.commit();
        return author;
    } finally {
        if (tx.isActive()) {
            tx.rollback();
        }
        session.close();
    }
}

@PUT
@Path("/authors/{id}")
@Consumes("application/json")
@Produces("application/json")
public Author updateAuthor(@PathParam("id") Integer id, Author updatedAuthor) {
    Session session = SessionManager.openSession();
    Transaction tx = session.beginTransaction();
    try {
        Author author = (Author) session.byId(Author.class)
                .with(LockOptions.NONE)
                .getReference(id);
        author.setName(updatedAuthor.getName());
        tx.commit();
        return updatedAuthor;
    } finally {
        if (tx.isActive()) {
            tx.rollback();
        }
        session.close();
    }
}
```

Our Book-related service calls are also very simple, with the caveat being that they also need to access the Author references in the Session. So we can't rely on the model sending us whole objects; we need to grab the Author references from the database, corresponding to what the service call requests, rather than just blithely assuming that the Book has valid data. Let's take a look:

```
@GET
@Path("/authors/{authorId}/books/{id}")
public Book getBook(@PathParam("authorId") Integer authorId, @PathParam("id") Integer id) {
    Session session = SessionManager.openSession();
    Transaction tx = session.beginTransaction();
```

```
    try {
        Query query = session.getNamedQuery("book.findByIdAndAuthor");
        query.setParameter("id", id);
        query.setParameter("authorId", authorId);
        Book book = (Book) query.uniqueResult();
        if (book == null) {
            throw new ObjectNotFoundException(id, "Book");
        }
        Hibernate.initialize(book);
        tx.commit();
        return book;
    } finally {
        if (tx.isActive()) {
            tx.rollback();
        }
        session.close();
    }
}


@GET
@Path("/authors/{authorId}/books")
@Consumes("application/json")
@Produces("application/json")
public Book[] getBooks(@PathParam("authorId") Integer authorId) {
    Session session = SessionManager.openSession();
    Transaction tx = session.beginTransaction();
    try {
        Query query = session.getNamedQuery("book.findByAuthor");
        query.setReadOnly(true);
        query.setParameter("authorId", authorId);
        @SuppressWarnings("unchecked")
        List<Book> books = (List<Book>) query.list();
        for (Book book : books) {
            Hibernate.initialize(book);
        }
        tx.commit();
        return books.toArray(new Book[0]);
    } finally {
        if (tx.isActive()) {
            tx.rollback();
        }
        session.close();
    }
}
```

```
@DELETE
@Path("/authors/{authorId}/books/{id}")
@Consumes("application/json")
@Produces("application/json")
public Book removeBook(@PathParam("authorId") Integer authorId, @PathParam("id") Integer id)
{
    Session session = SessionManager.openSession();
    Transaction tx = session.beginTransaction();
    try {
        Query query = session.getNamedQuery("book.findByIdAndAuthor");
        query.setParameter("id", id);
        query.setParameter("authorId", authorId);
        Book book = (Book) query.uniqueResult();
        if (book == null) {
            throw new ObjectNotFoundException(id, "Book");
        }
        session.delete(book);
        tx.commit();
        return book;
    } finally {
        if (tx.isActive()) {
            tx.rollback();
        }
        session.close();
    }
}


@PUT
@Path("/authors/{authorId}/books/{id}")
@Consumes("application/json")
@Produces("application/json")
public Book updateBook(@PathParam("authorId") Integer authorId,
    @PathParam("id") Integer id,
    Book updatedBook) {
    Session session = SessionManager.openSession();
    Transaction tx = session.beginTransaction();
    try {
        Query query = session.getNamedQuery("book.findByIdAndAuthor");
        query.setParameter("id", id);
        query.setParameter("authorId", authorId);
        Book book = (Book) query.uniqueResult();
        if (book == null) {
            throw new ObjectNotFoundException(id, "Book");
        }
        book.setCopiesSold(updatedBook.getCopiesSold());
        book.setEdition(updatedBook.getEdition());
        book.setTitle(updatedBook.getTitle());
        tx.commit();
        return book;
    } finally {
```

```
            if (tx.isActive()) {
                tx.rollback();
            }
            session.close();
        }
    }


    @POST
    @Path("/authors/{authorId}/books")
    @Consumes("application/json")
    @Produces("application/json")
    public Book createBook(@PathParam("authorId") Integer authorId, Book model) {
        Session session = SessionManager.openSession();
        Transaction tx = session.beginTransaction();
        try {
            Author author = (Author) session.byId(Author.class)
                    .getReference(authorId);
            model.setAuthor(author);
            session.persist(model);
            tx.commit();
            return model;
        } finally {
            if (tx.isActive()) {
                tx.rollback();
            }
            session.close();
        }
    }
}
```

Here's a fairly complete test suite for our services; note, however, that they're testing the services and they do *not* issue calls over HTTP. We're testing the services themselves; not the REST API. The test should make sure that the fields of the objects are accessed after the Session is closed to ensure that we have proper data isolation. This is, after all, why we keep calling Hibernate.initialize().

```
public class ServiceTest {
    ServiceImpl controller = new ServiceImpl();

    @BeforeMethod
    public void setUp() {
        SessionManager.deleteAll("Book");
        SessionManager.deleteAll("Author");
    }

    @Test
    public void testGetAuthor() {
        Author data = createAuthor("Test Author");

        Author model = controller.getAuthor(data.getId());
        assertEquals(data, model);
    }
```

```java
@Test
public void testGetAuthors() {
    Author[] authors = controller.getAuthors();
    assertEquals(authors.length, 0);
    createAuthor("First Author");
    createAuthor("Second Author");
    authors = controller.getAuthors();
    assertEquals(authors.length, 2);
}

@Test
public void testUpdateAuthorExistingAuthor() {
    Author data = createAuthor("Test Author");
    data.setName("Other Author");
    Author model = controller.updateAuthor(data.getId(), data);
    assertEquals(model.getName(), "Other Author");
    assertEquals(model.getId(), data.getId());
}

@Test(expectedExceptions = ObjectNotFoundException.class)
public void testUpdateAuthorNoExistingAuthor() {
    Author model = new Author();
    model.setName("My Test Author");

    model = controller.updateAuthor(15, model);
    assertEquals(model.getName(), "My Test Author");
    assertEquals(model.getId().intValue(), 15);

    Author data = controller.getAuthor(model.getId());
    assertEquals(model, data);
}

@Test
public void testRemoveAuthor() {
    Author data = createAuthor("Test Author");
    Author removed = controller.removeAuthor(data.getId());
    assertEquals(data, removed);
    try {
        Author check = controller.getAuthor(removed.getId());
        fail("Should not have found author " + check);
    } catch (ObjectNotFoundException ignored) {
    }
}

@Test
public void testCreateAuthor() {
    Author data = createAuthor("Test Author");
    assertEquals(data.getName(), "Test Author");
    assertNotNull(data.getId());
}
```

```java
@Test(expectedExceptions = HibernateException.class)
public void testDuplicateAuthor() {
    createAuthor("Foo Bar");
    createAuthor("Foo Bar");
    fail("Should not have been able to create authors with same name");
}

@Test
public void createValidBook() {
    Author author = createAuthor("Arthur Author");
    Book book = createBook(author, "Otter Ought To", 1);
    assertNotNull(book);
    assertEquals(book.getTitle(), "Otter Ought To");
    assertNotNull(book.getId());
}

@Test(expectedExceptions=HibernateException.class)
public void createDuplicateBook() {
    Author author = createAuthor("Arthur Author");
    createBook(author, "Otter Ought To", 1);
    createBook(author, "Otter Ought To", 1);
    fail("Should not have been able to create books with same name");
}

@Test(expectedExceptions = HibernateException.class)
public void createBookWithInvalidAuthor() {
    Book model = new Book();
    model.setTitle("Arthur Author");
    model.setCopiesSold(0);
    model.setEdition(1);
    Book book = controller.createBook(15, model);
    assertNotNull(book);
    assertEquals(book.getTitle(), "Otter Ought To");
    assertNotNull(book.getId());
}

@Test
public void testRemoveBook() {
    Author author = createAuthor("Arthur Author");
    Book book = createBook(author, "Otter Ought To", 1);
    Book persisted = controller.getBook(author.getId(), book.getId());
    assertEquals(book, persisted);
    controller.removeBook(author.getId(), book.getId());
    try {
        controller.getBook(author.getId(), book.getId());
        fail("Shouldn't have been able to get book " + book.getId());
    } catch (HibernateException ignored) {
    }
}
```

```java
@Test(expectedExceptions = HibernateException.class)
public void removeNonexistentBookWithValidAuthor() {
    Author author = createAuthor("Arthur Author");
    controller.removeBook(author.getId(), -1);
    fail("Should not have been able to remove book with invalid id");
}

@Test(expectedExceptions = HibernateException.class)
public void removeNonexistentBookWithInvalidAuthor() {
    controller.removeBook(-4, -1);
    fail("Should not have been able to remove book with invalid author and id");
}

@Test(expectedExceptions = HibernateException.class)
public void updateNonexistentAuthor() {
    Author author = createAuthor("Arthur Author");
    author.setName("Arthur Author II");
    controller.updateAuthor(-12, author);
    fail("Should not have been able to update nonexistent author");
}

@Test(expectedExceptions = HibernateException.class)
public void removeNonExistentAuthor() {
    controller.removeAuthor(-12);
    fail("Should not have been able to remove nonexistent author");
}

@Test
public void testGetBooks() {
    Author author = createAuthor("First Author");
    assertEquals(controller.getBooks(author.getId()).length, 0);
    createBook(author, "First Book", 1);
    assertEquals(controller.getBooks(author.getId()).length, 1);
    createBook(author, "Second Book", 1);
    assertEquals(controller.getBooks(author.getId()).length, 2);
}

@Test
public void testUpdateBook() {
    Author author = createAuthor("Arthur Author");
    Book book = createBook(author, "Otter Ought To", 1);
    book.setCopiesSold(1000);
    controller.updateBook(author.getId(), book.getId(), book);
    Book updated = controller.getBook(author.getId(), book.getId());
    assertEquals(updated.getCopiesSold(), 1000);
}
```

```java
@Test(expectedExceptions = HibernateException.class)
public void testUpdateNonexistentBook() {
    Author author = createAuthor("Arthur Author");
    Book book = createBook(author, "Otter Ought To", 1);
    book.setCopiesSold(1000);
    controller.updateBook(author.getId(), -1, book);
    Book updated = controller.getBook(author.getId(), book.getId());
    assertEquals(updated.getCopiesSold(), 1000);
}

@Test
public void testUpdateBookWithNewAuthor() {
    Author author = createAuthor("Arthur Author");
    Author author2 = createAuthor("Ronald Rhino");
    Book book = createBook(author, "Otter Ought To", 1);
    book.setAuthor(author2);
    controller.updateBook(author.getId(), book.getId(), book);
    Book updated = controller.getBook(author.getId(), book.getId());
    assertEquals(updated.getAuthor(), author);
}

private Book createBook(Author author, String title, int edition) {
    Book model = new Book();
    model.setTitle(title);
    model.setCopiesSold(0);
    model.setEdition(edition);
    return controller.createBook(author.getId(), model);
}

private Author createAuthor(String name) {
    Author model = new Author();
    model.setName(name);
    return controller.createAuthor(model);
}
}
```

So far, we've managed to not really address the client side of our web application; we discussed the services, tested them, and even provided working endpoints that a client-facing application could call. We've been mindful of how we initialize our data so that we don't get caught with a LazyInitializationException, and our tests should have done a good job of validating that our data should be initialized properly.

What we haven't done, however, is see how to actually access the services from the Web.

Because a JavaScript framework is a subject too complex for a single chapter in a book, we'll use a command-line tool, curl,[14] to interact with our application. Here's how curl would interact with our heartbeat service:

```
$ curl http://localhost:8080/app/library/hello
Hello, world
```

---

[14]http://curl.haxx.se/

Adding an author takes a little more doing because the call is simpler, but here's an example:

```
$ curl -H "Content-type: application/json" \
> -d'{"name":"Joseph Ottinger"}' \
> http://localhost:8080/app/library/authors/
{"id":1,"name":"Joseph Ottinger"}
```

This code submits an Author's data in JSON format and returns to us the same Author with the identifier assigned. We can validate the list of authors:

```
$ curl http://localhost:8080/app/library/authors
[{"id":1,"name":"Joseph Ottinger"}]
```

We can also look at a specific Author:

```
$ curl http://localhost:8080/app/library/authors/1
{"id":1,"name":"Joseph Ottinger"}
```

We can also update the Author and validate the new value:

```
$ curl -X PUT -H "Content-type: application/json" \
> -d'{"id":"1","name":"Joseph B. Ottinger"}' \
> http://localhost:8080/app/library/authors/1
{"id":1,"name":"Joseph B. Ottinger"}
$ curl http://localhost:8080/app/library/authors/1
{"id":1,"name":"Joseph B. Ottinger"}
```

If we're tired of this Author, we can always delete him:

```
$ curl -X DELETE http://localhost:8080/app/library/authors/1
"id":1,"name":"Joseph B. Ottinger"}
$ curl http://localhost:8080/app/library/authors
[]
```

Likewise, we can work with books in much the same way:

```
$ curl -H "Content-type: application/json" \
> -d'{"name":"Joseph B. Ottinger"}' \
> http://localhost:8080/app/library/authors/
{"id":2,"name":"Joseph B. Ottinger"}
$ curl -H "Content-type: application/json" \
> -d'{"title":"Otters Ought To", "edition":"1","copiesSold":"0"}' \
> http://localhost:8080/app/library/authors/2/books
$ curl http://localhost:8080/app/library/authors/2/books
[{"author":{"id":2,"name":"Joseph B. Ottinger"},\
"copiesSold":0,"edition":1,"id":2,"title":"Otters Ought To"}]
```

Summary

In this chapter, you learned how to define services with clear boundaries for `Session` access, exposed over REST. You also saw a handy way to use `curl` to interact with the web services, which demonstrates how to maintain loose coupling between layers of an application.

We've looked at a lot of things in this book, covering many of the use cases that Hibernate users will run into through the development of an application. We've seen ways to approach those use cases as well as tests that validate the solutions—a practice that, when applied liberally, will serve to improve programmers and their output throughout their careers.

Index

Get the eBook for only $10!

Now you can take the weightless companion with you anywhere, anytime. Your purchase of this book entitles you to 3 electronic versions for only $10.

This Apress title will prove so indispensible that you'll want to carry it with you everywhere, which is why we are offering the eBook in 3 formats for only $10 if you have already purchased the print book.

Convenient and fully searchable, the PDF version enables you to easily find and copy code—or perform examples by quickly toggling between instructions and applications. The MOBI format is ideal for your Kindle, while the ePUB can be utilized on a variety of mobile devices.

Go to www.apress.com/promo/tendollars to purchase your companion eBook.

Apress®
THE EXPERT'S VOICE™